❧ Praise f[...]

Yours is one of the most clear, concise presentations of dissociation I have found. I really liked it!

Doris M Wagner
Global Harvest Ministries
Co-founder, International Society of Deliverance Ministers
Colorado Springs, Colorado
Author: HOW TO MINISTER FREEDOM and other titles

Quinn Schipper has written a very valuable book dealing with an area that comes up frequently in inner healing. The book is based on a large amount of valuable and successful experience that will be very helpful both to those ministering to dissociative clients and to those facing dissociation internally. TRADING FACES is not a book merely of theory, though there is plenty of helpful theory presented. It is a practitioner's book. As a practitioner of inner healing myself, with hundreds of cases under my belt, I resonate strongly with the author's approach and am thrilled to see him have such success in an area where professional counseling tends to be weak and ineffective.

Charles H. Kraft
Professor Fuller Seminary
Pasadena, California
Involved in inner healing since 1985
Author: DEEP WOUNDS, DEEP HEALING, DEFEATING DARK ANGELS, I GIVE YOU AUTHORITY, and CONFRONTING POWERLESS CHRISTIANITY

TRADING FACES is very well written, and though exposing technical material, easily readable, and understandable. Quinn Schipper demonstrates a clear grasp of inner healing. He speaks, for example, to the supreme importance of fathers and the damage done when they fail. He makes good distinctions between what are "practices" a la Colossians 3:10 of putting on the new man and what is demonic, revealing that demonization is not the same as possession. He shows how to interrogate so as to uncover alters and how to minister to them. While focusing on common dissociation, he exposes the spectrum of the phenomenon including that which is highly complex.

For those intending to minister in this field, I recommend TRADING FACES as a basic text for learning.

John Loren Sandford
Elijah House Ministries
www.elijahhouse.org
Spokane, Washington
Co-authored with Paula Sanford: TRANSFORMING THE INNER MAN, GOD'S POWER TO CHANGE, and other titles

---

Donald Grey Barnhouse, the famous theologian, once said, "Get the hay down from the loft, and onto the barn floor where the cows can eat it." The subject of dissociation, or Dissociative Identity Disorder, as it is known in psychiatric circles, has become an increasingly puzzling concept for me. Working, as I do, with people who have been wounded in life, naturally places me in direct contact with those who suffer with dissociation. Quinn Schipper's book, TRADING FACES, gets the "hay down from the loft and on to the barn floor." He makes the complex simple and much easier to understand. While I feel there is still much to learn about the subject, Quinn has done us a great service in peeling away the mystery.

Quinn's book is rich with helpful information and personal stories - and his section on *Practical Application* is invaluable.

This book is a must read for anyone trying to help those in need of restoration.

Pastor Chris Hayward
President, Cleansing Stream Ministries
Van Nuys, California
Author: GOD'S CLEANSING STREAM and THE END OF REJECTION

As I was reading TRADING FACES by Quinn Schipper, I found myself nodding frequently in agreement with his statements and his revelations. This book is the clearest presentation of the very real effects of trauma in human lives that I have come across in over ten years of involvement in this essential ministry.

Many people suffer the effect of their soul hurts in their bodies and their spirits. Quinn's book contains very useful and practical guidelines on how to recognize and minister into these frequently misunderstood and often mishandled areas of counseling.

Real-life testimonies of both the effects of trauma, and the required ministry for their healing and wholeness, are found throughout this book. These are used to help us understand the issues, as well as to equip those called to deal with this deeper ministry.

TRADING FACES should be required reading for all Christians who minister, counsel, and provide hurting people with therapy in churches and communities. I highly recommend this book.

Selwyn R. Stevens, Ph.D.
President, Jubilee Resources International Inc.
Wellington, New Zealand
Author: UNMASKING FREEMASONRY - REMOVING THE HOODWINK and other titles

When I picked up to read Quinn's book, TRADING FACES, my immediate response after the first two chapters was, "Wow, where has this guy been in the last 18 years of my ministry?!" It was a book I couldn't put down.

Quinn has taken a rather complicated topic and ingeniously presented it in such a way that is easy to understand, practical, and applicable to everyone. At last, a laymen's approach which works!

This book is a must addition to any personal library, especially if you are called into the healing and deliverance ministry.

My prayer is that "Trading Faces" will receive the exposure and recognition it deserves. May the Lord use it mightily to bring a greater awareness to the hidden areas of dissociation in each of us.

> Reverend Dean Fujishima
> President, Laulima Ministries International
> www.laulimaministries.com
> Honolulu, Hawaii

Quinn Shipper has done an outstanding job of bringing simplistic understanding to the very complex subject of dissociation. The teachings in this book are well balanced and scripturally sound. I highly recommend this valuable resource to counseling, inner healing, and deliverance ministers.

> William Sudduth,
> Ambassador, International Society of Deliverance Ministers
> Co-founder of Righteous Acts Ministers
> Colorado Springs, Colorado

TRADING FACES

*Dissociation: A Common
Solution to Avoiding
Life's Pain*

By Quinn Schipper

NEW
FORUMS

Stillwater, Oklahoma
U.S.A.

TRADING FACES
Dissociation: A Common Solution to Avoiding Life's Pain
Second Edition
By Quinn Schipper © 2005

TRADING FACES by Quinn Schipper
Second Edition
Published by New Forums Press
1018 S. Lewis
Stillwater, Oklahoma 74074
Website: http://www.newforums.com

Library of Congress Cataloging-in-Publication Data Pending

ISBN 10: 1-58107-142-6

ISBN 13: 978-1-581071-42-9

The Cover: Designed by Casey Crowdis.

Contents

A Note from the Author

Many men, women, children, couples, and families have trusted me to enter into the private world of their pain, their fears, and their failures. I take this privilege seriously and protect each one fiercely. In recent years, I have discovered a theme of dissociation in hurting people. Simply put, dissociation is a natural response of the mind to aid survival in a trauma situation. It results in the condition of being divided within oneself, as well as separated from others. Psychiatry's restricted definition of multiple personalities does not allow for the fact that dissociation is far more common than is recognized. Dissociation can range from everyone's mild experience of briefly "spacing out" to the complex working of programmed mind control.

TRADING FACES reveals truths about dissociation and provides practical, helpful answers. Many real life illustrations of dissociation will be found throughout this book. Names, references, and details have been changed as needed to protect the identity of individuals. In some cases, a composite story has been created to best illustrate a familiar circumstance of dissociation. You may find yourself personally identifying with some of these illustrations. If so, take a deep breath and press on to discover how you, too, may become free of past hurts and be made whole.

As you turn the page, you will step into newly charted territory of a controversial subject that is rapidly gaining attention. A glossary is provided at the back to help you understand terms and definitions. I dedicate this book to the family members, friends, and associates who have helped me to walk out my journey of personal restoration as well as to write this book on the healing of dissociation.

Trading Faces

Bradley's Story

Dissociation Takes Root

Bradley recoiled when he unexpectedly found himself back in a terrifying memory of being bullied as a five-year-old on the school playground. He was even less prepared for the accompanying surge of shame and fear that rocked him emotionally. He remembered children gathering around, pointing and laughing. He heard the triumphant glee of the girl who had taken him down and now sat squarely across his back. Intense feelings of helplessness and embarrassment overwhelmed him. Body memories returned. Bradley grimaced, choking back dust. He sensed the grit against his face as he was pushed into the ground and felt the searing pain of his arm being twisted behind him.

Bradley sat across from me, fighting back tears, as he had done fifteen years before. He also struggled to resist a familiar, yet uncomfortable rush that coursed through his body. Anger uncontrollably surfaced. As his countenance darkened and his brow furrowed, I instantly recognized this as a side of Bradley I had never seen. I was now facing an alternate personality, who was making a mess of this young man's life. With an infuriated Bradley glaring and fuming across from me, I knew "five-year-old Bradley" might finally confront his place of woundedness and receive healing. But that was not going to happen without another kind of battle.

Perhaps like Bradley, you may struggle with "another side of yourself" that shows up at inopportune times, unpredictably, even against your will. Maybe you do not particularly like this side of yourself, yet seem powerless to change. Or you may live or work with someone who acts one way here, another way there, and a completely different way somewhere else. How does this happen? Why? What flips the switch that causes a person to "trade faces" and "become someone else?"

Extreme stresses such as abuse, trauma, or tragedy can cause a person to dissociate in several ways. For five-year-old Bradley, the horror of being bullied literally fragmented his young mind. A separate identity formed to help protect him from the pain of that dreadful experience. Bradley's story continues in Chapter 2. As you learn about the origin and outcomes of dissociation, stories like Bradley's will help explain the phenomenon of dissociation and connect you to a place of restored order, peace, and wholeness.

Part One
Vital Foundation

Trading Faces

Chapter One

More Common Than You Think

Overview of Dissociation

DANIELLE, A PERKY BLONDE IN HER LATE THIRTIES, MADE AN IMMEDIATE IMPRESSION AS SHE STRODE INTO THE STAFF MEETING. Her smile brightened the room, and she felt totally prepared with her contribution for the upcoming presentation. All was going smoothly until her boss expressed his preference for some of his own wording rather than hers. It was really no big deal, but she suddenly felt overwhelmed with shame in front of her colleagues. Out of nowhere, words exploded in her head, echoing the hidden pain of being yelled at by her mother and slapped around in front of her brothers. "How could you be so stupid? Only an idiot would do something like that!" Unable to control her tears, Danielle fled the meeting to pull herself together. In the safety of the ladies room, her heart pounding wildly, she felt like the stupid idiot she had been called as a child. How could such a simple suggestion from her boss elicit such a disproportionate reaction? Danielle was a capable, intelligent woman, yet the slightest criticism could send her into an uncontrollable, emotional nosedive. Who *was* this that responded so irrationally? It certainly was not the same woman who stepped so confidently into that meeting just moments before.

Living with dissociation

Your interest in reading this book is evidence that you want to be informed and aware of a timely subject that is rapidly gaining attention. Whether you know it or not, dissociation is happening all around you – possibly within you. Despite medical or psychiatric assertions to the contrary, dissociation is surprisingly commonplace and can be healed. Because so many live *in* dissociation, most of us live *with* dissociation to some degree. This chapter will give you an overview of dissociation. It will prepare the way for you to understand better the perplexity of and unique challenges linked to dissociation. As you navigate through this book, you will come to discover the hope that is offered, the very real solutions that are available, and the wholeness that comes in the process of inner healing.

Notes

TRADING FACES focuses on common dissociation, which primarily happens spontaneously as a consequence of unexpected trauma. Except for a brief overview in Chapter 4, this book does not detail the complexity of programmed mind control where a perpetrator's premeditated intention is to manipulate and control the behavior of his victim.

A glossary is included at the end of the book to help you understand various terms and definitions related to this topic. The first occurrence of a word or term found in the glossary will hereafter be noted in the text as **boldfaced** and *italicized*.

Grasping definitions

Simply stated, to *dissociate* means to "dis-unite," or separate, from association. The prefix "dis" itself denotes *separation* or parting from. If you dissociate from someone else, you separate yourself from him or her. You discontinue association. You go separate ways. You disconnect.

An individual may personally dissociate in the mind as the result of trauma such as abuse, fear, abandonment, or parental abdication. The corresponding pain of such an event may cause a person to disconnect mentally from that pain in order to survive. Should trauma result in *dissociation*, an encapsulated and separate identity splits off within a person's mind that holds its own memories, thoughts, feelings, attributes, and characteristics. Psychiatric terms for inner dissociated identities include "multiple personality," "alter identity," "alter personality," or simply, "*alter.*" An alter's primary role is to protect the person in order to avoid both hidden and present pain. Each alter that forms may be experienced as having a distinct personal history, self-image, and identity, including its own separate name. It seems that increasingly, psychiatric disorders are pinned to some form of dissociation, for example *Dissociative Identity Disorder*. This book will help you understand the limitations of a strictly psychiatric perspective. (See Chapter 3)

The psychiatric use of the word dissociation may help explain the concept of "double-mindedness." The dictionary defines *double-minded* as "having different minds at different times; unsettled; vacillating; also, deceitful." Dissociation is deceptive in appearances, causing an individual to contradict himself by being one way at one time and distinctly different, even quite opposite, at another time. A *switch* between these states may be prompted by circumstances, by other people, by decisions that need to be made, and the like. Such a person, being of two minds, may be perceived by others as confused, illogical, unreliable, unstable, unpredictable, and even hypocritical.

The opposite of association

The mind normally functions by association, which is why people remember a whole event, including sights, sounds, smells, feelings, and meanings. Dissociation usually occurs when a person experiences extreme stress physically, emotionally, or mentally. The mind then operates in a way to separate out things that are usually kept together. The mental process of dissociation is a way the mind records, stores, interprets, and retrieves information. For example, when a child is abused, the event may be experienced in a state of shock, stored in a different part of the mind, and recalled in fragments. Given the nature or focus of the stress, some information may be dissociated, or disconnected, while other information is stored as a congruent whole. In the case of severe abuse, part of the mind functionally "checks out" in order for the person to tolerate the pain of the abuse. Correspondingly, the person's mind may fragment and form a distinct, alter identity whose primary purpose is to protect the person from returning to that place of pain and being re-traumatized. This alter may hold selective information that is recorded in a dissociated state in another part of the mind. Mental data that may "go missing" might be detected later as the inability to show emotion or to respond to pain in a normal, healthy way. This might even include the threat of pain, as seen in Danielle's exaggerated reaction to her boss's comments. Fortunately, the mind is so intricately made that it is capable of separating in dissociation as the defense of choice in a traumatic event. Alternatives to dealing with the trauma include insanity, suicide, and *desertion*.

The *true person* is the actual person who has been born and presumed to be the "original" person in whose subconscious mind wounded parts are hidden and alter identities have separated. When a person is traumatized, memory data from the event will be recorded in a dissociated state in the subconscious mind. Distanced from the conscious mind, it is as though a *part* of the person "goes into hiding" at the subconscious level, holding the pain experienced during the trauma. Functionally, this wounded part of the true person "stalls" at that moment and in that memory, even though the person overall continues to mature. If this stalled part is accessed, it will likely have the same name as the true person at the age of the trauma. For example, the stalled part of Danielle may be acknowledged simply as "six-year-old Danielle" and interacted with accordingly. Alter identities may form to protect the stalled part in the subconscious mind from consciously reconnecting with the pain linked to the trauma. An alter serves as a sentinel, on guard to prevent, if possible, the pain from being accessed and the person from re-experiencing the trauma. To carry out its duty, an alter may defend the true person by protecting, controlling, or presenting – however it must – to help the stalled part avoid pain. It is important to understand that alters are not separate people. There is only one true person. Alters are merely "false images" of the true person, established for the primary purpose of protection and to aid survival. Alters are typically self-focused in their manner and limited in their function.

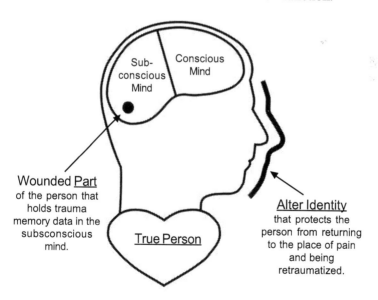

Sub-conscious Mind

Conscious Mind

Wounded Part
of the person that holds trauma memory data in the subsconscious mind.

True Person

Alter Identity
that protects the person from returning to the place of pain and being retraumatized.

Problem or solution?

As the mind's preferred defense mechanism, dissociation is a mental, inner solution to pain avoidance. Any outer representation of that solution may be maintained by an alter. At times, that representation may be incompatible with the person's basic nature. For example, an alter may help mask a person's hidden pain by habitually using drugs. It may be that the use of drugs is actually loathsome to the true person and perplexing to others. Typically, family, friends, and professionals will identify the drug addiction as the person's "problem" and focus on treating "the problem." Regrettably, the existing myriad of sophisticated self-help techniques and styles of therapy will fall short if the *real* problem is not dealt with: the underlying pain, lies, fears, and unforgiveness held tightly by a stalled part of the true person and buried in the subconscious mind. In summary, what is outwardly perceived as a person's "problem" may actually be his "solution" to cover, hide, control, manage, or in other ways prevent from recurrence, the pain that is deeply hidden away in the subconscious mind.

There will usually be some kind of lie established that corresponds with the trauma event. Danielle, who was repeatedly abused in early childhood, may have wrongfully concluded, "It was my fault," or "I deserved this," or "My life is ruined." No amount of logic or knowledge of facts will dissuade the part that holds that lie from believing it as anything but truth. If a child is repeatedly told she is stupid and as a competent adult feels disgraced by her boss, she may unexpectedly find herself feeling like, even acting like, that stupid child she subconsciously believes herself to be.

Trading faces

Why did Danielle react in the staff meeting? Because a present-day situation unexpectedly tapped into the hidden pain of a past trauma event. The wounded part of her true person, who holds the pain, was instantly alerted and responded. Any number of *triggers* could have caused this to happen – a touch, a smell, a visual cue, a sound, a voice. In Danielle's case, the boss's "correction" ignited something inside of her that *felt like* the verbal abuse inflicted by her mother many years before. Even though the boss was not abusing her and even though she may not at the time have been consciously connecting this to her childhood trauma, the *feelings* were the same. It was Danielle's own reaction, not her boss's words, which really took her by surprise. Instantly, a protective alter appeared to bail her out of the frightening situation. Unable to hold herself together, Danielle "traded faces" and quickly excused herself from the staff meeting and ran to find a safe place to hide.

In a similar way, as a child is being abused, the conscious mind "looks away" while the rest of the mind retreats in search of safety. Even in the ladies room she may not have connected her feelings to the childhood abuse. Regardless, the original trauma was once again being subconsciously reinforced each time this place of pain was mysteriously accessed. The first time Danielle was traumatized, the natural response of her mind was to escape mentally and to dissociate. As an adult, her solution was still to escape. However, until she was ultimately willing and able to go to the place in her mind where the pain was held, she would defer to a false trust in an alter identity to protect her, come to her rescue, and help her elude a threatening situation. To the dissociated individual, this alternate "person" is very real, even necessary – no matter how inappropriate, irrational, or even illegitimate the behavior of the alter.

When the protection of an alter is respectfully bypassed in order to get to and deal with the *real* problem of hidden pain and lies linked to the trauma, inner *restoration* can take place. When a wounded part of the true person is accessed at the point of pain, the mind returns to the "now" of what is happening, and the person responds accordingly. She is suddenly in the crisis again, connecting with the memory, feelings, emotions, and other circumstances surrounding the pain. She may even experience **abreaction**, which may include reliving a physical **body memory** of the trauma.

A trauma situation need not be long lasting or life threatening. More likely, it will be some circumstance a child was too immature to cope with. But once traumatized, a child is placed, as it were, on an ever-widening path of self-destruction. From that point on, the person may experience repeated forms of **sabotage**. Such acts of malicious injury will either replicate or reinforce the event linked to the initial trauma and dissociation. When she least suspected it during a staff meeting, adult Danielle found herself ensnared once again in the childhood memory trap of invalidation. Worst of all, she did not understand how she got there.

Examples

Dissociation thrives on mixed messages. Imagine a child with a father who loves, cares for, and plays with his child one minute and mercilessly beats him the next. The immature mind of the child cannot reconcile the incompatibility of this, so it dissociates. Consequently, the child will learn different ways of responding to the "loving" father and the "cruel" father. When "loving" father is around, the child may have no knowledge or thought of "cruel" father. But as soon as the father becomes violent, the child **switches**, and the mind defers to the functioning of the alter identity that knows how to react to "cruel" father in order to protect the wounded part of the true person. As the mind continually rehearses the double-minded activity around the unpredictable father, the dissociation gets reinforced. This example also helps you understand how this child's abuser is likely acting out of his own dissociation and unresolved pain.

Over the years, I have spent thousands of hours with dissociated people ranging in actual age from five to seventy seven years old. I have interacted with wounded parts linked to trauma-based experiences who are of a stalled age much younger than eight. I have discovered the distinct purposes and presentations of countless alter identities. For instance, once while speaking with a teenage alter of an adult man, he suddenly pulled the glasses off his face and declared with astonishment, "I don't wear glasses!" And that was correct. The true person did not start wearing glasses until he was in his thirties.

Alters may have dietary preferences, even restrictions. I recall being with a group at a restaurant where I was sitting across from a woman I knew to be dissociated and in whom several alters had been identified. I observed with interest a personal battle that ensued as she argued with herself over which dessert to order. The friend she had come with, irritated and embarrassed by her indecision, ordered for her once the waitress arrived. The woman became sullen. In hopes of salvaging an awkward situation, when the desserts were served, I looked at the unhappy woman – that is, her presenting alter – and said, "What a fabulous looking dessert! You are really going to enjoy that." Then, pointing to my choice added, "Look what I'm stuck with." As I suspected, this tapped into another alter that really wanted that particular dessert and was thankful she was not served what I chose. No one at the table was any the wiser as to what had transpired, although I did sense relief on the part of her friend that the woman's disposition had happily changed.

Many more examples will be shared throughout this book to help illustrate the diversity of dissociation as well as the ***inner healing*** and restoration that are possible for those who live a divided existence.

Finding oneself

Inside each of us, the "real me" is longing to be revealed and released. Years of my life have been devoted to helping people discover genuine peace that comes from deep inner healing. People have come seeking help for various "problems." As they learn that a perceived problem is actually their personal solution to avoid hidden pain, they are eager to pursue resolution so their true person might emerge and be made whole. The unique insights and style of guidance they receive often put them in touch with their dissociation and connect them responsibly to wounded parts hidden away in the subconscious mind. This *self-awareness* is key to unlocking the doorway to inner healing. People frequently exclaim, "You mean I'm *not* crazy?!" Expressions of joy as they come into healing include, "I feel whole!"

But this work cannot be done alone. As you continue reading TRADING FACES you will become aware that I unapologetically rely on God to provide answers that man simply cannot offer. Whether or not you affirm the presence and work of God in the world, it is my sincere hope that your entire mind will be opened to understand and apply truths found in this book. The outcome will be healing to hidden, wounded parts and restoration of the soul. There will be renewed energy as the true person emerges and indescribable peace comes to a formerly fragmented, troubled mind.

Chapter 2

The Origin of Dissociation

Roots of Relational Separation

THE COLOR DRAINED OUT OF MARK'S FACE WHEN TYRONE CONFRONTED HIM WITH THE PORNOGRAPHIC IMAGE THAT HAD SPAT OUT OF THE OFFICE PRINTER THEY SHARED. How had he failed to wait for the printer to produce that last picture which he had downloaded after everyone left the evening before? Mark squirmed under Tyrone's disbelieving gaze. Stammering with excuses and denials, Mark finally buried his face in his hands and admitted his guilt to Tyrone. "Finally, somebody knows." Certain that he would lose his position with the religious organization he worked for, Mark begged this man, who was both his boss and a close friend, not to expose his dark secret to others. Incredulous, Tyrone wondered why this respected family man, active in his community and church, would be indulging in such graphic, hard-core pornography. How could he possibly be living such a double life? This did not seem to be the same person Tyrone had come to confide in and trust.

The dilemma of dissociation

Dissociation is a natural function of the mind to aid survival during trauma. In psychiatric circles, dissociation is often classified as "separation within an individual diagnosed as having two or more distinct, alternate personalities." From this perspective, dissociation is considered a mental disorder, therefore treated accordingly. The familiar term *"Multiple Personality Disorder"* has, for the most part, been replaced with a more accurate term, "Dissociative Identity Disorder," along with a host of related dissociative disorders. Perhaps more accurately, dissociation ought to be viewed as a relational "dis-order" that distorts perceptions of self and others. Dissociation grotesquely misaligns and profoundly impacts relationships in three interrelated ways; not only does a dissociated person experience separation within his own mind, he will experience corresponding separation from other people and from God.

As human beings, we are designed to be single-minded. We are intended to be one in ourselves, with others, and with God. When wholeness and relational order are disrupted, spiritual discord follows. The mind becomes a battleground of conflict and *confusion*. Susceptibility to lie-based thinking creates further disharmony and puts one at risk to other undesirable influences. A person with the relational dis-order of dissociation becomes detached from his true person, disengaged from others, and has intimacy with his Creator interrupted. Disconnection from God distances a person relationally and spiritually from his ultimate source of truth and healing. Because dissociation creates a spiritual dilemma, spiritual solutions must be sought for healing those who are dissociated.

As a person is being traumatized, he will detach himself mentally from the source of his pain. That source may be another person who is abusing him, or it may be a tragic circumstance, such as a terrible accident. Regardless, in order to cope with the pressing fear and trauma of an event, the mind may dissociate to aid survival. If that happens, a wounded part of the person fragments and retreats to a hidden place in the subconscious mind. That part will generally stall at the occurrence of dissociation and retain certain thoughts, emotions, experiences, information, and relationships as if frozen in time. Whenever a person fragments in this manner for self-preservation, that wounded part may unintentionally cut him off from God. There is typically a lie he believes about himself or the circumstance such as, "I am no good," "I am dirty," "I deserve this," or "It's my fault." As more life experiences happen to reinforce the lie, truth becomes increasingly remote. After awhile, only darkness exists in that hidden place, and the wounded part may then be unreceptive, even hostile, toward God. This wounded part will subconsciously cause the person to function in relation to his embedded fears and lies. Often, a distinct alter identity forms to protect that part of the person, if possible, from being further wounded or traumatized. Alter solutions to avoiding pain may come in many expressions, including addictive behaviors.

Mark had repeated experiences of rejection and abandonment in childhood. At the breaking point of dissociation around age seven, Mark embraced the lie, "Nobody loves me." As he grew, even so much as a hint of rejection tapped into this wounded part of Mark hidden away in his subconscious mind. To avoid the hurt this caused, he would fantasize about people and situations where he was loved, accepted, and powerful. When Mark was introduced to pornography while playing at a neighbor's house one day, the arousing images fueled his fantasy world yet created a sense of inner conflict he could not avoid. Mark was no stranger to separating himself from others who had rejected or abandoned him. Fantasy and pornography simply became his preferred means of self-protection and comfort. Despite the sense he had that this was displeasing to God, he became driven to seek out pornography.

By the time he was in his teens, it had become an established addiction. Mark adapted to a double life. He openly lived for God among friends who had gotten him involved in a local church but secretly gratified himself in private. The more he indulged in pornography, the more his conscience became desensitized, and the more isolated the wounded part of himself became that was buried away in his subconscious mind.

Mark did not know that he had an alter identity who turned to pornography as a way to protect this deeply wounded part of himself. The more permission this alter was given to act, the more polarized became the God-focused and self-focused sides of Mark. The pattern of dissociation strengthened to the point that an addiction to pornography became his solution to skirting deep-seated issues of rejection. In response, his *dissociative system* would seek escape in pornography to salve the pain of loneliness and isolation he often felt. This cycle strengthened a common lie, "It's okay as long as I don't get caught," to the point this alter almost felt invincible.

When Tyrone confronted Mark at work with the pornographic image, it instantly tapped into Mark's hidden fears. Echoes of earlier life experiences made his head pound, terrified that he would be rejected by his friend, lose his job, and once more be abandoned. Because neither man had any knowledge of dissociation, Tyrone could not understand that Mark's true person battled constantly with this alter's repulsive quest for sexual thrills and false validation in an anonymous cyber world. Tyrone's instinct was to distance himself from Mark. Feeling hopelessly trapped, Mark's seven-year-old wounded part was glaringly exposed as he pleaded not to be hurt again. As a result of this confrontation, Mark lost his job and brought much shame and embarrassment upon himself and his family. The good that came of it was that Mark sought help, including inner healing. As fears were unearthed and dealt with, so were the numerous lies he believed, one being that he was the only man in his extensive circle of relationships who was snared in this duplicity. Coming to self-awareness of his dissociation did not excuse Mark's addictive behavior, but it did make it understandable and therefore redeemable. In the process of receiving healing, Mark was able to reconcile relational breaches within himself, with others, and with God.

A spiritual issue requires spiritual insights, for there is more to Mark's story than just relational separation. There is a subversive enemy of our souls in whom there is no truth. Although this enemy is known in the *Bible* by several names (Satan, the devil, the adversary, the accuser), one of his most telling names is "father of lies" (John 8:44). It is impossible for Satan to hold to the truth. It is not in him. He aggressively pursues anything that is in opposition to God and his plans. The devil is unrelenting in his work to deceive, disunite, and destroy. In whatever way relational separation occurs, this nemesis capitalizes on every opportunity to keep people divided within themselves, from others, and from their Creator. Deception and lies are among the tools Satan uses to capitalize on dissociative instability and to pry open doors for his diabolical influence. If these are not closed, a person may come to an end of utter ruin, as could have been the outcome for Mark had his addiction gone unrestrained.

Dissociation divides

Insights and answers to dissociation may be found in a variety of legitimate, authoritative sources. Rarely will you find dissociation interpreted from any kind of spiritual perspective. Fewer still will examine it through Biblical lenses. To present dissociation as a three-way relational dis-order is itself unique. A familiar story from the Bible will be referenced to lay a spiritual foundation for this view of dissociation – Adam and Eve and the circumstances surrounding their eating of the forbidden fruit in the idyllic Garden of Eden. In the very first book of the Bible, the book of Genesis, we see the story of Adam and Eve unfolding. In particular, in Genesis chapter 3, verses 1-13, we are given the account of how the antagonist, Satan, disguised as a serpent, goes about separating Adam and Eve from God, their Creator, and from each other.

Now the serpent was more crafty than any of the wild animals the Lord God had made. He said to the woman, "Did God really say, 'You must not eat from any tree in the garden'?" The woman said to the serpent, "We may eat fruit from the trees in the garden, but God did say, 'You must not eat fruit from the tree that is in the middle of the garden, and you must not touch it, or you will die.'" "You will not surely die," the serpent said to the woman. "For God knows that when you eat of it your eyes will be opened, and you will be like God, knowing good from evil."

When the woman saw that the fruit of the tree was good for food and pleasing to the eye, and also desirable for gaining wisdom, she took some and ate it. She also gave some to her husband, who was with her, and he ate it. Then the eyes of both of them were opened, and they realized they were naked; so they sewed fig leaves together and made coverings for themselves. Then the man and his wife heard the sound of the Lord God as he was walking in the garden in the cool of the day, and they hid from the Lord God among the trees of the garden.

But the Lord God called to the man, "Where are you?" He answered, "I heard you in the garden, and I was afraid because I was naked; so I hid." And he said, "Who told you that you were naked? Have you eaten from the tree that I commanded you not to eat from?" The man said, "The woman you put here with me – she gave me some fruit from the tree, and I ate it." Then the Lord God said to the woman, "What is this you have done?" The woman said, "The serpent deceived me, and I ate."

Elsewhere in the Bible it becomes clear that the **scheme** of this enemy, who is also known as the devil, is to "steal, kill, and destroy." (See John 10:10) 1 Peter 5:8 cautions, "Be self-controlled and alert. Your enemy the devil prowls around like a roaring lion looking for someone to devour." A lion stalks for small, weak, injured, or already isolated prey. Just as an ensuing chase may separate his prey away from the herd, it is not uncommon for Satan to isolate individuals in order to deceive them.

Genesis 3:1 speaks of the serpent as being "more crafty than any of the wild animals the Lord God had made." He apparently catches Eve alone and speaks to the woman, "Did God *really* say, 'You must not eat from any tree in the garden'?" (*Emphasis mine.*)

The woman, having been forewarned about the tree of the knowledge of good and evil, replies to the serpent that they can eat of every tree except one. If they touch or eat of that tree, they will die. Immediately the serpent lies, contradicting God's truth and challenging obedience to God's command. This allure by the enemy entices the woman to disregard God's command. She is baited into disobedience. When the woman saw that the fruit of the tree was good for food and pleasing to the eye, and also desirable for gaining wisdom, she took some and ate it.

Adam faced an alarming reality. Although the woman had eaten, she neither looked nor acted dead. Perhaps fearful that his Creator had lied and this creature seemed to have spoken the real truth, Adam may have reasoned that he *did* need this knowledge the tree was supposed to provide. Knowing full well what he was doing, Adam joined in Eve's disobedience and also ate of the fruit.

Up until this point, the man and woman were both naked and felt no shame. (Genesis 2:25) But once deception gave way to disobedience, they suddenly become conscious of something they had not previously known: "Then the eyes of both of them were opened, and they realized they were naked." This startling discovery caused them to do two things they had no reason to do before. They covered their nakedness with fig leaves and hid among the trees, thus attempting to conceal their shame from God as he walked in the garden in the cool of the day. In Adam's reply to God, we see that the chain of events had successfully linked deception, disobedience, shame, and fear:

"I heard you in the garden, and I was afraid because I was naked; so I hid." (Genesis 3:10)

Relational separation

Transcending the restricted definition of dissociation as being "that which occurs within an individual," relational separation from others is possible and does indeed happen. When an innocent child is unexpectedly abused, he reacts to the fear and may dissociate in his mind to bear the pain. He may also dissociate from his abuser in a situation where he is required to maintain some level of ongoing relationship with that person, for example, a child with a parent. Relational separation is brought about through dissociation when a person either believes or is made to feel he is unacceptable to others. Mark had neither sought rejection nor wanted to be abandoned by those who should have loved and cared for him. The pain of believing he was unloved, therefore unacceptable, translated into a shame that he wanted to keep hidden from others, including God. In order to do that, he relationally disconnected from all who made him feel uncomfortable and would not allow others to get close to his real hurt. Although years later he became a Christian, a wounded part of Mark still believed he was unacceptable to God. That hidden part was stalled in Mark's subconscious mind. A corresponding protective alter believed he did not matter anyway to God or to others and pacified Mark's pain through fantasy and pornography.

Satan preys upon a person's sense of being unacceptable. As an accuser, he lies to us and gets us viewing our unacceptable condition through lenses of overwhelming fear, shame, and hopelessness. A self-focused orientation was reinforced in Mark as he began operating from the belief that he was unacceptable.

Adam and Eve felt unacceptable around God after they disobeyed him. Their conscious rebellion against the truth God had spoken and the obedience he required separated them from God. When they were created, they were naked and unashamed. But now, their nakedness made them feel uncomfortable around him and around each other. Their circumstance exposes the three primary ways dissociation functions. These are explained more completely in Chapter 5.

1. To protect: Adam and Eve attempted to protect themselves from disgrace by hiding their nakedness behind coverings of fig leaves. (Genesis 3:7) These flimsy garments, coupled with excuses, were two of their solutions for masking the separation they felt from God and the discomfort they felt around each other.

2. To control: The pair made an effort to control their relationship with God by hiding from him among the trees of the garden. (Genesis 3:8) Fearful of being caught in the shame of their disobedience, hiding was another

solution for dealing with the predicament of being separated from God.

3. To present: The two, fearful of being caught naked, camouflaged themselves behind fig leaves and moved stealthily about the garden. (Genesis 3:7-8) No longer able to be who they had once been before God, this solution meant they now had to present themselves differently toward each other and toward God when they were with him.

When God questioned them about their disobedience (Genesis 3:11), they both resorted to replying out of a position of self-preservation. They distanced themselves from the serpent, who had duped them. They even showed signs of having relationally separated from each other, choosing the defense of blame as the means to explain and justify their sin: The man said, "The woman you put here with me – she gave me some fruit from the tree, and I ate it." (Genesis 3:12) Then the Lord said to the woman, "What is this you have done?" The woman said, "The serpent deceived me, and I ate." (Genesis 3:13)

God is merciful. Rather than condemning the man and the woman, he identified the real culprit in the story: So the Lord God said to the serpent, "Because you have done this, cursed are you …" (Genesis 3:14ff) Because the serpent deceived the woman, God cursed him. But the disobedience of the first man and woman also had consequences. The result of Adam's disobedience, of eating fruit from the tree he was commanded not to eat, was that God cursed the ground. For the remainder of Adam's days it would be through painful toil and by the sweat of his brow that he would eat. With pain Eve would give birth to children. The couple was banished from the Garden of Eden, driven out to work the ground from which Adam had been taken and to which he would return. (Genesis 3:16-24; see also Genesis 2:7)

God looked upon the desperate self efforts of Adam and his wife to hide themselves from their sin. He even made a way for them to be acceptable to him and comfortable around him once more: God compassionately took it upon himself to sacrifice an animal so that they might both be covered with garments of skin that he personally made for them to wear. This shedding of blood and covering of shame would foreshadow Christ's redemption to come.

Dissociation impacts relationships in all kinds of ways. As a person begins to operate out of his woundedness, alter identities may correspondingly form as an expression of the mind's defense mechanism to avert further pain. Mark's mind had formed an alter whose solution was to find a perverted comfort in fantasy and pornographic images. The more rehearsed and adept this alter got at furtively indulging in pornography, the more detached Mark was from his subconsciously hidden place of suffering. Despite all the confusion and conflict this created, he increasingly yielded to the control of this alter and to the addictive behavior. What began as a solution to mask pain had in fact become problematic. Meanwhile, his relationship with God was strained even as his need for inner restoration was continually overlooked. Mark was no stranger to distancing himself from others and hiding his addiction. Although Mark and Tyrone had appearances of a close friendship and worked well together, Mark had subconsciously kept Tyrone at a distance. At any time he might have been added to a growing list of individuals Mark had been forced to separate from for fear his addiction might be discovered.

When woundedness collides, the dissonance created can isolate people from one another, as regrettably happened between Mark and Tyrone. Mark initially reacted out of shame and fear to Tyrone's confronting him with the pornography. He had never before been caught like this. Out of desperation, he resorted to the deception of excuses and denial. Tyrone's incredulous response echoed from his own history of disappointments as well as his ignorance of Mark's hidden pain. Unsure of what to do with the deep sense of betrayal he felt, Tyrone's solution was to immediately terminate not only Mark's position but also their friendship. Not every relational disconnection may end with such finality. Others may learn to co-exist in disengaged, co-dependent, or dysfunctional relationships. Such liaisons usually exclude consideration of others' woundedness and are often void of the resources to truly help heal one another's pain. This is particularly tragic in a marriage or family.

As you might imagine, this experience played havoc with Mark's dissociation. The now gaping wound of rejection catapulted his deepest fears and perceived inadequacies to the surface. He had to face an uncomfortable confession to his wife and the dreadful anticipation that she, too would abandon him. Although they had some painful issues to work through, she chose to cover his shame and help him face up to his fears by encouraging him to seek help. When his woundedness was genuinely healed, the alter no longer had a purpose. The addiction immediately stopped and he was able to recover relational association with God, with himself, and with others who were estranged by his addiction. This eventually included reconciliation with Tyrone. However, the path to restoration was not walked out without contemplating some serious alternatives ...

Multiplied lies and compounded pain have the potential to result in three extreme outcomes: insanity, suicide, or desertion. These correspond to the enemy's scheme to steal, kill, and destroy. A person may become so deeply wounded and divided that his mind "snaps." This reactive solution to the pain is to disintegrate mentally into insanity, stealing the mind. If a person becomes so deeply deceived through dissociation so as to believe life is no longer worth living, he may end it in suicide. Still for others, living in double-mindedness might become so torturous that a choice is made to desert significant relationships or responsibilities to pursue self-focused and often compromised lives. Friendships, marriages, businesses, churches, and reputations may be destroyed through desertion. All three of these outcomes are unnatural:

Insanity: the stealing of the mind and separation from oneself, or mentally giving up.

Suicide: the killing of self and separation from others, or physically giving up.

Desertion: the destroying of relationships and separation from God, or relationally giving up.

Dissociation and double-mindedness

James, who authored a book in the latter part of the Bible, gives us insights into the understanding of what it means to be double-minded. He writes in James 1:6, "But when he asks, he must believe and not doubt, because he who doubts is like a wave of the sea, blown and tossed by the wind." The phrase "and not doubt" is translated from the Greek New Testament words *meedén diakrinómenos*, describing someone who wavers between two opinions. That is, one divided in mind. In the context of this passage, someone seeking wisdom must not vacillate between believing God for it and doubting it will be given. James goes on to explain: "That man should not think he will receive anything from the Lord; he is a double-minded man, unstable in all he does." (James 1:7-8) The Greek word *dipsuchos*, translated "double-minded," in its literal sense, means "two-souled" or "double-souled," as though having two independent wills. A person who is divided in mind and two-souled operates out of his dissociation and double-mindedness with resulting confusion. No longer whole, the person may function in irrational, even unpredictable ways that are not only against fusion but also oppose unity.

Dissociation as a relational dis-order began in the Garden of Eden. Man was designed to be an image bearer of God, his Creator. God is whole. God is not dissociated. He is not double-minded. It was not God's original intent for man to be separated from him. But this intent was intercepted by disobedience. Satan goes to great lengths to keep a person separated from God. When the deception of the enemy entices a person to disobey God, that person separates himself from God and becomes conflicted in both focus and allegiance. One side of him may adhere to the truth of God. Another side may succumb to the lie of the deceiver. A battle of the wills erupts when a dissociated person is confronted with choosing either obedience to God's truth or submission to the enemy's lie. Together, dissociation and double-mindedness create instability, relational dis-order, and chaos.

A picture of dissociation

The very first chapter of the Bible tells how "God created man in his own image, in the image of God he created him; male and female he created them." (Genesis 1:27) Distinctly different from all other creatures, man is essentially a spiritual being confined to a physical body into whom God breathed the breath of life. (Genesis 2:7) Jesus teaches that "the thief (Satan) comes only to steal, kill and destroy; I (Jesus) have come that they (man) may have life, and have it to the full." (John 10:10) From the first deception in the Garden of Eden, Satan has been hard at work to distort that original image of man created in the likeness of God.

A photograph, also known as a "snap shot," captures in a split second a specific image representing a distinct moment in time. Whenever we attend a family gathering, inevitably photograph albums appear out of nowhere. Admittedly, I will spend my share of time over certain pictures, studying faces, recalling settings, and reviving memories. On the afternoon of a recent get-together, an adept digital photographer among us opened his laptop in the evening and delighted everyone with a slide show highlighting the day's events. I am aware that, with the right software, these pictures could have also been masterfully, even amusingly, altered to modify or distort the original image.

Satan targets innocence. He knew he could not deceive God, so he sabotaged man's relationship with God by deceiving God's prized creation – man, whom God had created in his own image. The enemy stepped into the purity and wholesomeness of intimacy with God in the garden and began disfiguring that image. Still today, the devil starts subversively working away on people as early in life as possible, often before they have developed their own set of defenses. This can begin at conception, in the womb, from birth, or any point that follows. If I were to take a penknife to this picture and slice it into vertical strips, the picture would become marred but still recognizable. At first, the slicing may appear to have little impact on the image. But repeated slicing, distorting, and separating will create something quite unlike the original image.

Satan's scheme has not changed. While his ultimate goal is to steal, kill, and destroy, he callously strikes the innocent and begins slicing them to shreds. Typically, the first cut is made in early childhood as a result of some outside force over which a child has no control. Perhaps the child has been abused, or abandoned, or invalidated in some way. If that cut is deep enough, the child may dissociate within herself to deal with the pain. Little by little, the enemy cuts away at that precious image. As he does, it seems as though he tugs at one piece one way and another piece another way. Before long, the picture is so out of alignment it becomes difficult to identify the original image.

As you can see, the picture is now very confusing. While the image may still be in consecutive order, it is no longer a fused whole. Satan hopes that, throughout her life, this person will remain in a state of "con-fusion." That is, to live in a way that is against fusion and resists wholeness.

These figures help illustrate how the devil works to destroy the image of God that man is created to bear and to obstruct the true person from emerging. The original picture is now a misaligned mess. No one fragment can stand alone as a complete representation of the girl. The enemy, who capitalizes on dissociation, not only brings "con-fusion," he also makes a mess and a mockery of the original image a person is intended to convey: the image of God. God is not a mess! God is in the business of restoring divine order and redeeming people so they may reflect his likeness and pursue their spiritual potential.

Spiritual gifts are inherent within a person, although few adults seem to have a grasp of their spiritual gifts, much less how those are to be used for the common good. The Bible explains that these gifts are uniquely distributed as the Holy Spirit determines (See 1 Corinthians 12:1-11), awaiting activation as one comes into a personal relationship with God. Spiritual gifts are supernaturally powerful and pose a tremendous threat to the enemy. Consequently, one bulls-eye that the devil takes direct aim at is the unique spiritual gift-mix intended for individuals. He also wants to impede the way these gifts are to be used to benefit others. As a ploy, Satan attacks in childhood in order to hinder, prevent, block, or otherwise intercept spiritual gifts from being discovered, developed, and used. If successful, he will keep a person separated from his spiritual potential and impede him from fully representing God's original image. It is difficult to function in the supernatural gifts of the Spirit if one is kept dormant spiritually, fragmented internally, and disconnected relationally.

But the enemy is not content to stop there. Satan wants to totally destroy a person at the core of his being. The devil will take advantage of any opportunity that brings harm to a person. This includes abuse, abandonment, rejection, trauma, the occult, generational inheritance, and abdication of the parental role, in particular that of the father. Once the way is opened, willful sin will eventually follow. Not only is the individual set on a path of destruction, but others associated with him may also become damaged and possibly destroyed as well. Left unchecked, a person's rightful connection with God, with self, and with others may never be realized.

The damage of dissociation: Bradley's story continues

To support his overall scheme of destruction, it is common to find that Satan somehow orchestrates a recognizable *theme* against a person. A destructive theme may be identified by repeated, characteristic patterns exercised in ways that bring harm. Both the scheme and theme will be directly linked to and reinforced by a demonic stronghold. These will be elaborated on in Chapter 6. Bradley's story, introduced at the beginning of this book, illustrates how the enemy's scheme of destruction, the theme of bullying, and the stronghold of anger worked together in a bid to conquer and destroy one particular individual.

Satan's scheme was activated against Bradley from the time he started school. The humiliation of being pinned beneath a six-year-old girl on the school playground, face rubbed in the dirt, was compounded by the laughter and ridicule of surrounding children. While he was being robbed of his dignity, the stress, fear, and shame of that degrading situation caused Bradley to dissociate within himself. A separate part of Bradley fragmented, envisioning himself to be a weakling, a pansy, a wimp, a loser. At the same time, he mentally and physically distanced himself from the other children who made fun of him. In this way, he could cope with having to see and interact with them on a daily basis. The subsequent lies he believed about himself began to slowly eat away at him like a cancer. These lies included, "I am too weak to resist," "There is no one to protect me," and "I am worthless." These lies cut him off from accepting the truth, thus creating a spiritual dilemma for Bradley.

From that incident forward, the enemy used a theme of bullying to slice away at Bradley, bringing ever-increasing emotional and physical pain to this sensitive child. Repeatedly the target of unexpected and undeserved attacks, it was as if he carried the scent of fear and shame that attracted aggressors. Even though he was being raised in a loving Christian home with caring parents, Bradley's dissociative system carefully guarded his fears and embarrassment. Ironically, he hid these best from those who could have helped him. Overwhelmed one day in ninth grade by the dread of going to school and being bullied, a desperate appeal to his parents alerted them to the suffering he had endured over many years. Although his parents intervened, the bullying continued.

By this time, repeated assaults ever widened the dissociative gap between Bradley's true person, who was a calm, God-focused "Likeable Bradley," and an explosive, self-focused alter, "Angry Bradley," who vehemently protected the wounded five-year-old part of Bradley that had sought refuge in the subconscious mind years before. This double-minded conflict tormented Bradley. Each act of bullying incited Angry Bradley to contemplate revenge, which in childhood was never carried out for fear of greater retaliation. Little by little as Bradley matured into young adulthood, Angry Bradley began asserting himself unpredictably and often at inappropriate times. This usually resulted in a discrediting of Bradley's character. Particularly hurtful to Likeable Bradley was the shame he felt when he realized that his behavior had somehow dishonored God or embarrassed someone he respected. This troublesome conduct was effectively separating him from others, causing relational dis-order in every direction.

Without realizing it, Bradley was being imprisoned in a stronghold of anger. Any expression of anger, which was incompatible with the belief system and ways of Likeable Bradley, kept him in unresolved tension. Whenever a situation arose that triggered Angry Bradley, especially if it had to do with bullying, the internal conflict Bradley went through became almost as terrifying as the initial experience of being bullied on the school playground. As he got older, he began to clash with others as pent up anger eventually started erupting. Anger slashed like a double-edged sword that not only kept Bradley divided within himself but also successfully cut Bradley off from others.

Bradley lived in a bewildering world of dissociation until he found his way to an inner healing session. Once exposed to the understanding of what dissociation is and how it affects people, he honestly exclaimed, "You mean I'm *not* crazy?" Bradley was then able to quickly differentiate between his true person, whom he referred to as Likeable Bradley, the wounded five-year-old part of himself, and the ferocious alter identified as Angry Bradley. To facilitate communication during the session, he would actually hop between two chairs to present himself as either God-focused, Likeable Bradley or self-focused, Angry Bradley. The distinction was so clear between the two that there were noticeable switches in demeanor, attitude, voice, and posture. This also became evident through his rapidly awakening self-awareness. Following a trail of several particularly painful memories, Bradley found himself back where the fear, shame, dissociation, and lies originated: with a little tomboy on his back, his face in the dirt, one arm painfully pinned behind him, and surrounded by mocking laughter.

As he recalled that terrible experience, Bradley was overcome by intense feelings of fear and shame. He began abreacting and was thrown into physical reenactments as though the experience on the playground was happening all over again. Bradley was asked to state aloud each lie linked to this memory, which verified the power they held over him. In the pause that followed a moment of prayer for Bradley, God revealed truth to him in a very personal way. All the lies Bradley had identified in the context of that memory were instantly dispelled. Wounded, five-year-old Bradley was able to forgive his offenders in the context of that memory and in each memory that was revisited up to the present time. Likeable

Bradley forgave Angry Bradley for causing him to appear a hypocrite and for the ways he had discredited him in front of others. An unfamiliar yet welcomed sense of peace and calm suddenly washed over Bradley. In a most supernatural instant, Bradley's dissociation was remarkably healed and fused. When asked where Angry Bradley was, he thoughtfully looked at the empty chair next to him. As a symbolic gesture, he knocked the chair over and reported that Angry Bradley was not there anymore. With a heartwarming grin, Bradley joyfully announced, "I feel complete!"

Double-mindedness appears as hypocrisy

A person who is double-minded, or double-souled, is often perceived as a hypocrite. Likeable Bradley was a sensitive, compassionate young man whom many admired and sought to emulate. On the other hand, Angry Bradley did not hesitate to offend others if it meant protecting himself from being humiliated. For fifteen of his twenty young years, Bradley's self-worth had been relentlessly battered. Every time a threatening person caused Angry Bradley to flare up, it only added to an already mountainous heap of shame. Angry Bradley had almost completely shut down Bradley's inherent gifts and was blighting any consistent representation of whom he believed he was to be. Feeling crippled by the inability to control his anger, Bradley would hide behind either a flimsy covering of justifying his outbursts or the safety of close friends "who understood."

As one indicator of double-mindedness, a hypocrite is unstable, saying one thing but doing another, claiming freedom but living in bondage, espousing victory but wallowing miserably in defeat. While hypocrisy is rampant, it seems to be spotlighted among people who claim to be Christians. Jesus himself denounced hypocrisy, especially among those who were religious leaders. It was his intent that those who followed him be whole and complete, of soundness and singleness of mind. The deception of hypocrisy is exposed by revealing what is at its roots: double-mindedness that relationally separates a person from being one with God, one with self, and one with others.

God heals dissociation

Bradley was frustrated by the conflict and confusion he often lived with, not realizing he was dissociated within himself. Before his own dissociation and double-mindedness were identified, Bradley did not consciously understand where his anger originated. Neither could he explain how Angry Bradley was able to "take over," effectively forcing his way to the forefront when the need arose to protect a younger, wounded part of Bradley from further pain. As soon as Bradley recognized his own double-mindedness, he was immediately able to distinguish Likeable Bradley from Angry Bradley. No one before had ever distinctly identified Angry Bradley, much less directly interacted with him by name. This caused him to feel both threatened and fearful. Once the dissociation and double-mindedness were revealed, the scheme, theme, and stronghold of the enemy were simultaneously exposed. All this information helped Bradley to walk through a tangible experience of inner healing that was life-changing and lasting.

From the beginning, the devil has capitalized on lies to deceive people, to distort the truth, and to alienate people from God. The initial deception began with the first man and woman, who lived free of shame and fear. They were strangers to failure, doubt, and despair. They walked with God in the garden he had made for them. They talked with him. The devil had lost all rights to such closeness with God through his own pride and rebellion against God. Perhaps jealous of what Adam and Eve had, he deliberately and aggressively set about to destroy intimacy and association between the Creator and his creation.

Seeking an opportune time, Satan seized the chance to sidle up to Eve near the forbidden tree. This allowed the serpent occasion to challenge the truth of God and deceive the woman into disobedience. Immediately this spilled over onto Adam. Using building blocks of shame and fear, the enemy crafted his first strongholds around man. Still today, it is with shame and fear that much of his fraudulent work continues to be built.

God responded to the failure of the first man and woman by doing a remarkable thing. As already noted, there were consequences to their disobedience, but God did not destroy them. He cursed the serpent, and he cursed the ground, but he clothed the man and the woman he had created in his image. It has always been God's purpose to "cover over our nakedness," to protect us, to provide for us, and to help us best reflect the original image for which we were created: to represent God so that others may believe on him and experience eternal life in heaven with their Creator.

Summary

1. Dissociation is a relational dis-order that separates a person within himself, from others, and from God. *Psychiatry* classifies dissociation as a mental disorder peculiar to an individual and does not take into account the spiritual implications of relational separation.

2. Deception is the #1 tool of the devil. His native language is lying. (John 8:44) Satan is no silent foe. He speaks deceptively to contradict, twist, challenge, or negate the

voice of the Lord. His goal in deceiving people is for them to disobey God.

3. Disobedience brings about the exchange of the natural for the unnatural and causes disorder, chaos, and confusion. While in the Garden of Eden, it was natural for Adam and Eve to converse with God. It was natural for them to be unashamed and unafraid. It was natural to be in God's presence and for him to walk among them. But as happened with Adam and Eve, once disobedience opens a doorway for Satan's influence, a person will begin acting unnaturally toward God, himself, and others.

4. Shame and fear are the first evidence of demonic influences found in the Bible. It is common still to discover shame and fear imbedded in people's fragmented minds. These two factors, along with others, keep people relationally separated from God, from themselves, and from others. Shame and fear dominate the power platform from which Satan operates to steal, kill, and destroy.

5. The enemy sabotages the innocent to replicate dissociation, both multiplying and compounding its effects. Adam and Eve, in their innocence, were targeted for destruction. However, Satan first had to isolate and sabotage Eve in order to capture them both. The ploy of sabotage is to act at an opportune time. The enemy is patient. The enemy is watchful. The enemy is cruel. At the right moment he will assault the innocent.

6. By exploiting a person's dissociative system, the enemy can attack, manipulate, influence, and subjugate parts and alters for unholy and unnatural purposes. Capitalizing on dissociation, the enemy may exercise a measure of control over an individual and, in so doing, cause damage to others.

7. Satan is not satisfied to strike a person once. As soon as he has his foot in the door, he orchestrates a theme against the individual, relentlessly playing on that to bring further separation within a person. Every blow is like a hammer to a wedge that splits wood. As the individual fragments, he also dissociates from others.

God is in the business of putting things back the way they were originally intended to be: whole and complete. He alone can ultimately renew the mind, restore the soul, and redeem the loss that accompanies relational separation because of dissociation. Psychiatry offers many answers that are time tested and scientifically proven. Many contemporary therapy, counseling, and self-help options abound that genuinely improve the quality of a person's life. Some measure of self-effort is often expected or required if a person is sincerely going to change. In the next chapter, you will better understand both the benefits and the limitations of these approaches in helping those with dissociation.

Chapter 3

Psychiatry and Self Effort are Not Enough

No Knot at the End of the Rope

"WHAT HAVE YOU DONE TO MY WIFE?" DEMANDED THE MAN ON THE OTHER END OF THE PHONE. Sensing the agitation in his voice, I braced myself and calmly asked what he meant by that question. His wife, an attractive woman in her mid-forties, had come for her first session the day before but with the reluctant consent of her husband. During our afternoon together, she had experienced several points of tremendous breakthrough and significant healing from traumatic events suffered throughout her childhood. I soon realized this man's irritation was displaced. He resentfully explained that for five years he had been paying for regular counseling for his wife but saw more change in her after one inner healing session than he had ever seen in all her years of therapy. I tried to help him understand that "I" had done nothing to his wife. In fact, it was God who had revealed truth to dispel lies she believed about herself and who had freed her from paralyzing shame and fear. While he seemed to have difficulty comprehending this concept, her undeniable and lasting transformation eventually turned him into an advocate of God's way of restoring order to his troubled wife. Subsequent, periodic sessions continued to help put this fragmented woman back the way she was originally intended to be: restored and whole.

Detecting dissociation

Everyone experiences some degree of dissociation in its mildest forms as brief occurrences of mental escape. These may include normal day dreaming, "zoning out," or momentarily losing track of time. On the opposite end of the spectrum, some people will be targeted victims of atrocities that result in extremely complex dissociation with extraordinarily intricate inner systems. But the majority of people will be familiar with common dissociation, which is the normal response of the mind to cope with unexpected pain and to survive acute distress. When faced with an overwhelmingly traumatic situation from which there is no physical escape, the person will mentally flee. The mind's ability to dissociate is an extremely effective defense against severe physical and emotional pain, or even the anxious anticipation of that pain. Because memories, thoughts, feelings, and perceptions of the traumatic event can be separated off, the person may function as though the trauma had not occurred. As dissociation becomes reinforced and conditioned, dissociative escape may become somewhat automatic if a trauma is repeated or there is even a threat of anxiety or harm.

There is no people group or level of society immune to dissociation. From the homeless to the wealthiest to the best educated and everywhere else across the social strata, people dissociate routinely to deal with stress and hurt. A person does not need to be diagnosed with a complex disorder to have experienced or to live in dissociation. To have common dissociation is not rare but more widespread than realized or accepted.

Common dissociation often has an accompanying system of alter identities that have formed to help protect the person from being re-traumatized. Distinctions between common and complex dissociation are further explained in the next chapter.

Even though dissociation is a prevalent condition, it is generally viewed by the psychiatric world as a rare disorder that is difficult to treat. Some will go so far as to say it is incurable. This is due in part to the belief that dissociation is atypical – for example, that Dissociative Identity Disorder (DID) may affect only 1% of the general population in the United States and only 5-20% of those in psychiatric hospitals. Dissociative disorders may be misdiagnosed or go undiagnosed as survivors flounder within the mental health system. Many people with a dissociative disorder have spent years in the mental health system prior to accurate diagnosis. Meanwhile, they may have gone from therapist to therapist, changed from one medication to another, and received treatment for symptoms but have made little or no actual progress. This is due, in part, because the breadth of symptoms that cause a dissociated person to seek treatment parallel those of so many psychiatric diagnoses. Dissociation may also go undetected because the average person, with common dissociation, may not be able to afford therapy. It is the "rare" cases that seem to catch the attention of the psychiatric world.

Psychiatry's contribution

It is generally agreed among therapists that the majority of individuals who develop dissociative disorders have experienced repetitive, overwhelming, and often life-threatening trauma at a sensitive developmental stage of childhood. In our culture, the most frequent causes of documented dissociative disorders are physical, sexual, and emotional abuse in childhood. But survivors of other kinds of acute trauma include those impacted by war, natural disasters, survivor guilt, divorce, invasive medical procedures, and torture. For example, ***Post Traumatic Stress Disorder*** (PTSD) is widely accepted as a major mental illness and is often closely related to diagnosis of dissociative disorders. PTSD is an anxiety disorder associated with serious traumatic events and characterized by such symptoms as reliving the trauma in dreams, numbness, lack of involvement with reality, or recurrent thoughts and images. Research suggests that among people with trauma disorders there are higher rates of suicide attempts, alcohol and drug addiction, chronic mental illness, and abusiveness in succeeding generations than among those with less complicated mental disorders.

In terms of understanding dissociation, the field of psychiatry has helped to differentiate the diversity of symptoms and experiences among the array of dissociative disorders. *The Diagnostic and Statistical Manual of Mental Disorders, Version IV* (***DSM-IV***), a publication of the American Psychiatric Association, is the handbook most used in diagnosing mental disorders in America and other countries. The DSM-IV, which may be found in a local library, includes a compilation of dissociative disorders. In this manual will also be found a perspective on dissociation as it relates culturally in other parts of the world. War-torn nations, societies ravaged by disease and death, and the impact of various shared factors of trauma contribute to widespread psychological and dissociative conditions that may be peculiar to certain cultures or nations.

What is the difference?

For many of us, the differences between a psychiatrist, a psychologist, and a psychoanalyst are unclear. We know they all work to help people deal with their lives, especially the mental and emotional aspects. We know that a psychiatrist often gets paid more! But the distinctions grow blurry beyond that. The word *psychology* is a combination of the Greek word *psycho* (meaning "mind") and *logy* (a Greek suffix meaning "the doctrine, theory, or science of something.") So, psychology could simply be called "the science of the mind." Psychologists have extensive training in therapy and psychological testing. Their focus tends to be on how a person's behavior either fits or is out of sync with conditions surrounding him. They then seek to find ways an individual can modify his behavior to better fit his surroundings. Psychiatry, by comparison, is a branch of medicine that studies and treats mental and emotional disorders. The word psychiatry is derived from two Greek words: *psuche*, (which means "soul") and *iatros* (which means "physician"). Thus, the word psychiatry means "soul-doctor." Psychiatrists not only have a strong background in psychology and counseling, they are required to hold a medical degree. Psychiatry generally attributes mental illness to organic or neurochemical causes that can be treated by individual therapy and medications for specific symptoms. The extensive medical training comes into play when diagnosing and treating individuals. *Psychoanalysis* is a method of counseling developed by Sigmund *Freud* who believed all behavior is influenced by unconscious wishes and fears. The counseling goal of psychoanalysis is to bring to the client's consciousness any repressed or subconscious feelings and conflicts from the past. This is accomplished through several techniques, including free association of thoughts and interpretation of dreams. A plan would then be devised to help the individual deal with his conflict or fear.

Therapy scenarios

To further understand the differences between these three fields of therapy, let us see how they might each approach the same client. In the previous chapter, I shared about Bradley, who, as an adult, had an increasing problem with anger. You will remember he had been humiliated on the playground as a child when a girl beat up on him. All three (a psychologist, a psychoanalyst, and a psychiatrist) would undoubtedly provide an atmosphere in counseling where Bradley would feel accepted and supported and be free to discuss his problems. All would seek to develop a level of trust.

A psychologist might spend a little time "in the past," listening to "stories from childhood," but would not necessarily link past events with present behavior. Instead, he would primarily focus on the anger issue because it would be the behavior causing the current social problems. Supportive measures might include education about Bradley's own anger and lifestyle adjustments such as social skills training, improved communication and coping skills, and group support. The psychologist might help pinpoint the "triggers" for Bradley's anger then draw up a plan to help Bradley either avoid those triggers or deal with them more responsibly. Progressive meetings would fine-tune the process to the point that fewer and fewer triggers would be apparent in Bradley's life, consequently reducing the frequency of angry outbursts. In addition, anger management meetings with others may be recommended. This "you are not alone" approach might yield advice Bradley could apply to his own situation, along with making Bradley feel more comfortable with his problem. If Bradley was still having problems with outbursts of anger, the psychologist might help Bradley realign his personal goals. Reasonable and acceptable behavior may be measured as "having fewer outbursts now" compared to "many outbursts in the past." But to expect no outbursts would be unrealistic.

A psychoanalyst, on the other hand, might spend nearly all his time in the past, looking for a link between the angry outbursts and events that happened in early childhood, especially with sexual overtones. He would then develop an intricate system of theories that would explain the present behavior. To help Bradley deal with the angry outbursts, the psychoanalyst might convince Bradley to transfer his anger to another person (for example, the analyst himself) or some inanimate object. The thought here is that if Bradley can act out enough of the anger through transference, his "well of anger" will run dry, and he will not have as many outbursts.

Lastly, the psychiatrist might employ a combination of both "then-and-now" focused counseling, but he would also be looking for any hint of a medical problem or chemical imbalance that may be causing or augmenting the angry episodes. He might determine, for example, that added stress at work seems to bring out more frequent outbursts. He may then prescribe a medication to help him deal with stress and encourage Bradley to change some behavior to reduce stress even further.

While this may be an oversimplified interpretation of the three fields of therapy, there is one major point to be made: at no time do any of these three forms of analysis consider that Bradley's anger might be rooted in the spiritual dilemma of being both relationally separated from God and antagonized by the devil. It might be uncommon for any of the three fields to make the connection between the playground incident of early childhood and the present-day anger. If they did, they would be reluctant to diagnose and treat it as dissociation. If they were to diagnose Bradley as dissociated because of the trauma of that event, it is unlikely that their approach to treating him would take into account the spiritual implications of dissociation. None of them would attribute dissociation as operating in the three, interrelated ways explained in Chapter 2: separation within oneself, from others, and from God. In fact, Freud, the founder of psychoanalysis, was an atheist who had abandoned not only his Judaic heritage but all religious beliefs. Because he did not believe in God, he would have had no reason to bring a "nonexistent God" into the psychoanalysis treatment plan. In the fields of psychology and psychiatry, you might find professionals who have deep personal religious beliefs, but their counseling methods rarely differ from those of their non-religious colleagues.

Seeking help

Individuals with dissociation may seek out therapy or counseling, not knowing their condition but because depression, mood swings, memory loss, confusion, or addictions compel them to look for help. Since psychiatrists generally do not anticipate dissociation or understand it as a three-way relational dis-order, it goes undiagnosed and therefore untreated, or mistreated, as the case may be. One psychologist I consulted has worked for years with sexual abuse survivors. To my surprise, he reported never having diagnosed dissociation among them. My experience suggests that every person who has been abused – particularly if linked to the psychiatrically recognized consequences of physical, sexual, or emotional abuse – will have some level of dissociation and likely have a corresponding alter system to aid survival. I would go so far as to say that anyone who has endured extreme trauma will have dissociation with alter identities to help them cope. For example, I have yet to work with a survivor of divorce, whether a child or an adult, who does not exhibit some level of dissociation caused by the trauma of that relational separation.

It is not unusual for me to work with people who have also seen or who are currently seeing a therapist. I first met Anita immediately after a seminar workshop I had conducted on dissociation and inner healing from a spiritual perspective. I had noticed this woman, who had isolated herself from the rest of the audience, constantly nodding her head in agreement throughout the presentation. I consented to meet with her that afternoon, along with a female friend who also had done a presentation that morning. Anita, a well educated intellectual in her forties, explained that she had been in therapy for nearly twenty-five years and had come to the seminar out of desperation and waning hope. Disclosing that she had been clinically diagnosed with dissociation, I did not hesitate to venture tapping into her dissociative system. Anita fully cooperated, as did several alters we met, and within a couple of hours we had gleaned much helpful information while applying principles from the seminar she had attended. We agreed to work with her further, as she perceived we had a valid contribution to make toward her quest for wholeness.

With appropriate treatment, most people with dissociation greatly improve their level of functioning and personal comfort. But "greatly improved" is not genuinely healed. Better is not best. I am grateful for psychiatric research and information that is available to bring understanding to the realities of mental illnesses and disorders. I endorse working cooperatively as needed with professionals to facilitate a person's healing and restoration. Support groups are often a necessary and important component of a person's recovery. However, it is my premise that because dissociation is fundamentally a relational dis-order with spiritual implications, remedies are limited if offered only by counseling or medical professionals. Only supernatural intervention will ultimately bring authentic restoration of a dissociated person to wholeness in mind, body, soul, and spirit. Psychiatry does not consider God to be a solution. I cannot fathom a solution apart from God.

Anita was open to spiritual applications of healing, something she had not previously experienced under conventional methods of therapy. No one before had initiated this level of interaction with her dissociation, which proved to be a key to her rapid progress. She continued with her prior regimen of weekly counseling and arranged with us a monthly, half day session of inner healing. We were able to help her integrate into a supportive and nurturing church environment. Within six months, Anita had made remarkable strides, which she claimed had never been possible before. This was attributed to the added treatment of her dissociation from a spiritual perspective, along with both ongoing counseling and newfound support. While there were many evident changes, one of the most visibly noticeable was in her personal care. When we met Anita, she was disheveled and had become accustomed to hiding herself inside dreary, oversized clothing. Before long, her wardrobe had been completely exchanged, and for the first time in years she resumed wearing smart outfits, jewelry, and makeup, as well as caring for her hair. Her outward transformation mirrored the inner change and healing she had longed for. As well, her level of functional social interaction improved markedly, particularly in groups. Anita's motivation to change, combined with the cooperative strengths of counseling, support, and spiritual intervention, all contributed toward her healing journey.

Alter polarity

Every alter is encapsulated with characteristics that make up its unique identity and purpose. Within a person's dissociative system a fascinating array of "personalities" can be found, some with conflicting functions. Monty's traumatic childhood was typified by repeated emotional and sexual abuse. From the first session of inner healing, a range of common dissociation had been mapped. Around fifteen distinct wounded parts and polarized alter identities had been identified within the man. After several sessions of inner healing, Monty disclosed that he was simultaneously meeting with a psychiatrist in another city and had been doing so regularly for several years. This whole time, the psychiatrist had only interacted with a severely depressed alter identity who spent most of the hour in his office curled up in a fetal position, virtually incapable of normal function or response. For years, this alter had successfully prevented the psychiatrist from getting to a deeply wounded part of the man traumatized by abuse. The psychiatrist, not recognizing dissociation in the man, prescribed ever-increasing doses of a potent anti-depressant.

Meanwhile, Monty had made a recent visit to the family doctor. His physician was alarmed to discover the high dosage of medication he was taking. The doctor, who happened to also be a fellow club member, only saw Monty as a well-presented, happy man who appeared to have absolutely no reason to be on an anti-depressant, much less one so strong. Our team had interacted with both the fetal position, non-functioning side of Monty, only seen by the psychiatrist, and the confident, active club member known to the physician. Additionally, we were aware of other dissociated parts and alters neither of these professionals knew about or were likely to encounter. I use this example to further illustrate how dissociated parts and alters within a person can operate so distinctly that what impacts one of these dissociated entities physically or mentally, even spiritually, may not even register with another *entity*. It also punctuates my astonishment when I learn that professionals are not suspecting dissociation in patients, therefore it is not being diagnosed, dialogued with, or treated.

It is fascinating how the anti-depressant influenced the man. One of the side effects of the medication was drowsiness. The medication had only been prescribed for the man's severely depressed alter, and it only appeared to work on behalf of that alter. As evidence, when the depressed alter was accessed, Monty exhibited symptoms expected of the medication. He immediately appeared drowsy, and his speech slowed to the point of slurring. Moments later, when a different alter was presenting, he immediately became alert and articulate. His eyes brightened. This other alter showed no effects of either depression or the influence of the medication. In fact, this buoyant alter had no conscious knowledge that another alter existed who was on an anti-depressant.

In the process of dialoguing with Monty's dissociation, he came into self-awareness of the coexistence of not only these two alters but also of other dissociative entities. With God's help, Monty came to a place of restoration that dispelled lies, pain, and fears. He was also redeemed to a level of wholeness and well-being no amount of therapy or medication had previously been able to achieve. To the bewilderment of the psychiatrist and despite his protests, Monty ceased seeing him and gradually came off the anti-depressant under the guidance of his physician. To my knowledge, Monty told neither the psychiatrist nor the physician about his dissociation, which had been identified, mapped, and ministered to with measurable success. Regrettably, they remain ignorant of information and answers that would benefit both in their respective practices, as well as those they seek to help. If dissociation is either not diagnosed or misdiagnosed, or if only one entity within a person is known and treated, healing and restoration will be severely restricted.

In another example of alter polarity, Dana was conflicted over rejection issues rooted in her childhood but magnified by a recent divorce. The stress of the divorce triggered her dissociation in a variety of ways. One expression was a relapse to alcohol usage by an adolescent alter, who had all but ceased to function. This alter not only resumed drinking but also returned to smoking cigarettes as before. It seemed impossible, but another of Dana's alters was allergic to cigarette smoke. The two coexisting alters were operating entirely independent of one another. Furthermore, the dissociation barriers were so well established, the one did not know the other existed until Dana's astonishing self-discovery in a session where she pointed it out to them both.

Dissociated identities within a person are separate from each other. Some may work cooperatively, but generally they function autonomously. Various alters within a person are so distinct they may be transgender. It is usually quite a surprise for a man to find out he has a female alter, or vice versa. Dana came to herself in one session realizing she had been referring to herself (i.e. an alter) in masculine terms. Alters may be multi-cultural. One man, sodomized in a gang rape, assumed an ethnic alter because "this doesn't happen to white people." Monty and Dana are both examples of biochemical extremes among alters. Alters may be alcoholic or have a drug addiction not shared by the rest of the body and change body chemistry in severe ways.

One way to recognize alter activity is handwriting. Nathan showed up to a session one day bringing with him a journal he had kept for several years. He excitedly flipped through its pages to show us the four strikingly dissimilar styles of writing he had discovered. Each style he could attribute to a different alter. Carol, whom you'll meet in Chapter 5, had two different alters who shopped. It was easy to see which alter had made which purchases based on the handwriting in the check register. Cindy signed her third grade son out of school one day thirty minutes early for an appointment. Two hours later she arrived again to sign him out of after-school care, which she occasionally used. Distressed that her son was not there, Cindy had no recollection of having picked him up earlier in the afternoon and never returning him to the school. A secretary, perplexed that she did not remember this, later compared the two sign-out clipboards and was confused to find Cindy's signature appearing in two distinct cursives. Chapter 4 gives other examples of alter polarity.

Skeptics and other viewpoints

Many therapists and investigators are skeptical that there could be widespread occurrences of dissociation, claiming that it is extremely rare, if not non-existent in North America. Some professionals hold to the belief that multiplicity (the presence of alter identities) in dissociation does not exist unless it is fabricated by the therapist. While there may be recognition of the suffering of those diagnosed with Dissociative Identity Disorder, they are regarded simply as victims of misguided therapy. This may be linked at times to **False Memory Syndrome** that occurs through suggestive therapy techniques.

Some raise eyebrows at the beliefs of both Roman Catholics and Protestant Christians who claim that symptoms of dissociation are created by multiple, indwelling demons or "unclean spirits" as mentioned in the New Testament of the Bible. Those who subscribe to this belief deem that the appropriate method of treatment is to exorcise (expel) the demons in order to cure the dissociation. This is a faulty spiritual perspective because dissociated entities within a person are *not* demons and therefore cannot be cast out. Although demons might indeed be influencing the individual, they are not the source of the dissociation, and their absence does not mean the dissociation leaves with them. (See Chapter 4)

A few individuals believe that dissociation is a natural occurrence neither related to childhood abuse nor created by therapists. The presence of alter identities is viewed as a gift. Those who hold this position are empowered by their dissociation and consider it normal. This is also explored more in the next chapter.

Self effort's popularity

Go to any bookstore, and you will be amazed at the overabundance of books in the self-help section. There is a plethora of "how to's" on every kind of topic imaginable. By and large, the theme of a self-help book is to identify a problem and then explain how, with self-effort, you can overcome and live a better quality life. A book may be full of sound research, proven methods, and step-by-step recommendations to becoming a newer, healthier, smarter, faster, wiser, slimmer person who, with a little effort, will change remarkably. How is this possible? The common denominator in all self-help books is one little word: self. Admittedly, I have read a variety of self-help books and have attended a number of self-help seminars, applied their principles, and have found many of them helpful. What I have *not* always found their advice to be is sustainable, because self-effort and self-control cannot be prolonged indefinitely. This has been repeatedly confirmed to me by those struggling with dissociation. One side of a person may earnestly subscribe to a particular self-help goal. Another side? Forget it!

Research bears out that motivation and support exponentially increase the ability to overcome certain behaviors and addictions. Success increases with accountability. As humans, we were designed by God to function optimally in community and relationship. In a culture that prides itself on independence and individualism, interdependence is almost frowned upon. Even among writers of religious "how to" books, self-effort apart from the help of others is encouraged. One self-help book I thumbed through in the religion section of a bookstore even touted a chapter called "Self Control to the Rescue!" While that sounds noble, even Biblical, when a person is fractured by dissociation, one entity may embrace change; another may resist. It is hard for a person to find self-help success if not "every self" on the inside is in agreement or willing to participate. It is one matter to determine to change; it is quite another to follow through if the only person you have to depend on for success is yourself, and there is internal conflict or disagreement about the goals. Self-effort implies that all change is up to me; if any good happens, it is because I do it. Self-effort ignores connection with God or others and keeps a person relationally separated from those who might otherwise aid him.

Pop psychology and many talk shows have ignited a "tell it like it is," get-real approach to overcoming problems and issues. This has brought every kind of person and predicament imaginable into our daily lives through television, radio, magazines, internet, and other media, making them hot topics of debate and discussion. There is appeal in audience identification, causing people to tingle with anticipation that they, too, might be helped as are those being interviewed or spot-lighted. This help may include many valid suggestions that truly make a difference when applied, such as the importance of support in reaching goals. However, much advice relies entirely upon the ability of the individual to muster sufficient fortitude to conquer his highest personal mountain on his own. Occasionally there is emphasis on identifying and getting to the source of a person's problem rather than focusing solely on symptoms. However, popular self-help approaches lack the resources to assist a person to identify lie-based thinking, sin issues, or dissociation, much less ways to resolve them. These approaches abound in self-talk techniques that may include acknowledging deceptive thinking in order to break its power and consciously disengaging from internal voices that clash with positive affirmations or compete with personal endorsements of well-being. Other self-help strategies include ways to positively direct energy that was previously expended negatively. Different ways of "reprogramming" one's mind and lifestyle are all self-persuading steps toward triumph.

It is the rare individual who can actually get himself to the top of his own mountain and plant a victory flag there. I have never heard of an expedition-of-one to the top of Mount Everest. I am not suggesting that self-effort is wrong or bad. There needs to be some measure of personal commitment and self expenditure to move forward. But unless an individual seeking healing is responsibly connected with others, the degree of success may be arguable. So for many, their trekking comrades become doctors, therapists, medications, self-help resources, and talk show hosts. The common thread in the majority of these options is that they do not consider God to be the ultimate answer to restoration, peace, and wholeness.

The knot at the end of the rope

Sigmund Freud, by his own admission, called himself a "completely godless Jew" and a "hopeless pagan." Another psychoanalyst, Carl Jung, said of Freud, "He has devoted his life and his strength to the construction of a psychology which is a formulation of his own being." In his study of pagan and other religions, Freud discovered that demonology and evil spirits were frequently blamed for abnormal behavior. He sought to dismiss such notions as primitive and unsophisticated figments of men's imaginations. Freud's writings are often mocking, critical, and arrogant in condemning religious beliefs of any kind. In his book, *Totem and Taboo*, he says, "We have succeeded, as it were, in getting behind the demons, for we have explained them as projections of hostile feelings harbored by the survivors against the dead ... it would be another matter if demons really existed. But we know that, like gods, they are creations of the human mind." Because of Freud's influence in shaping modern psychiatry, there is no consideration that sin could be a cause of a person's emotional problems and psychosomatic illnesses. Neither is thought given to the possibility of Satanic oppression as a reason for abnormal behaviors, physical maladies, emotional disorders, or mental illnesses. This is because no school of psychiatry accepts Biblical truths or spiritual realities as being true or having any validity.

Disparity exists in the thought that Christians are to deal with spiritual matters, and psychiatrists are to handle emotional issues, thus seeking to separate the spirit from the soul. Christians subscribe to the belief that the Bible is the authoritative text written by the Creator of man's soul. Psychiatry, largely influenced by Freud, has defined "soul" in its own terms, with corresponding therapies that exclude God, the Creator, and reject spiritual solutions. Freud, if he were alive today, might find it a curious anomaly to think there are even those who claim to be "Christian psychiatrists."

The main issue in therapy is not how much has happened to a victim, but how he will deal with trauma. The two primary options will be to address his trauma either in a way that includes God or in a way that excludes God. Man's way to deal with dissociation is found in psychiatry, medicine, support groups, and self-effort, which all lead to a more tolerable existence. These reinforce dissociation because they only help a person cope.

God's way to heal dissociation is personal, spiritual, and supernatural, which leads to true healing, renewal of the mind, peace, and wholeness. He restores the soul, drawing a person back together through right relational connections within himself and with others. As the true person emerges, God redeems the losses incurred because of dissociation.

People need counseling. God knew this, so he has provided us with supernatural counselors. The Psalmists David and Asaph acknowledged God's guidance and counsel in places like Psalm 16:7 and 73:24. Foreshadowing the birth of Christ, the prophet Isaiah revealed that "he (Jesus) will be called Wonderful Counselor … Prince of Peace." (Isaiah 9:6) On numerous occasions, Jesus referred to the indwelling Holy Spirit of God as the Counselor. (John 14:16, 26; 15:26; 16:7) God has also provided insights and knowledge to understand the mind and the body. In cooperation with him, various tools may be applied through human counselors to heal fragmented and broken lives. The knot at the end of the inner healing rope is trust in God for authentic healing.

Spiritual matters require spiritual intervention

The spiritual side of a person is very real. There are even scientists and psychiatrists who would agree that humans are incurably religious and increasingly seeking answers that have some kind of spiritual source. Most people do not object to looking at the spiritual side of life unless it conflicts with their view of what is spiritual. Many people are uncomfortable with both the mystery of God and the mess they find themselves in. Both may be avoided by subscribing to programs and therapies that provide a defined structure, attainable goals, and hope of finding evidence of change. When it comes to treating disorders that affect the mind, therapy options abound, but there are no quick fixes. Treatment is often done by accessing the conscious mind and seeking to "reprogram" patterns, habits, behaviors, and attitudes in order to improve the situation and, if possible, to bring these under control with the appearance of having ended. Other remedies are to medicate people or hospitalize them. Regrettably, the existing myriad of sophisticated styles of therapy and self-effort techniques will fall short if the real problems are not dealt with: the underlying hurts, lies, and fears tightly held by a stalled part of the true person and the relational dis-order that results.

Many individuals with dissociation struggle with anger toward God for allowing their abuse or trauma. Many feel relationally alienated from God, believing that he could never accept them. During inner healing, a qualified and experienced *facilitator* can enable people with dissociation to work through their spiritual issues in a safe, non-judgmental environment. This allows them to openly discuss the many questions they have of God such as, "How could he let this happen to me?" Individuals will also be helped to face issues of fear, shame, and distrust and to restore belief in their acceptance by God.

Components of spiritual intervention may include:

1. Acknowledging God as the ultimate counselor.

2. Cooperating with the leading of the Holy Spirit as he guides the course of inner healing.

3. Getting out of the way of what God wants to do to bring inner healing in the manner of his choosing.

4. Accepting the truth God reveals at the experiential memory level to dispel lies and heal dissociation.

5. Utilizing prayer as a powerful, two-way communication tool that connects a person with God.

6. Forgiving those responsible for offense and pain.

7. Being restored in right relationship with God and others.

Summary

Modern neuroscience is a fascinating discipline that has made great progress in helping us understand how the mind works. In seeking resolution to man's inner woundedness, the science of psychiatry has been helpful by developing terminology and definitions. Yet despite all the empirical research and information, it has provided few viable answers that help people reconcile deep pain or overcome dissociation. Psychiatric and medical professions offer little or no hope of recovery for people diagnosed as dissociated. At best, their remedies help people compensate for and cope with dissociation. This includes prescribing medications to treat chemically the seemingly growing range of dissociative-based disorders. Popular self-effort resources offer many viable and valid programs for self-improvement. Support groups are another form of available help. With appropriate treatment, self-effort, and support, people with dissociation may enhance their level of functioning and personal comfort. But "greatly improved" is short of God's best. That is because solutions are sought apart from relational connection with God from whom truth and healing come.

The reason the psychiatric and self-help models have no genuine cure for dissociation is because they cannot remove dissociation. Only God can genuinely eliminate emotional problems and heal the dis-order of relational separation. The tendency is to rely upon professionals as if they have some secret method that can bypass God's wisdom. This may give a false hope that, in the end, does not deal with a person's lie-based thinking, relational separation, spiritual dilemma, or dissociative system. Psychiatry views any potential for healing dissociation as long and complicated, with different outcomes for different people. By trusting God, healing is possible and can be accelerated by divine intervention and supernaturally inspired solutions.

Trading Faces

Part Two
Helpful Information

Trading Faces

Chapter 4

Degrees of Dissociation

Mild to Wild – and Places In Between

IT WAS NORMAN WHO DISCOVERED HIS MOTHER DEAD ON THE FLOOR OF THE BARN. With dinner cooking on the stove, Norman's dad had sent him down to the barn to see what was taking his momma so long to collect the eggs. No one had heard the gunshot from the house. In stunned disbelief, Norman's eight-year-old mind desperately wanted her to be alive. His only prior experience with death had been earlier that year when he found a bunny that had been shot. Now his momma, like the bunny, had gone away and was not coming back. "I'm so scared," whispered eight-year-old Norman. "What am I going to do? I don't think daddy is going to take care of us."

As you continue reading through TRADING FACES, many more examples will be given of circumstances that brought fear, shame, and pain to people. These illustrations, based on actual cases, will expose you to details about the trauma and abuse of others. They are also shared to demonstrate there is hope for healing, wholeness, and peace. If you feel uneasy about or become triggered by a particular account, it may be

Dissociation: A Common Solution to Avoiding Life's Pain   **65** advisable to bypass that one for the time being. It may also be helpful for you to process those feelings in the company of someone you consider safe and trustworthy. The following prayer is offered to help prepare you for stories to which you may personally relate.

Prayer Pause

"God, as I read about people who have been hurt to the point of dissociating, I invite you to be near to me. Should I personally identify with any stories, examples, or information, help me to understand my own feelings and not be afraid. Give me courage to look inside myself. Give me strength to forgive. Give me hope that will lead to my own healing. Reveal your truth to dispel lies I may hold. Restore my soul, I pray. Amen."

The dissociation spectrum

Dissociation comes from the Latin prefix *dis* meaning "not; absence of or opposite of; deprive of," and *socire* meaning "to unite" – from *socius* "companion." In other words, it means not to be united, to be absent of companionship, to deprive oneself of association. Dissociation separates people relationally, depriving them of personal unity and distancing them from right relationship with others, including God.

Dissociation exists on a spectrum of severity that reflects a wide range of experiences, symptoms, and presentations. At one end are the mildest of dissociative experiences that are familiar to most people. These include "highway hypnosis," "zoning out" during a dull sermon, or "getting lost" in a book or movie. All of these are momentary mental breaks that involve briefly losing touch with conscious awareness of one's immediate surroundings. Close to this mildest end of the continuum may be found those who live in some degree of common dissociation, caused by the normal response of the mind to cope with unexpected trauma and to aid survival. Those with common dissociation may function with a few or up to several dozen wounded parts and alters in their system. To family, friends, and others with whom they daily interact, they may appear quite ordinary. At the other end of the spectrum is extremely complex, chronic dissociation that results in serious impairment or impedes the ability to function normally. Those who are on this extreme end exist in a highly intricate world of complicated dissociation with literally hundreds or thousands of alters in their system.

I have had people argue that they could not possibly be dissociated because they had a stable upbringing and were never abused. But not all dissociation comes from abuse. Ryan recalled a frightening experience that happened one summer at the public pool. He had plunged merrily into the water off the slide, but the next child did not wait for Ryan to surface before taking his turn. As Ryan was about to break through for air, the next child hit the water, his spread legs catching Ryan at the neck and shoving him back to the bottom of the pool. With his breath nearly expired, the force of impact, the inability to pull away from the other child's legs, and the fear that he was drowning instantly caused Ryan to dissociate. In fact, he held no conscious memory of what happened after that. His wounded part that held the rest of the memory data believed the lie, "If I get in deep water again I will die," and thereafter refused to return to a pool. Later in life, this translated into a disproportionate fear of taking any kind of risk.

After sharing a similar illustration, a ministry *recipient* protested that such an example was too light, fluffy, and not possibly representative of "real" dissociation. She then proceeded to report her perception of what *real* trauma was and relayed story after story of horrifying abuses she had personally suffered that contributed to her clinical diagnosis of Dissociative Identity Disorder. The nature of trauma that comes upon a person is irrelevant, whether being chased by a Chihuahua results in fear of all dogs, or being raped as a preschooler initiates a protective alter system. To the person who was traumatized, the experience is real, and it is huge. No matter how insignificant, even laughable, it may seem to another, if the trauma results in dissociation, a person will live conflicted until the memory is confronted, lies are dispelled, and fears are vanquished. Until that time, wounded parts and alters may be either working quietly in the background or actively presenting to avoid re-traumatization.

Examples of alter polarity given in Chapter 3 hinted at the spectrum of dissociation represented by what would seem to be impossible opposites and extremes. Two instances of biochemical dissociation were observed in Monty and Dana. Monty only had one part that was influenced by the antidepressant he was taking. Dana was allergic to cigarette smoke, yet there was an alter who smoked as a solution to relieving her pain. Alters can be transgender, even multi-cultural. The latter circumstances may occur if the nature of trauma or abuse is seen to the child as "I would not have been treated this way if I were a boy/girl" or "If my skin were a different color this would not have happened to me."

Polarity within a person's dissociative system can be detected in many other ways, whether expressed by a wounded part of the person or by an alter identity. A sudden switch in personality may betray dissociation, observed as noticeable changes in facial expression, speech, posture, mannerism, and behavior. Unique handwriting styles have already been mentioned. An individual's parts and alters may have different voices and accents. Some can be left-handed, others can be right-handed. One likes her hair one way, the other another way. Dietary preferences and eating habits may vary. One may be stalled as a single, even though the person is married. Conflict may occur because a gay alter is present within the system of a straight person. Unbelieving parts and alters may clash with the true person who is a professing Christian. One likes wearing baseball caps. Another hates wearing caps. The true person needs glasses. A younger part does not. Internal age discrepancies can cause turmoil as was the case with a mother of three young children. She wrestled with an angry, fourteen-year-old alter who was sick and tired of having to "baby-sit" those perceived by her as three little "siblings."

Most alter identities are characterized as human, although some will have a different representation. One woman's alter system was a menagerie that corresponded to the personalities of her various alters: a tiger, an eagle, a chimpanzee, a snake, a goat, a skunk, a rat, a shark, and others. One man portrayed a kennel full of alters with an English Sheepdog, Great Dane, Doberman Pinscher, Pekingese, Beagle, Corgi, and a Dachshund, each with unique characteristics and duties. Another person expressed her alter system as an ocean liner with identities including the captain, crew, guests, and stowaways. An individual's dissociation may be conveyed as plants, rocks, or any variety of things. As a person comes into self-awareness and *co-consciousness* of his dissociation, he will expose his system in his own terms. Ministry facilitators must never suggest to or superimpose upon a recipient their interpretation of his dissociation. Although dissociation is far more common than most people realize, the diversity of personal expression and exhibition will be as unique as the individual.

Common dissociation

Common dissociation is a typical reaction to unexpected trauma. The intensity of the trauma contributes to the mind's inclination to dissociate in order to cope with the accompanying pain and to help the person survive. Common dissociation will occur spontaneously in a trauma situation, causing certain information to be separated to a different part of the mind. This is why, for example, a person may exhibit no feeling associated with recalling a trauma memory. Even though the experience may have been accompanied with intense emotion, that component of the ordeal may be relegated elsewhere in the subconscious. In other cases, memory data of an event may appear to be absent. Ryan's last recollection was being forced to the bottom of the pool. A protective *amnesia* wall went up around the event to keep his mind from going there again.

Trauma comes in many forms and is not limited to abusive circumstances. A tragic accident, divorce, death, and abandonment may all intensify stress to the point of dissociation. The level of dissociation may correspond to the level of loss sustained – whether that is loss of innocence, physical or mental functioning, or a significant relationship. No two people are going to respond to trauma in the same way. However, as the severity of trauma increases, so do the likelihood of dissociation and a compensating alter system.

Norman's story continues

With vivid memory recall, eight-year-old Norman stood motionless over his momma's dead body. Unfamiliar thoughts invaded his mind. Too scared even to cry, a gateway to his emotions became blocked by companion lies: "Crying is bad," and "It's not okay to cry." The thought that "I'm going to be good from now on" flashed through his head. He suddenly remembered his dad and two younger siblings back at the farmhouse. "I don't want Rhonda and Donny to be afraid." Looking away from her face, Norman concluded, "Momma doesn't love me or she would have stayed." Although he ran back to the house, the path never seemed so long as a new framework for life was being subliminally erected. "I don't need anyone to take care of me." As he gripped the handle of the screen door, he said to himself, "No more being a kid."

As details of the memory burst forth, Adult Norman was rapidly coming into co-conscious awareness of his dissociation. He shared a surprising, personal revelation: "When I stepped back into the house through the kitchen door, I was not the same person who had approached the door from the outside." With no show of emotion, Norman calmly told his dad why momma had not come back to the house with him. Then he walked to the stove to do his best to finish the meal and begin taking care of his little sister and brother. Eight-year-old Norman remained outside. Childhood was over.

Most professionals will agree that dissociation is typically rooted in early childhood and often the outcome of severe physical, sexual, or emotional abuse. In Norman's case, it was created by the overwhelming distress of discovering the lifeless body of his momma lying in a pool of blood. Regardless of the source, if the nature of the trauma causes dissociation, this characteristic response of the brain will help a person get through the suffering they are experiencing. For Norman, his eight-year-old self collected what data he could, along with lies he believed, and retreated for the safety of his subconscious mind. The creation of an alter identity in conjunction with a trauma is also a usual occurrence. Because Norman believed he could no longer be a child, a protecting alter would not only thereafter look after Norman but also his sister and brother. The next morning, this alter was up early to prepare breakfast and, a few days later, remained with his siblings in the care of others during the funeral. Norman never got to tell his momma goodbye.

The true person has always been and will always be "one." Dissociation creates alternative images of the true person, molded to disguise pain and mask lie-based thinking. As the dissociation is developed and reinforced, without realizing it, an individual puts increasing trust in these false images of his true person. This only distances him from those who might otherwise be able to help, including God. Eventually, it may be these created likenesses that are most commonly interacting with others and most frequently operating to keep the person going. The true person may not be consciously aware of this or realize he is being overshadowed by the working of his dissociative system. Until or unless there is co-consciousness, an alter who is not in contact with other alters may adamantly believe he is "the only one there."

The innocent child who found momma dead stalled that day along with several lies, including, "Momma doesn't love me or she would have stayed." Alternate, false images of Norman grew up as others developed a relationship with the person they perceived him to be – a basically good kid who helped others. As a teenager, Norman got involved in church and decided to become a Christian. However, life did not noticeably change or improve because of that decision. In fact, pent up anger began leaking out, and Norman's reputation changed to match that of a violent young man who smoked, drank, and got into fights. At thirty-five, Norman experienced a rekindled desire to go to church. He began reading his Bible. It was during this period that he decided to go for the first time to the place where his momma had been buried. Not realizing it at the time, it was eight-year-old Norman who openly mourned at the graveside, crying for the first time in twenty-seven years since finding his momma's body in the barn. This episode added to a number of life-changing events around that period in his life that compelled him to pursue God all the more.

As degrees of dissociation increase, more energy and brain activity is required to manage and maintain the system. It is suspected that dissociation starts to break down as a person moves into his late thirties or into his forties. The mind gets tired and the ability to "hold it all together" diminishes. While I have worked with people of all ages, the majority have been in their forties. It is in this decade of life that people are also experiencing physical and other changes. They may become aware of personal inconsistencies and internal conflicts for which they find no logical explanation. For some, the reason may be attributed to dissociation. Another sixteen years passed before Norman sought inner healing. He came seeking insight into conflicted feelings of hypocrisy and suppressed violence. Little did he expect to end up not only in the single most horrific memory of his life but also to encounter an eight-year-old part of himself who was still stuck there.

There are a number of ways to help facilitate self-awareness and restoration, many which will be illustrated and explained throughout this book. It is essential for a person to get to the place of pain and, in that memory, to allow the wounded part that is there to receive healing. It is important to identify specifically and to state lies held by that part. Forgiveness is often a powerful factor in the healing process. When Norman understood that his present-day conflicts might be echoes of past experiences, he was willing to explore what could be at their root. The alter system built around protecting eight-year-old Norman cooperated with the ministry facilitators and agreed not to interfere. Timid at first, eight-year-old Norman began telling his story, unwittingly stating lies:

"Crying is bad."

"Momma doesn't love me or she would have stayed."

"I don't need anyone to take care of me."

Although each of these lies registered very strong with eight-year-old Norman, the most potent and painful one was his belief that momma did not love him or she would have stayed. Eight-year-old Norman was invited to forgive his momma. In the terror of that memory, he forgave momma for abandoning him. He started weeping. Along with the trickle of tears, other expressions of forgiveness came seeping out – toward his momma, his dad, even himself. Many things that had not been fully dealt with at her gravesite came gushing out, along with a flood of tears and deep sobs. As the statements subsided and his tears eventually stopped, eight-year-old Norman became still. In the quiet, I asked him if I might pray for him. He nodded his head. "Jesus, Little Norman believes that his momma doesn't love him or she would have stayed. Is there something about this you would like for Little Norman to understand?" We waited together in silence.

Suddenly, as though a light went on in a very dark place, eight-year-old Norman's countenance brightened. He excitedly blurted out, "Momma loves me!" He went on to explain that momma felt all alone. She had to be very sad to go away, but this was as long as she could hold on. He realized for the first time that he could not have helped her. "What can I do? I am just a kid. No one else she knew could help either." I tested the strength of the other lies. "Is it okay to cry?" With cheeks still wet, Little Norman grinned and said, "Yes, it is okay to cry!" "Do you need anyone to take care of you?" Little Norman paused for a few moments and then thoughtfully replied, "Jesus will take care of me."

How is it that Little Norman came by these remarkable insights? As ministry facilitators, we had applied components of spiritual intervention mentioned in the previous chapter. Because Norman's eight-year-old wounded part was made to feel safe, he became receptive to God's counsel. We cooperated with the leading of the Holy Spirit. In this case, we simply listened to his story, with ears alert to possible lie-based statements. We were directed to guide Little Norman in expressions of forgiveness, which he did. Now that Little Norman was engaged in the process, we prayed and quietly waited on the Lord to bring inner healing however he might choose. This childlike part of Norman was positioned to accept truth directly from God while experientially back in the context of the memory. He suddenly had an "Ah ha!" moment and spontaneously began sharing what he was sensing. We explored his reaction to the lies he had previously embraced. Each one had been firmly dispelled but not by any suggestion on our part. All of Norman was firmly persuaded that the Lord would take care of him. Any feelings of abandonment vanished.

Typically, a person will be fairly exhausted after a session of this nature. This was certainly true for Norman, who had expended a great deal of physical, emotional, and mental energy. We would see Norman a couple of more times to address other issues that helped his true person emerge and become strong. Norman was one who would contact us years later because something else had surfaced he wanted help dealing with. But he would not return this time with a need to focus on any feelings of hypocrisy, violence, or abandonment. Since we had last seen Norman, his self-awareness and co-consciousness motivated him to explore other memories, lies, places, and parts of himself. Doing so had resulted in continued personal experiences of inner healing and peace.

Complex dissociation

Induced dissociation

Complex dissociation is on the extreme end of the dissociation spectrum. It differs from common dissociation, which happens spontaneously, in that complex dissociation is the result of intentionally traumatizing victims to control them. It is possible to induce and program dissociation. Program Based Mind Control is the deliberate conditioning of a person's mind through repetitive trauma events. These are designed to impart a belief that can be used later to get a person to do something he would not normally do and at the same time not remember what he has been through or done, thus creating the ultimate slave and spy. The concept of induced dissociation is sometimes relegated to debatable conspiracy theories involving Nazis, Satanism, child pornography, and government mind control. Cults have induced dissociation for centuries to control people, with brain washing techniques that fracture minds, suppress wounded parts, and indoctrinate alter identities to do their bidding. Sophisticated techniques engineered by Nazi Germans took programmed dissociation to a whole new level with the aid of scientific technology. The atrocity of Hitler's Nazi death camps, as well as live medical research and experimentation on humans, contributed to the deliberate formation of alters through the use of emotional and physical trauma. The goal was to subjugate people by forcibly creating and encoding alters for specific tasks and purposes. Today, some believe forms of mind control programming may play a part in the strategy of military and government agendas for intelligence, espionage, and other purposes.

Some cases of common dissociation are the result of habitual or persistent cruelty by an abuser. While this may not come in the form of calculated, deliberate mind control programming, the frequency of a particular pattern of abuse may result in behaviors akin to those experienced by victims of induced dissociation. Whether encountered periodically or systematically, repetitive experiences of abuse can fragment and demoralize their victims, thus compounding their dissociation as well as contributing to the control held over them by others.

Satanic Ritual Abuse (SRA)

Satanic Ritual Abuse (SRA) is a category of trauma-based mind control programming that merits attention because of its spiritual aspect. The goal of Satanic Ritual Abuse, as a method of mind control programming, is to deliberately traumatize the mind into fragmenting in order to control the victim by dissociated states. Common dissociation may exhibit relatively few alters, but the alter system of an SRA victim is highly elaborate and may operate with hundreds, even thousands of alter identities. With common dissociation, perpetrators of abuses do not victimize with the express purpose of causing dissociation. With SRA, dissociation is calculated and expected so that emerging alter identities can be dominated. Alters are trained to perform tasks and behave in ways desired by the abusers, to support the agenda of their programmers, and to assure loyalty to the cult.

Ritual abuse narratives given by supposed victims are controversial. There is skepticism about recovered-memory therapy which directs patients to search inside themselves for "proof" of abuse. A variety of techniques may be used to aid this quest including stream-of-consciousness writing, dreams, art therapy, and age-regression hypnosis in which patients are temporarily taken into childhood. Many therapists dispute the reliability of most so-called recovered memories. Regrettably, False Memory Syndrome has been linked to wrongful accusations of innocent people who have been fabricated as abusers, perpetrators, and tormenters. The FBI and police claim there is insufficient evidence of a widespread satanic cult or proof of an underground satanic conspiracy. This is not to suggest that all Satanic Ritual Abuse reports are untrue. Although presumed rare by both therapists and civil authorities, there are reports based on reality and some cases of sadistic ritual activity in a cult setting that have been proven in courts.

Satanic Ritual Abuse survivors tell of dehumanizing cruelties and degrading sexual molestations deliberately imposed upon them in order to exercise control over them. Animal and human sacrifices are reported among the ceremonial rituals that are both grim and appalling. Other brutal and torturous experiences are part of the mind control and encoding techniques used to bring about dissociation. This is done in order to manipulate the victims' minds and bodies for unnatural purposes. Occult ceremonies and ritual abuses may include alternating, or simultaneously imposing, pain and pleasure as a means of forcing dissociation. This is particularly effective in young children but also possible in adults. For example, a child's mind can neither comprehend nor process sexual stimulation happening concurrently with inflicted pain. Such techniques may be synchronized with words, phrases, or threats, as well as colors, lights, sounds, smells, or symbols that become triggers used later to evoke previously implanted responses. When a programmed alter is triggered, the rest of the mind and body do not have to think about or participate in what is happening.

The horrors that ritual abuse victims endure – if they ever come to a place of disclosing these without fear for their lives – are extreme enough that they are not to be ignored. Rather than being disregarded, a ritual abuse survivor needs to be seen as someone in deep pain who is crying out for help. If in fact a survivor is authentically a ritual abuse victim, the complexity of dissociation requires the attention of qualified professionals. Help and treatment should not be attempted alone or even with a well-meaning, untrained support person. Satanic Ritual Abuse is occult based. It will result in dissociative disorders and is directly linked to demonization of victims. Due to the spiritual implications of working with SRA survivors, intervention and healing must include a spiritual component. As one of the most extremely complex dissociation issues, those engaged in the "helping professions" must be prepared for a long-term commitment with Satanic Ritual Abuse survivors to help unravel the mind-boggling multitude of alters interwoven in intricately tiered systems.

Empowered multiplicity

Empowered multiplicity is a term coined to describe people who are multiple but do not feel they fit into the classic definitions of Multiple Personality Disorder (MPD) or Dissociative Identity Disorder (DID). Emphasis is placed on the word "empowered" in recognition of their ability to take responsibility for their own lives without dependence upon outside support. Empowered multiplicity may also refer to a system that is no longer living in victim mode, but where individuals have learned to manage their lives and behaviors in ways that maximize the strength and potential of their multiple selves. Other terms found for this classification include non-disordered multiples and self-invented multiples. Within this trend are various views of what it is to be a multiple, not all of them in harmony with one another. However, four basic tenets appear common among those views:

1. Empowered multiplicity promotes the concept that there are literally many real people sharing the same body, each with independent wills, emotions, abilities, interests, and rights. They do not subscribe to the traditional view that there is only one true person who has multiple parts and alters formed in dissociation.

2. Empowered multiples do not need a doctor or therapist to diagnose them because they do not consider themselves

disordered. They will not sacrifice their individual parts, capabilities, and potential to the notion that they are sick or in need of cure. They generally believe the medical and therapeutic communities encourage dependence upon experts, pharmaceuticals, hospitals, and other external controls simply because a person is multiple. As no model for healthy plurality exists in our society, there is disgruntlement that DID/MPD is still listed in the DSM-IV. This is seen by empowered multiples to promote dissociation as dysfunctional and pathological. Many empowered multiples live functional, productive lives but keep their multiplicity secret, rather than risk being labeled mentally ill.

3. Empowered multiples argue that multiplicity is natural, and not everyone is born with a single original person. They hold that multiplicity is pre-existent at birth and not necessarily connected to abuse or trauma that results in alter identities. This suggests a biological component to their multiplicity, which has not been substantiated by research. Empowered multiples promote diversity rather than *integration*, which some claim is not possible for natural multiples.

4. Empowered multiples believe true resources for help and healing come from within. They believe an empowered multiple system takes steps to help its members change negative behaviors, both past and present. However, given the potential diversity within a system, there are limitations to self-effort when it comes to multiplicity. They recognize without shame that multiplicity may result in mixed messages. They are happy to live as they are, making the best of life without being desperately dependent on outside support. Empowered multiples want to explore and

celebrate multiplicity as an extraordinary advantage, promoting ways to make it acceptable within the wider culture by advocating its recognition and support.

Dissociation and demonization

A controversial subject both within and outside of religious circles is that of demons and whether or not an individual can truly be demonically influenced. The New Testament Greek verb, *diamonizomai*, means "to have or to be afflicted by the presence of a demon, or **demonized**." This definition is a more accurate translation than "demon possessed," as possession implies ownership. If the true person is a Christian, the true person cannot be demonically inhabited. However, wounded parts and alter identities, separated from the true person because of dissociation, can be hosts to the demonic. Demons need deception (lies) in a person for habitation to be possible. Demonization occurs when a door for the devil's activity is opened, allowing evil spirits access into a person's life. This may happen because he is victimized by an evil person. Demons and dissociation are not the same thing and are not to be confused. Demons are external entities that seek entry into a person in order to bring about spiritual destruction. Dissociation creates internal entities that help a person survive.

One astonishing account of demonization found in the Bible is recorded in Mark 5:2-15:

> When Jesus got out of the boat, a man with an evil spirit came from the tombs to meet him. This man lived in the tombs, and no one could bind him any more, not even with a chain. For he had often been chained hand and foot, but he tore the chains apart and broke the irons on his feet. No one was strong enough to subdue him. Night and day among the tombs and in the hills he would cry out and cut himself with stones.

When he saw Jesus from a distance, he ran and fell on his knees in front of him. He shouted at the top of his voice, "What do you want with me, Jesus, Son of the Most High God? Swear to God that you won't torture me!" For Jesus had said to him, "Come out of this man, you evil spirit!" Then Jesus asked him, "What is your name?" "My name is Legion," he replied, "for we are many." And he begged Jesus again and again not to send them out of the area.

A herd of pigs was feeding on the nearby hillside. The demons begged Jesus, "Send us among the pigs; allow us to go into them." He gave them permission, and the evil spirits came out and went into the pigs. The herd, about two thousand in number, rushed down the steep bank into the lake and were drowned.

Those tending the pigs ran off and reported this in the town and countryside, and the people went out to see what had happened. When they came to Jesus, they saw the man who had been possessed by the legion of demons, sitting there dressed and in his right mind.

There are several clear indications in this passage that the man was demonized. He not only had an evil spirit, a multitude of demons inhabited him. The spokesman for the many demons was named Legion, a legion being 1,000. The demons had to be in the man because the passage says they came out of him.

There are also some possible hints of dissociation. The man was a cutter, or self-mutilator, who may have inflicted self-abuse as a solution to manage his hidden pain. Kaylie's story in Chapter 9 gives an example of self-abuse directly linked to alter activity. Dissociated people often struggle with loneliness. An alter will go to great lengths to protect a wounded part, causing both internal seclusion and detachment from others. Anger is the most common expression of resistance by alters. The man lived in isolation and distanced himself from others by his behaviors. His display of superhuman strength, crying out, and self-mutilation could possibly be expressions of both dissociation and demonization.

There is a danger of committing *spiritual abuse* if either a wounded part or an alter is treated as a demon. Dissociation is internally created in the mind. Parts and alters cannot be cast out or expelled from a person as can demons, which gain access from outside. When ministering to dissociation from a spiritual perspective, it is imperative that facilitators are trained to accurately distinguish between dissociation and demonization in order to avoid contributing further to suffering. The approach to inner healing for these two conditions is exactly opposite. On the one hand, renewal of the fragmented mind may conclude with the integration of dissociated parts. On the other hand, restoration of the soul may necessitate the expulsion of demons. To disregard the potential to be dissociated, demonized, or both may greatly hinder a person who is seeking help. Failure to differentiate between the two may only add to inner conflict as well as cause resistance to healing.

Summary

1. Dissociation exists on a broad spectrum ranging from common to complex.

2. In its mildest form, dissociation is as simple as "zoning out" in a brief mental escape.

3. Everyone has the potential to experience common dissociation as the result of uninvited abuse, unexpected trauma, or exaggerated stress.

4. Some people are forced to dissociate as victims of Programmed Based Mind Control.

5. Dissociation and demonization are not the same. Although they may be interrelated, they are to be treated distinctly.

Chapter 5

Functions of Dissociation

Dissociation Protects, Controls, and Presents

As HER TWENTY FIFTH BIRTHDAY WAS BEING CELEBRATED AMONG FAMILY AND FRIENDS, ASHLEY COULD NOT ESCAPE THE THOUGHT, "IT WOULD BE BETTER IF I HADN'T BEEN BORN." How could she even think such a thing when surrounded by those who genuinely loved her, or were they only pretending as well? Other taunting thoughts clamored in her head. "If they only knew what happened, not one of them would want to even be near me." As her best friend chatted excitedly across from her, Ashley could feel herself mentally slipping away. Realizing her happy face may be rapidly disappearing as well, the only way she could protect herself was to turn from the circle and retreat to the house. She hated who looked back at her in the mirror. Was it true? Would it really be better if she had not been born? Ashley drew a deep breath and said to herself in the mirror, "Let's go back out there, get through the party, and we can deal with this later."

Functions of dissociation

Dissociation is a natural occurrence in the mind that helps a person cope or survive. Most people can relate to one of the mildest expressions of dissociation, normal daydreaming, as a mental alternative to a particularly mundane task or boring event. But in response to acute stress or extreme trauma, dissociation becomes more diverse and complicated. When a child is being beaten, the true person receives the physical blows while an "alternate person" takes the mind somewhere else in order to mentally escape the painful experience. The mind separates itself from the abuse and distances the person from the pain, the memory, and any perceived lies. Wounded parts of the true person and alter identities form within the mind to aid survival and help avoid further pain. While being sexually abused as a child, Ashley's mind had turned away so as not to consciously think about or participate in what was happening at the moment. But lies and fears mired in her subconscious began haunting her in adulthood.

Some people in a dissociative state report that they seem to be out of their body observing the incident from a distance, as though they had floated to the ceiling or are watching from elsewhere in the room. During the abuse, a child may fixate so intently on a particular object, sound, or smell that he tunes out everything happening to him or any other feature of his environment. For example, the ticking of a clock may become the object of fixation. As an adult, the same sound could affect a person in one of two ways. It could be a comfort because it is associated with taking him away from the pain, or it might be a trigger that causes him to subconsciously connect with the trauma.

In Chapter 1, the Biblical example of Adam and Eve helped illustrate how dissociation is established to protect, control, and present. These three functions may work separately or in combination with one another. As a person is ministered to and layers of dissociation are peeled away, wounded parts and alters will be revealed. These entities are aware of their origin. Alters, especially, have a well-defined purpose. They have distinct names. Discovering their purpose and names will aid dialoguing with the dissociation and help facilitate healing.

Dissociation protects

The dominant function of dissociation is to protect a wounded part of a person from connecting again with the shame, fear, or pain of a damaging experience. Adam and Eve sought to protect themselves by attempting to conceal their disgrace behind fig leaves. Amnesic walls may go up that totally block the conscious mind from accessing certain information, memories, lies, and other data hidden in the subconscious mind. An alter identity, functioning in the present, may aggressively guard a wounded part who is stalled in the past. A protecting alter will do everything possible to defend a wounded part either by shielding him when an abuse is repeated or by attempting to prevent it from happening again. That includes staving off anyone who seeks access to the wounded part, even for the purpose of bringing genuine healing. For example, an alter may presume that a ministry facilitator, like others before, will bring harm.

Alters have a limited range of functioning and thinking. By acknowledging and affirming an alter's role and purpose – whether you agree with it or not – a facilitator is more likely to get the cooperation of an alter. An alter will resist being told what to do but may be persuaded to work with you if convinced you will not harm either him or the wounded part he guards. Despite important information an alter may have, much energy and time can be consumed in dialogue or negotiation with alters. At times, this may be their ploy to put off or hinder getting to the wounded part. Usually, the protecting alter must agree to cooperate in order to reach and minister healing to the wounded part of a person.

One possible indicator of dissociation is the inability to convey appropriately a healthy range of emotions. This may include emotional voids or a disproportionate display of emotions. An outburst of anger may signal that dissociation is activated to protect. The Bible cautions, "In your anger do not sin. Do not let the sun go down while you are still angry, and do not give the devil a foothold." (Ephesians 4:26-27) When abuse has caused a person to dissociate, resentment and anger can easily take root as the devil furtively gains access through the gateway of dissociation. Fear and anger become a destructive duo to alienate the person in his dissociation further from himself and from others. Anger creates fear, whether it is internally or externally directed. When anger is turned inward among the dissociated parts, it may be likened to a raging alcoholic father whom everyone else in the house scurries to get away from in hopes they will not get hurt. When anger is expressed outwardly, it seeks to keep others from getting close. Not all anger is demonstrated aggressively. Anger can be passively displayed through "the silent treatment," body language, facial expressions, the eyes, and by cunning acts of sabotage.

Anger leads to destructiveness perhaps more than any other pathway. When a child is severely abused, he may not be in any position to express his true fears and feelings, including anger. Eventually, anger may be displaced through an alter who will hate his abuser, be furious with God, and even react violently to the name of Jesus. Well-meaning Christians might misinterpret the latter response as demonization, not dissociation, and wrongly attempt to cast out an evil spirit. Adding spiritual abuse to the weight of a pre-existing abuse only compresses anger. Most people are hesitant to admit anger toward God for not protecting them in an abusive situation and, if they do, are often shamed back into silence. Others may feel alienated from God, believing that he does not love them or could never accept them again because of the nature of abuse they experienced. Unresolved anger and unforgiveness toward an abuser also stoke anger and keep it burning. An experienced ministry facilitator will enable a person with dissociation to work through his personal and spiritual issues in an environment that is safe, non-condemning, caring, and confidential. Linda had a remarkable encounter that helped her move away from the fear and pain that had been so integral to her makeup, into a true experience of God's love, acceptance, and healing.

Linda's story

Linda's perfectionist mother was overly strict and demanding. Even though Linda grew up poor, one way her mother attempted to hide their poverty was by always keeping her daughter beautifully presented. Five-year-old Linda loved it when her mother braided her hair, dressed her up in frilly clothes, read her stories, and sang with her at the piano. Mother would occasionally get cross with Linda, but nothing prepared her for the day she came in soiled from a fall in the yard that had torn her new blouse. Without warning, her mother flew into a rage, grabbed the fly swatter, and began mercilessly beating Linda with it as she fled to her room in hopes of escape. With no place else to go to avoid the relentless blows, Linda dissociated in her mind to endure what was happening. As the abuse escalated, Linda clutched her pillow and fixated her attention on a favorite teddy bear until her mother's wrath was gratified.

From that day, it seemed her mother would not hesitate to strike Linda if something was deemed inappropriate or inexcusable. Years passed, but a deeply wounded five-year-old Linda was stuck in the moment of the first abuse. This stalled part would remain mentally disconnected during subsequent thrashings, subconsciously distanced from the intolerable physical pain and accompanying emotional trauma. A corresponding alter identity, established to protect five-year-old Linda, despondently took the beatings. Fearful of exacerbating her mother's anger, Linda silently endured the vicious attacks. She eventually stopped crying and grew up devoid of a normal range of emotions. Thirty years later, Linda portrayed stability and confidence. This well-educated, professional woman made a stunning fashion statement and kept her tresses carefully braided. Despite appearances, deep inside a sense of worthlessness nagged at her. No amount of money, praise, or recognition had ever been able to erase the persistent echo of invalidation and incompatible feelings about her self-worth. Mysteriously, she could not pinpoint where those feelings came from.

As Linda was brought into self-awareness of her dissociation, she made two common responses. The first was admitting the notion that she might genuinely be going insane, something she secretly feared. This tormenting thought was abated by reassurances that what she was discovering about herself was not unusual and that her mind was working normally. This led to the second typical response, which was one of overwhelming relief. Finally there was someone she could talk to who truly understood the mental conflict and torment she had lived with for decades. Not only that, Linda found there was actually hope for freedom from the confusion, bitterness, hatred, and fears that bound her.

Linda visited several memories linked to the compounded pain in her life. Each stop provided an opportunity to clear some clutter of lies and fears. All this helped free her up to face the most hurtful wound first inflicted by her mother when Linda was five years of age. A guardian alter threw up a battery of defenses, angrily saying no one was allowed in the "room" where access was sought. Once the alter was persuaded that no one was going to hurt five-year-old Linda, she reluctantly agreed to allow us entry with the proviso that she come along. It soon became apparent that an amnesic barrier prevented Adult Linda from having any conscious awareness of this five-year-old part. When this hidden part of Linda revealed herself, she immediately began talking and behaving like a five-year-old. I responded by interacting with this part of Linda as I would a young child. When I asked five-year-old Linda what happened when she came in with soiled clothes and a torn blouse, she vividly recalled the experience of being beaten with the flyswatter. She became terrified and grabbed a pillow off the couch, gripping it tightly as she sobbed. When I held out a tissue box to her, unexpectedly she stopped crying. She gingerly took the box in her hands and began examining it as well as the curious, soft paper protruding from the opening on one side. Eyes brimming with moisture, she surprised us by asking, "What is this?"

At age five, Linda had never seen tissues before and was enthralled. I pulled one out and explained she could use it to dry her eyes when she cried. I told her that the box was full of these soft little hankies, and she could use as many as she needed and then simply throw them away. I reminded five-year-old Linda that she had been telling us the story about when her mother got so angry because her new blouse was torn. Instantly, she returned to the terror of that moment but chose the familiarity of a pillow over the tissues to absorb her tears and muffle her wailing.

We offered to pray for five-year-old Linda and together invited the Lord to reveal truth to her in whatever way he chose. Linda's sobs subsided and she became quiet, her face still buried in the pillow. I asked her if she could tell us what was happening. With eyes shut, and in five-year-old vocabulary, she described how, from a distance, she could see herself on the bed with her mom striking her backside and bare legs with the flyswatter. All of a sudden, a "man who looks like he has a light on inside him" came between her and her mom. He appeared to be taking the blows instead. She went on to say that he whispered in her ear, "It's okay. It's not your fault. I'm here to protect you." Five-year-old Linda reported her mother was no longer in the room with her, only the nice man who came to help her.

I asked five-year-old Linda if she knew who this man was. She replied, "Oh, yes. This is Jesus. I see his picture every week at Sunday School." With eyes still closed, she asked if she might stay with Jesus so her mother could not hurt her any more. We prayed with five-year-old Linda so we would all know what Jesus wanted done in this situation. She sensed him telling her, yes, she could stay with him. Five-year-old Linda at once let out an enormous sigh and slumped back into the couch, her whole body going limp.

Momentarily, Adult Linda was present again with us. At first, she seemed vaguely aware of what had transpired, so great was the mental chasm that had kept her separated from five-year-old Linda. She explained it was though she had been looking on from a distance, knowing she could not interfere, yet somehow being able to take in all she had observed. As the reality of what had just been experienced sank in, Linda jubilantly exclaimed, "It's gone!" At a loss for other words, Linda could only happily repeat, "It's gone, it's gone!"

In fact, several things were gone. As the Lord brought deep healing in such a personal way, Linda was released from all the anger and fear she held toward her mother. In testing lies she had earlier articulated, she was no longer able to connect with any of them. Remarkably, five-year-old Linda was "gone" as well. Neither was there an alter needed anymore to protect this part that was no longer present. In the totality of what God did for Linda, he restored that young, wounded part to her original place, *merging* her back to wholeness, and bringing peace in this area of Linda's mind.

A session follow-up was made by phone several days later. Linda had stopped on the way home to buy something she had never owned before – a flyswatter. Hanging next to her kitchen door, it served as a constant reminder of the Lord's intervention and the healing she had received from him. As well, the tattered old teddy bear that had continued to comfort her these many years was no longer to be found on her pillow. It was retired to a special place on a shelf across the room where it could symbolically keep watch from a distance as she slept peacefully.

Dissociation controls

Another function of dissociation is to control, often demonstrated in efforts to manage relationships in such a way as to avoid being wounded. Adam and Eve endeavored to control their relationship with God by hiding from him. This proved impossible. Control may operate in tandem at times with the dissociative function to protect. What may sometimes be wrongly interpreted as a "strong personality type" may in fact be an alter identity that is well-trained and well-rehearsed to control. As learned in the previous chapter, dissociation may open the door to demonic influence. Once the enemy gets a foothold, it is not unusual to trace a repeated theme set up against a person. In the following example, that theme is bullying.

Sean's story

Several years ago, a self-confident and handsome university senior came to see me. Sean was well groomed and stylishly dressed, having the appearance of one accustomed to affluence. He exhibited refined manners and spoke with utmost respect and courtesy. Sean held offices in his fraternity both locally and nationally. His academic performance was unparalleled. His peers respected Sean, although many felt intimidated by him.

As he journeyed through inner healing, protective layers were gradually peeled away, and his guard began to come down. In the process, going to a succession of painful memories exposed a pattern of abuse. Throughout Sean's childhood and youth, he was repeatedly, and at times mercilessly, bullied, beginning in grade school. For him, this typically happened without warning or provocation and usually involved some form of physical harm. One of the most agonizing memories was an attempt to protect another, weaker child from being bullied, then taking the pounding himself. It was soon discovered that most people never saw or interacted with Sean's true person. Instead, they interacted with the facade of a strong-willed alter that had been established to control relationships in a way that kept others from getting too close. No way would he allow the wounded part who held so much pain to be hurt again.

In Sean's case, two alters shielded the wounded part that had been so mistreated by others: one, a protecting alter formed the first time he was bullied and eventually a second, dominant alter, created to control. The goal of the latter was to manipulate and manage both his environment and those who were allowed access into his structured world. By being the best at everything – superior grades, highest office in the fraternity, best athlete on the team – he had made himself unapproachable. This brusque control alter went by the fitting name of Curt. He admitted to even deliberately bullying others if necessary to keep Sean from being bullied.

The wounded part that suffered the first attack at an early age had separated off into the subconscious. Once located, and without interference from either of the two alters, this part could receive ministry and healing. At the experiential memory level, lie-based thinking was exposed, and truth was revealed that dispelled those lies. Forgiveness was specifically spoken by this wounded part in each situation and by name for every person that could be remembered. One of the astonishing and uncontrollable

94   *Trading Faces*

things that happened at several points was the eruption of pent up emotion in the form of anguished crying with floods of tears. Sean honestly could not remember the last time he had cried. As an adult, Curt restrained Sean's emotions so strictly that he was sometimes accused of having no feelings. Another way this alter controlled was that everything had to be perfect – Sean's appearance, his performance, his behavior. To a certain extent, this also corresponded to a need for the approval of his aloof father.

The final outcome for Sean was that this dissociated part expressed heartfelt forgiveness, received deep healing, and was renewed to singleness of mind. The strengths of that part were rightfully integrated as Sean's true person was made more complete. Sean had numerous behavioral adjustments to make after that because Curt was no longer present to supervise his performance. However, the "real Sean" emerged and proved to be every bit as friendly and competent, only without the negative characteristics of a controlling alter. With restoration of the soul comes redemption of the authentic, true person. This also included redemption of relationships that had been kept distant because of Sean's dissociation.

Dissociation presents

The third primary function of dissociation is to present. All dissociation presents in some way as required or when triggered. Adam and Eve no longer wanted to be caught naked by God. After separating themselves from him, thereafter they presented themselves covered. Presenting alters may be recognized by their distinctive role and purpose. Sometimes a presenting alter may act on behalf of, or work in cooperation with, other parts or alters in a person's dissociative system. A presenting alter may regulate the expression of others in the system by filtering the display of emotions or the choice of words. Such false representations of the true person may operate on his behalf to help him survive and function in everyday roles.

Whenever an alter identity is presenting, it represents who the person appears to be at that time. A person will literally switch from one alter to another depending on a range of needs, circumstances, and variables. For some people, as with Sean, there may be a dominant alter like Curt who presents consistently and becomes so domineering that the true person is greatly minimized or seemingly nonexistent. In multi-faceted dissociation, where there are a large number of parts and alters within a person, a well-developed internal system makes it both necessary and possible for alters to independently and distinctly present themselves. To illustrate, it may be discovered that within one person there are individual alters such as a

Home alter, who takes care of certain domestic or family duties.

Work alter, who fulfills responsibilities in the work place.

Church alter, who attends church and related functions.

Shopping alter, who shops and purchases.

Driving alter, whose only task is to drive the car and responsibly transport the person.

This is not referring to normal transitions of a healthy, mentally sound person operating in various, familiar environments. These are distinct alters all within the same person that stand alone, each with a clearly defined job. Just because parts and alters are quiet or unknown to one another does not negate their existence. They likely are unaware of others operating within the system in their own respective roles. That is, they are not co-conscious; there is no awareness or acknowledgement of, nor interaction with, one another. Therefore, it is not expected or even possible that they might cooperate together or be in agreement. A person may come into co-consciousness of his dissociation. When that occurs, there may be shared consciousness of or cooperation between certain parts, alters, and the true person. This will become the case once they are separately distinguished, and barriers between them have been removed. Bringing a person to self-awareness of his dissociation helps isolate the entities that need to receive individual and personal healing leading toward wholeness. It also paves the way for association between the conscious and subconscious mind and facilitates ongoing restoration and integration.

Carol's story

Carol has numerous parts and alters in her dissociative system. Five of these correspond to the five examples of presenting alters noted above. Each of these five alters has a function name attached to the name of her true person. To focus your attention on the working of presenting alters, details of how and when each of these five alters formed are not included.

Home Carol

At home, this alter manages the household reluctantly, but dutifully, and engages the help of husband and children to minimize the necessity of it all. If things are partially done, that is good enough for her. Home Carol exhibits a lot of lethargy, lack of energy, fears, isolation, and frequent depression. Operating exclusively at home around immediate family members only, this part has very low self-esteem, often dresses in drab clothing, is critical of the family, withdraws, and avoids responsibilities as much as possible.

Work Carol

Work Carol thrives as an elementary teacher. Carol becomes a totally different person once on the school property, even more so behind the closed door of her classroom. Work Carol is a perfectionist, evidenced by her appealing dress, meticulously decorated room, and contented, disciplined children. Teaching dominates Work Carol's world. Work Carol is so absorbed in teaching that inordinate amounts of time are spent outside of teaching hours, either at the school or at home, in preparing, grading, studying, and such. Like Home Carol, this alter loathes domestic obligations and does not participate in them. She prefers the fulfillment of spending time on teaching related tasks. During the summer, or even on school holiday breaks, Work Carol compounds Home Carol's depression because she has no teaching job to perform.

Church Carol

Church Carol is always bubbly and presents at church with an exaggerated joy. She is well-versed in Scripture and its application, sings on one of the worship teams, and is involved in drama. She will readily volunteer wherever needed, especially if teaching children is involved. In this instance, there is co-conscious and cooperative working of two of Carol's alters when Work Carol and Church Carol team together at times. Church Carol and her family stride through the church doors impeccably dressed, faces shining, others looking to them with admiration as a "model family." They sit near the front and are surrounded at church by friends. Church Carol is proud of her husband's leadership position. Her effervescence belies the hurts, fears, and pain held by deeply recessed, wounded parts. Except for Work Carol, other entities are *not* allowed to present at church. Church Carol is disgusted with Home Carol and often berates her depression and slovenliness.

Shopping Carol

Actually, Carol has two distinct alters who go shopping. Because these two are so incompatible, shopping is a love-hate experience for Carol. One is a miser, the other a spendthrift. Miser Carol counts every penny and is overly mindful of the family's financial constraints. Spendthrift Carol is known to come home occasionally with luxuries and indulgences that exceed the family budget. Spendthrift Carol's solution to masking inner pain is by treating others to gifts in hopes they will be compelled to accept and appreciate her. Often, Carol's embarrassed husband must return these items.

With "four hands on the shopping cart," a trip to the store is draining and filled with conflict. When the two, constantly battling shopping alters arrive home, their job is done, and Home Carol is expected to take over. Home Carol usually deserts the responsibility to unload the car and restock the pantry. The now exhausted woman tries to recover by napping in the isolation of her darkened bedroom, seeking relief from a pounding headache brought on by another stress-filled shopping experience.

Driving Carol

This alter's only job is to drive the car. She knows all the road rules and obeys them without question, getting Carol from one place to another safely and courteously. All the other alters like it when Driving Carol is active because they get a break and can rest. Besides, Driving Carol really has to concentrate hard when doing her job and will not tolerate distractions in the vehicle. (While it may seem astonishing, even alarming, that a person can have an alter whose sole duty is to drive, it is not uncommon. One recipient could not tell me how she got from her home to my office for a session. That is because whoever stepped through my door had not consciously participated in the drive across town. On the bright side, the driving alters I have met claim to be extremely conscientious behind the wheel and may be some of the safest drivers on the roads.)

To those unfamiliar with dissociation, the possibility of such distinct alter identities may seem bizarre or impossible. Examining Carol's dissociative system sheds light on how a person might act a certain way in one situation (competent Work Carol or the battling Shopping Carols) and completely different in another (vivacious Church Carol or despondent Home Carol). However, to those who live with dissociation internally, in another family member, or in a friend, autonomously functioning alters are decidedly real and often perplexing. It is beneficial to those closest to a dissociated person to understand her dissociative system. Carol's husband was eventually brought into awareness of her dissociation. This led to positive interaction as they could then journey together toward her deeper inner healing.

Chapter 6

What Keeps You Fragmented

Conspiracy of Schemes and Themes

JARROD'S COUNTENANCE INSTANTLY DARKENED AND IN A SINISTER VOICE HE MENACINGLY GROWLED, "I'M GOING TO KILL YOU." The session had been progressing well when something triggered this fearsome change. As though to demonstrate his ability to fulfill his vow, Jarrod seized the trash can next to his chair and crumpled it into a wad with his bare hands. Jarrod was larger in size than his two facilitators put together. My immediate thought was, "This guy *could* kill me!" Thankfully, my ministry partner had already bypassed that consideration and had taken up an authoritative position to resist his threat. Was this dissociation, or was something else provoking this intimidating outburst?

Authority clash

Jarrod's family and mine had been acquaintances for several years through the church we all attended. I knew him as a gentle giant of a man with a rousing sense of humor. Needless to say, I was not expecting this kind of behavior. I was fairly new to the ministry of inner healing at the time he asked for a session. If there was ever a moment when fear could have persuaded me to stop doing this, the threat on my life would have been it. Satan pulled out all the stops. If I held any doubt about the reality of the devil and demons, all disbelief vanished during that particular session. In hindsight, I realize the enemy's surprise attack was twofold in hopes of stopping my pursuit of inner healing ministry: to cause fear of the demonic and to provoke a sense of failure in my ability to help people. The urgent reliance upon the presence, protection, and guidance of the Lord brought quite an opposite outcome. I knew nothing at the time about dissociation or lie-based thinking. So my ministry partner and I did the only things we knew to do: utter a quick prayer (HELP!), take spiritual authority over the situation the best we could, and command the presence of evil to leave in Jesus' Name. I learned more about getting out of God's way that evening than I had ever learned before, one of the most important lessons the Lord has taught me in this ministry. When the session ended, big Jarrod was not unlike the Gadarene whom Jesus healed, peacefully sitting there in his right mind. (See Mark 5:15) He even straightened out the trash can. After that experience, I plunged even deeper into inner healing.

Authority has a voice

God has a voice. Satan also has a voice. The voice of the devil comes as invasive thoughts in the mind. These are easily recognized as being diametrically opposed to the Word of God. Therefore, it is advantageous to know the Word of God in order to accurately distinguish truth from lies. Satan's native language is lying. Jesus declared him to be a liar and the father of lies in whom there is no truth. (See John 8:44) Satan operates by deception leading to disobedience and resulting in destruction.

Through the lies and deceptions of the devil, one is tempted to sin. Sin, full grown, brings forth death. (See James 1:13-15) People are "deception-ized" before they are demonized. Evil spirits may gain right of entry through the seedbeds of trauma and abuse where lies are implanted. Eight-year-old Norman, whose story you read in Chapter 4, was deceived into thinking it was his fault that his momma committed suicide. The intruding thought in his mind was "Momma doesn't love me or she would have stayed." This deception eventually led to rebellious and damaging behaviors as solutions to avoiding the hidden pain associated with finding his mother dead in the barn. Over forty years passed before he encountered truth at the experiential memory level that nullified this and other lies.

As the enemy's territory is encroached upon, he will use various lines of attack to hold his ground in an effort to impede inner healing. Three typical maneuvers he attempts to implement in a session are fear, confusion, and mockery. Fear may come against a person if he feels vulnerable or exposed. (For example, when a three hundred pound man is demonstratively threatening to kill you, believe me, that strikes a bit of fear in the heart!) It is common during a ministry session for the recipient to become confused. This may be experienced as foggy thinking, scattered thoughts, jumping erratically between memories, blurring of vision, or a feeling of mentally shutting down. Mockery is typically first seen in the face by a jeering smile and scornful look before any contempt is verbally expressed. These three tactics of the devil, and all others for that matter, are halted in relation to the strength of a person's spiritual authority exercised in Jesus' Name.

God's kingdom is built on the authority of the Lordship of Jesus Christ. In Matthew 28:18, Jesus declared to his followers, "All authority in heaven and on earth has been given to me." Conversely, Satan's counterfeit "kingdom" is built on rebellion.

The following diagram helps illustrate that everything Satan stands for is the "flip-side," or reverse, of God's original intent, plan, and purpose for people.

Counterfeit "Kingdom" of Satan	True Kingdom of God
Rebellion	Authority
Lies	Truth
Confusion	Peace
Disorder	Divine Order
Fear and Oppression	Faith and Obedience
Guilt and Shame	Forgiveness
Bondage Leading to Slavery	Release Leading to Freedom
Destruction	Deliverance
A Destroyer	A Deliverer
Eternal Damnation	Eternal Life

Many do not understand spiritual authority exercised in the name of Jesus. They wrongly think submission to authority is submission to a man. It is those who have passed the test of submission to the authority of the Lordship of Jesus Christ who truly understand authority. A person is given authority as he comes under the Lord's authority. History with the Lord builds authority, develops tenacity, and increases boldness. By steadfast submission to the Lord, one stays in authority. Growing in authority involves exercising God-given responsibilities and facing spiritual conflicts with confidence.

Authority is primarily exercised through the mouth. A good sequence of examples of this is found throughout the fourth chapter of the gospel of Luke. Jesus exercises his authority over the devil by quoting Scripture to refute his temptations. Jesus, in the power of the Spirit, taught authoritatively in his hometown of Nazareth. He rightfully declared himself to be the fulfillment of Old Testament prophecy. Those offended by the truth rejected him and, with ill intent, drove him out of town. When he next taught the people in Capernaum, "they were amazed at his teaching, because his message had authority." (Luke 4:32) They also observed with astonishment his command over the demonic and declared, "With authority and power he gives orders to evil spirits and they come out!" (Luke 4:36) By the authority of his words he rebuked sickness and healed people. He also rebuked very vocal demons who "knew he was the Christ." (Luke 4:41)

The enemy exercises counterfeit authority to attack and destroy whereas Jesus demonstrates his true authority to rescue and save, to heal and restore. True authority is prophetically declared through the mouth revealing truth, healing illness of mind and body, silencing the enemy, and putting him to shame. This is not referring to a "lord it over others" type of authority but a "Lord in me" authority humbly demonstrated by those in submission to him. (See Colossians 1:27)

God will not allow true spiritual authority to be maligned by mockery. Galatians 6:7 clearly states, "Do not be deceived: God *cannot* be mocked." (*Emphasis mine.*) Those who exercise authority illegitimately are ones who have authority by title but not by relationship with Jesus Christ. The evil spirits threatening us through Jarrod sought to control the situation and incite fear and failure. But when authority was exercised in submission to the Lordship of Jesus Christ it brought about the release of this captive who was in bondage to Satan's schemes, themes, and strongholds. It also strengthened our confidence as facilitators. In hindsight, I realize that the authority clash experienced years ago with Jarrod could have stopped me from pursuing part of God's plan for my life. It also could have stopped Jarrod from receiving freedom and having his life transformed. At the time, I never fathomed it was imparting valuable lessons that in turn could be shared with others.

It is important to provide a safe environment for inner healing. When people come under the authority of the Lordship of Jesus Christ, they come under an umbrella of safety and *confidentiality*. Ministry recipients are to be schooled not to be dependent upon their facilitator team. Unhealthy bonds can grow through co-dependency between facilitator and recipient. I neither desire nor expect recipients to look to me as though by human ability I can do anything for them. When I minister to people, it must be the "Christ in me" that people encounter and with whom they connect. (See Colossians 1:27) True inner healing is a supernatural work. Whenever a team facilitates a session, it is made clear to the recipient that their job is to get out of the way of what the Lord wants to do, yet at the same time be so close to him that they represent him with confidence and authority. (See *Procedures: Prepared Facilitator; Prepared Recipient* in the Appendix)

Schemes, themes, and strongholds of the enemy

Satan is a schemer, that is, "one who forms schemes; especially, a plotter; an intriguer." To intrigue means "to cheat, trick, contrive, entangle; to complicate; to puzzle or perplex." These definitions help us comprehend how Satan operates. The Bible says "we are not unaware of his (Satan's) schemes" (2 Corinthians 2:11), and we are to arm ourselves "against the devil's schemes" (Ephesians 6:11). Satan plots and plans, tricks and traps, engineers and ensnares, complicates and confuses, baffles and bewilders, and in other ways conspires against God's prized creation, man, who is made in God's likeness. Satan hates all mankind, in particular those who are God's image bearers to a lost and dying world. The devil opposes the Lord's representatives, who offer salvation, hope, and eternal life with God in the name of Jesus. On the whole, the church today seems unaware of Satan's schemes, therefore neither alerts people to their dangers nor arms people against them. Ignorance of the devil and his ways does not negate the reality of who he is and what he does to keep people separated from God, divided within themselves, and alienated from others.

The schemes of the devil are succinctly stated by Jesus in John 10:10: "the thief (Satan) comes *only* to steal, kill and destroy." (*Emphasis mine.*) Satan is aggressively pursuing this agenda while he can. Revelation 12:12 reveals "the devil ... is filled with fury, because he knows his time is short." He intends to rob people of everything rightfully theirs, including fulfillment of their destiny, single-mindedness, spiritual gifts, and life to the full. He desires to kill them in whatever manner possible, whether it is to put an end to joy or an end to life.

Years of ministry in inner healing have helped me understand that, alongside Satan's schemes, he will introduce a theme or themes against an individual. By accessing a child at the earliest age possible, Satan can commence his work in hopes of ultimately bringing destruction. Bradley and Sean, whose stories you have already read, were both targets of bullying. Their experiences of unsought and undeserved mistreatment became a common theme played out over, and over, and over in their lives. The power of this theme reinforced dissociation in them both, creating internal conflict and frustration. Each traumatic abuse further distanced them within themselves and from others.

Linked to Satan's schemes and themes, corresponding strongholds such as anger, confusion, perversion, infirmity, despair, sabotage, or fear may keep a person debilitated by the enemy. A person begins operating out of lies he believes about himself that relate to the schemes, themes, and strongholds Satan has set up against him. For example, every abuse of bullying (a theme) was building a prison of anger (a stronghold), in which both Bradley and Sean were held captive. As a demonic stronghold, anger destroys both internally and externally. Reinforced through dissociation, anger operates to the destruction of both the person in whom anger resides as well as his targets of displaced anger. For instance, it is not uncommon for a victim of bullying to eventually victimize others, as Sean found himself doing. An unnatural *soul tie*, connecting both the perpetrator and victim, may be used by the devil to replicate the stronghold of anger in others, thus multiplying its destructive influence.

Two more demonic strongholds will be expanded upon for further illustration: perversion and sabotage. These will each have a corresponding story, the second one being my own.

Sample stronghold: Perversion

The word perversion means "a turning from truth or right, a perverted or corrupted form of something." Lying is a perversion of truth. As the father of lies, Satan seeks to pervert truth and prevent truth from being revealed. Ministering spiritually to people in their dissociation offers the potential for God to present truth that dispels lies held about themselves because of trauma, abuse, or some other contributor to dissociation. Things can become perverted for many reasons, but sexual perversion consistently links back to abandonment and/or rejection. The abdication of a father to protect and provide for his children is a common way Satan gains access to abandoned or rejected people. Abdication can also be the failure to protect one's children from exposure to sin or by approving of evil, even by the error of remaining silent about its influence. Perversion may also exploit involuntary inheritances through the bloodline. For example, a propensity toward adultery can often be traced to a generational history of adultery. The deception (lie) that perversion will satisfy often fuels an ever-escalating appetite for more. Voids created by the wounds of abandonment, rejection, and abdication will never be filled except by an experiential relationship with Jesus Christ.

As a stronghold of the enemy, perversion often works in secret, relishing attacks in isolation and behind closed doors. Whether the enemy's invasion of the conscious mind is able to be thwarted or not, during sleep the subconscious mind often comes under assault. Perverted sexual dreams may climax in night emissions, masturbation, terror, fear, depression, shame, and guilt. The most common lie associated with perversions is "It's okay as long as I don't get caught." Exposing hidden perversions removes the covering of secrecy that holds many in bondage. This can be very difficult for people. Therefore, it is imperative that they are protected in a safe, nonjudgmental atmosphere where they know their disclosures will be kept confidential. People are set free by the power of God, by the light of his truth, by the authority of our words to renounce secret and shameful ways (See 2 Corinthians 4:2), and by severing ties with all associations to perversion.

Dissociation may result from sexual perversion forced by a perpetrator against a person's will, such as being raped or molested as a child. Dissociation may also occur because of unintentional sexual perversion such as stumbling upon pornography or accidentally being exposed to another's nakedness. Repeated experiences may result in a person having several self-focused alters that are perversion oriented.

The more a dissociated person yields to sexual perversion as a solution to his pain, the greater the tendency for that to become an uncontrollable addiction, for example, to pornography. The addiction also may be linked to the irresistible urges of ***besetting sin***, typically experienced as an overwhelming repeated compulsion over which the true person seems to have no choice but to succumb. A pattern of besetting sin may cycle around in somewhat predictable time periods, perhaps weekly, or monthly, or every few months and usually culminates in acting out in some perverse activity. Afterward, the true person may be remorseful and feel even more wounded, fearful, confused, shameful, dirty, or guilty.

As another example, a person may seek to ease the pain of abandonment by repeated fornication. Through the fragmentation of dissociation, Satan retains his grip and maintains besetting sin cycles along with the accompanying feelings of defeat and despair. Even though the true person has repeatedly repented, some entities in the dissociative system holding onto the same sin may provoke the person to act upon it again. Regardless of its origin, the perplexity and mystery of besetting sin is rooted in the subconscious and linked to dissociation. Self-effort programs and works-based theological plans might help for a time but are usually unsustainable to the dissociated person because not all parts or alters agree with or cooperate with the recommended strategy for overcoming. If repeated failures are experienced, the person may be shamed into no longer dealing with it openly. A sense of hopelessness and rejection may cause already low self-esteem to spiral downward further.

Besetting sin is closely linked to the work of alters, which is why no amount of knowledge, logic, reason, or self-control will completely release a person from sexual bondage and related addictions. Self-awareness that one is dissociating may come by invasive thoughts, unnatural desires, or physical sensations that intensify to the point a person feels driven to find relief. Not all besetting sins are perversion oriented. But all perversion spirits are liars, promising pleasure but ultimately bringing pain. Those in bondage to sexual perversion will only overcome by the power of Jesus Christ, who reveals truth to dispel lies held in dissociation and who expels related evil spirits.

The Bible says "There is no fear in love, but perfect love drives out fear, because fear has to do with punishment." (1 John 4:18) The key to the *deliverance* of one shackled to the stronghold of perversion is love. Lust, the perversion of love, is often kept secret out of fear. Many in bondage to the stronghold of perversion have never known genuine love which is ultimately found in Jesus Christ and demonstrated in right relationship with others. When Jesus destroys the enemy's lies with truth, all pain and fear are also annihilated. Personally receiving his liberating truth at the experiential memory level sets people free from lies and demonic strongholds.

Carl's story

Carl is a naturally curious, seven-year-old boy being raised in a Christian home. His mother plays piano at church, and his father is an elder and chairman of the board. Bored one day, Carl wanders down to the basement and notices the cupboards he has never thought before to inspect. He begins innocently opening doors, one after the other, and peering inside. When he opens the last one on the far right, its overstuffed contents tumble out, and into view slides something he has never seen before: several pornographic magazines.

At seven, Carl has no context to understand what all is happening or what is going to subsequently occur. He picks one up, attracted to its glossy cover. There is a strange picture on the front of a nearly nude woman. He starts to thumb through the magazine and, for the first time in his well-protected life, is exposed to all sorts of perverted sexual images. These images cause arousal, fear, and confusion, yet scream for his attention.

Questions fill Carl's tender mind. "How did these get here?" "Whose are these?" "Why would these be in my house?" He guesses they must be his father's because everything else that spilled out with the magazines is literature he has seen his dad with before. Carl suddenly becomes conscious of noise upstairs and comes to himself. He scrambles to collect the pornography and other magazines, newspapers, and stuff it was hidden among. He crams it all back into the cupboard and quietly shuts that last door on the right. Already Carl is tormented by thoughts, as though a switch has been flipped on inside of him for the first time. He somehow knows that the first chance he gets he will come back and steal another peek, especially of the other magazines he did not get to this first time.

The mix of fear and stress cause a part of Carl to stall in the state of innocence that existed before that last cupboard door was opened. But somehow, Carl has to deal with this new experience and information. An alter identity forms and comes to his aid for the primary purpose of protection. In this case, the protection mechanism works two ways. One, it is there to protect Carl from ever getting caught with pornography. Two, it is there for Carl to protect his dad from being exposed. After all, what would happen if other family members found out about dad's secret stash or worse yet, that Carl knew about it? Besides, if the pornography were to disappear, he could no longer secretly indulge in it.

Through exposure to pornography, a stronghold of perversion is under construction. Pornography becomes the open door to allow evil spirits access into Carl's life. Through the schemes and the sabotage of the devil, every possible opportunity will now be exploited to reinforce perversion in Carl, establishing in him a base of operation for unholy and unnatural purposes. Pornography is simply serving as an entry point. But this large gate opens onto a broad path that will become ever-widening as Carl grows up. Little does he know that this first unsolicited exposure to pornography will become a theme in his life. Tragically, pornography will eventually become an addiction that leads to other sexual perversions.

Several other things are going on in this picture. Mixed messages are already causing Carl some internal conflict. Although a seven-year-old may not be able to articulate them in this way, such messages include, "How can a Christian man be hiding something that looks bad and makes me feel funny inside?" (Confusion) "Why is this hidden with dad's stuff in our basement? Maybe this is a mistake." (Denial) "Maybe it got here some other way, or dad just had to put it there until he figured out how to get rid of it." (Rationalization) "If dad is hiding this and looking at it, it must be all right." (Justification) Even more specifically, the memory may hold a precise lie-based statement such as, "It's okay to look at pornography as long as I don't get caught." Those in bondage to pornography typically state this lie. As an addiction to pornography often escalates into corresponding actions or other perversions, that same lie gets transferred to various situations, such as "It's okay to masturbate (have premarital sex, commit adultery, etc.) as long as I don't get caught."

At another level, something of an even more subversive nature is at play in this scenario. God has set fathers in place as spiritual authorities and protectors over their children. Any time a father abdicates his responsibility to shield his children from the enemy, he relinquishes his position to the devil. Abdication of either parent is damaging, but particularly ruinous if exercised by the father, whose role is to represent the heavenly Father to the family as provider, protector, and spiritual leader. Father abdication may come in a variety of ways. A man may never marry the woman he conceives a child with, so the child is raised without a father. He may desert the family in divorce. He may be emotionally absent or a workaholic who is physically absent most of the time. Or, he may be absent for other reasons such as incarceration. I have yet to see where a history of father abdication has not resulted in harm and devastation. Whether done actively, passively, or absently, whenever a father relinquishes his position, his authority, or his parental responsibility, the enemy immediately steps in to fill the void. In effect, the enemy says, "I will gladly stand in for the father." I have repeatedly observed that a father's abdication may result not only in a child's dissociation but also in corresponding demonic influence. Satan fervently pursues anyone that will falsify, nullify, tarnish, or degrade God's presence within a family. He especially targets fathers, who are to represent the heavenly Father.

Involuntary inheritance is another component in the mixture of what Carl unsuspectingly stumbled upon. Involuntary inheritances include generational curses and ancestral sins evidenced by certain predispositions, habits, patterns, and behaviors. These all have roots in parental lineage and are transferred through the bloodline of father or mother or both. Carl's paternal grandfather was not a Christian. He was an angry and perverse man who conceived Carl's father in an adulterous relationship with a woman whom he would eventually marry. Carl's father did not outwardly exhibit signs of a perverse history. However, pornography had become one solution to dull his own inner pain of rejection, invalidation, and abuses by his father. Unwittingly, he was passing on a heritage of perversion to Carl by his furtiveness, even boldness, to hide pornography in the house. Carl's father lived in the conflicted state of professing to be a Christian yet secretly engaging in pornography and other perversions. This inconsistency is indicative of his own struggle with both dissociation and demonization. It also hints of the reality that both dissociation and demonic spirits can be generationally imparted. An established, generationally-based stronghold is easier for Satan to replicate. Therefore, cases abound of strongholds being replicated in children and grandchildren. Furthermore, generational curses and strongholds may merge, align, or link through marriage. (See *Pointers: Curses* in the Appendix)

Sample stronghold: Sabotage

Sabotage is a working of the enemy that awaits an opportune moment to act. Perhaps one of the best illustrations of this in Scripture is found in Mark 6:14-29. Usually titled something like "John the Baptist Beheaded," this account says far more about sabotage of the enemy than about the decapitation of Jesus' cousin. Only two verses are given to the death of John while fourteen verses illustrate the work of sabotage through an offended woman. This passage might be more appropriately named "Herodias the Saboteur" after the woman whose selfish character and wicked influence dominate the story. When the opportunity presented itself for her to call for John's head, no regard was given for the many people who would be impacted by this, from the guests at her husband's birthday party to John's devoted followers.

One way that Satan sabotages is to destroy trust by repeatedly violating trust. For example, any untrustworthy actions by a father toward his child will ultimately devastate that child's trust not only toward his father but also toward others, including the heavenly Father. Satan seizes such moments to infiltrate a person and establish a demonic presence. Sabotage may then become a theme running through a person's life, doing everything possible to disrupt, intercept, or stop God's plan and purpose for his life from being fulfilled. In the event of resulting dissociation, alter identities will be set up to protect or control. Such alters will function to continually sabotage trust within a person's inner dissociative system or between the person and others. "I can never trust again" is a common lie associated with sabotage.

Like Herodias, the enemy is crafty. He is patient. He stays alert for the exact moment to attack not only to destroy an individual but also to bring harm and destruction upon others. While it appears that Satan works suddenly, often his assault comes after imperceptible preparation. In that sense, Satan works like an earthquake. Below the surface there is a shifting of plates over time that leads to an unannounced jolt of the earth, taking everyone by surprise.

In our sixth year of marriage, my wife and I moved to New Zealand. School lessons, milk cartons, and backs of phonebooks gave instructions about what to do in the event of an earthquake, volcano, or tidal wave. We weathered two earthquakes while living there, the second sending wave after wave of earth rolling beneath us. Our house was built on low concrete piles. Once we realized what was happening, our best recourse was to huddle together in a doorway in the center of the house, pray, and wait until the tremors ended. From the vantage point of this central doorway, we could both watch and feel the house heave and fall from one end to the other with each aftershock. Our hearts seemed caught up in this rhythm as we anxiously waited for this unfamiliar and surprising activity to subside, then eventually cease. Despite all the warnings, lessons, and precautions, one is rarely ready for such an unnerving experience!

God's Word is full of instruction alerting us to be prepared for the attack of the enemy. Ephesians 6:13 explicitly points out that the day of evil will come. This same passage warns us to put on the full armor of God in readiness, so that we may stand our ground. While the enemy wants to, and often does, take us by surprise, prepared and equipped believers are ready for the shock and upheaval his attacks bring. Knowing that one way Satan operates is to strike when least expected, wise spiritual warriors are in a constant state of alertness and readiness.

One way the enemy quietly sets the stage for sabotage is by gradually estranging relationships. He is not content to wound individuals, but also to fragment and destroy friendships, marriages, families, churches, communities, and whole nations. Often, what an individual is personally experiencing may mirror parallel activity in other relationships.

Quinn's story

I had a great imagination as a child and still do. But if imagination could be bottled and sold, my son would have made me a millionaire by the time he was five. I can relate to his inventiveness and creativity, his ability to "make something out of nothing" then play with it for hours on end, and have a whale of fun in the process. His mother and I have sought all kinds of ways to encourage and foster his ingenuity.

When I was growing up, my dad subscribed to a magazine whose ideas I would take and either embellish in my mind or try to replicate in some way with my hands. Occasionally, inspiration needed outside help to become reality. One particular issue presented the step-by-step procedure to transform an ordinary bicycle into a stunning, low-slung two-wheeler pedaled as one sat inches from the ground with feet extended forward. I *had* to have that bicycle! But I also had to have help.

Raised on used bicycles, I reckoned there were enough raw materials lying around to build one of these unique cycles. I presented a game plan to dad, who would be enlisted to cut metal, weld tubing, and fine-tune the running gear. I stripped a suitable candidate and separated out bits and pieces for later use. Dad began reconstructing the frame to the desired shape. As I watched him work, I could almost feel the road whizzing beneath me. Shaping extended forks would demand a bit more time than that day held, so the project was set down.

Unfortunately, it was never picked up again except to be moved from the workbench to the floor, to the other side of the shop, to under another bench, to eventually being obliterated by sundry items piled on top of it. Decades later, it was still buried there.

At the time, I could not realize that similar, repeated disappointments were at work below the surface of my life, like shifting plates beneath the earth. I knew my dad to bend over backwards to do things for others, even driving great distances or devoting long hours to them. I do not know when Satan first drove a wedge between us, but each delay or personal denial was like a sledgehammer blow on that wedge. But the enemy awaited this opportune time to strike forcefully.

The stage was set. What was meant to be a rewarding dad and son project provided his chance to sabotage our relationship with a double blow: one to definitively separate my dad and me, the other to divide me within myself.

Through inner healing ministry as an adult, I discovered this dissociation: a twelve-year-old part of myself stalled on the inside who believed some lies about himself. Not only had the enemy successfully separated me from my dad, he continued to work his sabotage in and through me by these lies of invalidation:

I'll never be good enough for dad.

Others are more important to dad than I am.

Dad always does things for others but not for me.

Dad always gets my hopes up then disappoints me.

Dad makes promises but never keeps them.

I can't trust dad to keep his word.

I don't deserve dad's time and attention.

The greatest harm perhaps came in how these lies would later influence how I perceived my relationship with others, in particular my heavenly Father. Through Satan's twisted distortions, my relationship with God came to be interpreted through the paradigm of faulty relationship with my earthly father. Now reread those same lies stated about my dad, replacing "dad" with "God."

I'll never be good enough for God.

Others are more important to God than I am.

God always does things for others but not for me.

God always gets my hopes up then disappoints me.

God makes promises but never keeps them.

I can't trust God to keep his word.

I don't deserve God's time and attention.

Because I learned that I could not trust my dad to keep his promises, the twelve-year-old boy inside had to protect himself from being hurt or disappointed by others. One way he succeeded was to determine never to trust anybody ever again. Although my true person came to know, love, and trust God, this wounded, twelve-year-old part did not. Despite a personal relationship with God, knowledge of his word, and history of his faithfulness, the enemy repeatedly exploited me by tapping into the disappointments and pain held by this twelve-year-old part. I became self-aware of this when I experienced a devastating loss. Alert to the enemy's ways, I was not going to let this sudden "earthquake" rock my world. As the spiritual ground beneath me began to heave, I grabbed for the stability of faith, hope, and love and cried out to God. I immediately understood that my faith was not under attack, for I had no doubt that God was at work and had everything under control in the situation. Neither was it love being assailed, for I sensed neither fear nor failure about the loss. Clearly, it was hope the enemy had targeted. He strategically assaulted me with feelings of disappointment, despair, betrayal, and hopelessness.

Grabbing pen and paper, I determined to apply for myself familiar components of spiritual intervention that I was accustomed to using with others. (See Chapter 3) I found a quiet place to reflect on what was happening to me. I prayed for direction from my trustworthy counselor, the Holy Spirit. I was able to identify and write out the seven lies that appear above. While they all felt very true to me, the one that caused the most intense feeling of distress was "God always does things for others but not for me." I began listening for echoes of that, traveling back through memories, desperately searching to find the first time I felt that could be true. I suddenly discovered myself in a memory as a twelve-year-old boy, standing in my dad's shop, staring at the pile of parts that were supposed to be my new, cool bicycle. Each moment in this memory was like another aftershock of an earthquake. My eyes began to burn with tears and an intense anger rose up in me.

I felt mad at God. Knowing that anger toward God is always rooted in something that is not true, I combed back over my list of lie-based statements. I knew the safest place I could go right then was to the doorway of forgiveness. Realizing this had nothing to do with God, but everything to do with my dad, through my tears I asked my twelve-year-old self if he would be willing to forgive this man who had so deeply disappointed him. A torrent of forgiveness expressions flooded from me. Twelve-year-old Quinn named specific things that had repeatedly happened leading up to this event of dissociation then continued building to this breaking point of despair in adulthood. I found myself being jolted to numerous memories and events. As circumstances or faces came to mind, forgiveness was sincerely expressed. I made notes in my journal as all this transpired.

Then it was over. I cautiously stepped away from the doorway of forgiveness. There were no more aftershocks. In the peace and calm my heart turned to thanksgiving. I began praising God for his presence, his power, and the truths he revealed to me in this situation. Despite all the forgiveness I had expressed toward my dad up until this time and the genuine contentment I have in our adult relationship, this twelve-year-old part had never before participated in any of it. Instead, he held on to deep resentment and hurt, as well as several lies. Forgiveness dispelled every one of the lies, healed the pain, and drove out the darkness with the light of truth.

My personal inner healing journey has included both going to others and, at times, going personally to God as I did in the account you just read. But up until this time, this twelve-year-old part had never been tapped into nor given an opportunity to experience renewal and healing. It was as though the devil awaited an opportune time to repeat what he had done thirty-four years earlier when he separated me from my dad: to sabotage me, only this time in hopes of separating me from my heavenly Father. Thankfully, my journey of inner healing to that point had prepared me to stand against this acute and unexpected attack. As I reflect on this over a year later, I have paused to review the seven lie-based statements above. Not one of them causes me to feel anxious, angry, or afraid. God restored this part of me, renewing my mind and redeeming this slice of relational loss with my dad that was stuck back in time. Through the ministry of inner healing, I have watched him do likewise for others. If you are willing to let him, he will do it for you.

(Thanks, dad, for permission to share this personal story.)

Deliverance reservations

There is much debate about whether there is a Satan, much less a host of demons he commands. Doubters are generally uninformed of Biblical truth or the realities of unholy spiritual realms either in their own or other cultures. In Haiti, for example, the majority of people claim Voodoo, called Vaudou, as their religion. Dissociative techniques are used to make a person vulnerable to trances and rituals that invite demon possession. In other cultures where shamans, witch doctors, and mediums are considered the religious leaders and influencers, it is the norm to be possessed by evil spirits. Demon possession therefore fails to be looked upon as an abnormal behavior. But in many western cultures, psychiatrists and many religious leaders regard demon possession as rare or impossible.

My personal conviction is that a Christian cannot be demon-possessed because possession implies ownership. I do believe a Christian can be demonically oppressed, or "demonized" as explained in Chapter 4. A misconception exists that once a person accepts Jesus Christ as Lord and Savior he is no longer subject to the influence of the devil. If that were true, the Bible would not admonish believers in Jesus to "work out your salvation with fear and trembling" (Philippians 2:12) nor would it alert them to "be self-controlled and alert; your enemy the devil prowls around like a roaring lion looking for someone to devour." (1 Peter 5:8) Christians would not need to be told to "put on the full armor of God so that you can take your stand against the devil's schemes … so that when the day of evil comes, you may be able to stand your ground, and after you have done everything, to stand." (Ephesians 6:11,13) If professed followers of Jesus were unphased by the enemy, none would be living in double-mindedness and exhibiting hypocrisy.

Some Christians may remain stymied because they have self-focused parts and alters acting in disobedience, continuing in addictions, or maintaining relational separation on all three levels because of the phenomenon of dissociation. DISSOCIATION DOES NOT EXCUSE SIN, nor does it negate a person's responsibility for his sinful behavior. However, dissociation does help explain why some believers can claim personal relationship with Jesus Christ and have knowledge of truth, yet persist in disobedience. Perhaps this is how it was possible for Judas to be a chosen disciple of Jesus, betray him for a paltry sum, and then commit suicide upon coming to himself and realizing what he had done. (See Matthew Chapters 26 and 27)

Dissociation is the natural response of the mind to aid survival in the event of extreme stress or trauma. Dissociation buries lies and fears in the subconscious, creating dwelling places for Satan to infiltrate and reside. The enemy will do everything he can to keep a person from receiving healing and restoration. Within a person's dissociative system will be found both God-focused and sin-focused parts and alters. Demonic influences attached to the dissociation are like time-bombs waiting to go off when a person turns to God for help. This can include inner abusers who oppose God and work against healing and a return to single-mindedness. As subconscious dissociative activity is brought to the attention of the conscious mind, a connection can be made that leads to mind renewal and restoration.

Common entry points of demonization are abandonment, rejection, abuse, terror, trauma, abdication, generational inheritance, the occult, and willful, deliberate sin. Many think that the most common way to invite the enemy's presence is through sin choices. This is actually the least common because access by the devil most often comes in early childhood. When an innocent child is subjected to trauma that results in dissociation, demonization becomes linked to the lies and fears held about the experience.

The power of continual trauma through a repetitive theme, such as bullying, reinforces those lies and fears and keeps a person's mind divided, compartmentalized, and amnesic. A wounded part of a person may play host to demons attached to lies held in the dissociation as well as the anger, bitterness, shame, and fear surrounding the dissociative event. No child makes a willful choice to be abandoned, abused, or traumatized. But once subjugated by such things, a child is unwittingly set on a path of self-destruction. It then becomes possible for him to begin making willful sin choices.

There are many valid reasons for having reservations about deliverance ministries and the concept of casting evil spirits out of a person. A lot of bizarre, unruly, even harmful things have been done under the guise of deliverance or exorcism, as is it is known in some religious circles. This includes the spiritual abuse of ignorantly mistaking dissociated parts or alter identities for demons and attempting to cast out what is in fact part of the person. The customary approach to deliverance is to identify demons and order them out in Jesus' Name. This technique can be a very powerful, real experience that brings a measure of freedom and relief. Going through deliverance radically changed my life. I engaged this method for many years because that is all I knew and had been taught. But I was puzzled as to why some people had symptoms return even though demons had been expelled.

You can shoo flies away from an open wound, but if the wound is not treated, the flies will keep coming back. For example, treating a person's addictive behavior as his "problem" without ever getting to the dissociated place of woundedness is like casting out demons without ever getting to the lie-based source of their presence. People do not need a remedial encounter with a therapist or a power encounter with the devil. People need a truth encounter with Jesus Christ. When the authority of the Lordship of Jesus Christ sheds the light of truth into the dark places of a person's subconscious mind, lies are dispelled, and all corresponding demonic attachments simultaneously disappear. Demons do not leave because they have been cast out; they go because they no longer have a lie to justify their present habitation. Addictive and other behaviors that have been a person's solution for masking pain will cease. As wounded parts of a person receive truth, corresponding alter identities no longer have a function. Both the parts and the alters integrate as a consequence of mind renewal and restoration of the soul. The end result is a genuine healing experience that is all-encompassing because it involves a divine encounter with the living God.

It may appear that Satan is totally indiscriminate. Not so. Satan is both deliberate and strategic, engineering all kinds of tactics that, unchecked, lead to destruction. One way that Satan and his minions function are as snipers. A sniper is "one who shoots at detached men of an enemy's force at long range, especially when not in action." Immediate parallels can be seen in the spiritual realm. First, from Satan's perspective, the people of God are "the enemy," his number one target. Heather, a good friend and ministry associate, was on a commercial flight several years ago. She noticed that a woman ahead of her appeared to be praying throughout the flight. Assuming the woman to be a Christian, Heather approached her to make a positive comment about the woman's activity. To my friend's surprise, the woman brazenly admitted to being a witch and that she was praying for the downfall of pastors and the breakup of Christian marriages. Heather, who is rarely at a loss for words, was speechless! Second, among his enemy, Satan targets "detached men," that is, Christians isolated or separated from other Christians for whatever reason. This can include separation within themselves or from others because of dissociation. Third, Satan zeroes in on believers "when not in action," or not actively engaged in spiritual warfare.

Is Satan real? Do demons inhabit people? I have personally experienced enough to convince me that both realities are true. Societal mores and cultural beliefs do not negate the truth. There is an enemy. He hates mankind. He destroys people. He keeps them fragmented. The good news is there is one with spiritual authority and power to both rescue and to save. His name is Jesus, who is the Christ, the Son of the one true and living God.

Chapter 7

What Keeps You Free

*Victory Over Doubt, Despair,
Fear, and Failure*

BOB LOOKED PUZZLED. "HOW DID YOU *DO*
THAT?" HE ASKED WITH ASTONISHMENT. "Do what?"
I replied, as though I did not understand what he was talking
about. "You know," he insisted, "*that* ... how did you *do that*?!"
Bob was clumsily attempting to pull himself back together in front
of me, wiping his face and recapturing his composure. This
respected businessman in his mid fifties did not remember the last
time he had cried, but his embarrassment was overshadowed by
the life-altering experience he had just been through.

Bob had phoned that morning and asked if he might come by
my office on his lunch break. I only knew of Bob from a brief
introduction months previously. Not knowing why he had come
to see me, we were exchanging pleasantries when I was alerted
to a lie-based statement he absentmindedly made about himself.
"I'll never amount to anything." "*Really?*" I thought, as I sat across
from this distinguished man who had every appearance of success.
So I interrupted him. "Bob, I just heard you say something that
surprised me," and repeated the vow back to him. "When is the
first time you believed that was true?"

Instantly Bob was in a teenage memory. As he began describing the circumstance, he stopped himself and leapt even further back into his childhood. Bob, now acting very much like the seven-year-old of the second memory, vividly recalled the berating he had received from his drunken, alcoholic father. "Little Bobby" burst uncontrollably into tears as he remembered hearing his father's stinging words, "You'll never amount to anything." Shattered, this wounded part of Bob retreated into hiding. Now that this particular door of invalidation had been opened into his life, he became a regular target of his father's undeserved scoldings. However, an alter, created to protect Little Bobby, was determined that Bob *would* amount to something. By all appearances, he had done a pretty good job.

To be honest, I was taken by surprise at the instantaneous access into this man's deep pain. As I gently interacted with Little Bobby, I asked him if he would be willing to forgive his father, which he agreed to do. Between subsiding sobs, Little Bobby forgave his dad in tender seven-year-old vocabulary. Next, I asked if it was okay if I prayed for him, which he accepted. When I ended the prayer, I suddenly had Adult Bob back, self-conscious that he had been crying in front of me. Trying to grasp what he had just been through, he sincerely wanted to know how I had "done that." The only thing I had really done was to ask him a simple question about a lie he believed about himself, listen as he recounted two distant memories, and offer to pray in the context of the place where the lie originated. Neither of us expected the dialogue with Little Bobby, of whom adult Bob, until that moment, had no conscious awareness.

I asked Adult Bob to restate the lie. He cautiously said, "I will never amount to anything," and paused to think. Then, with yet another look of surprise, he exclaimed, "That's not true!" A smile lit up his tear-stained face. Adult Bob accepted my offer of another prayer. Then looking down at his watch, he jumped to his feet and announced he had to get back to work. As he hurried to the door, I followed him out and waved as he left in his red sports car.

I rarely frequent Bob's place of business, but about two weeks later I had to go in for something I needed. Bob spotted me from across the store. He hastily approached me and, in the middle of the store, threw his arms around me. Holding me by my shoulders, he excitedly told me about attending a family reunion the previous weekend in another state. It had been some time since he had seen his father, who had always made him feel like an incompetent child. It was not until the drive back that it dawned on him that absolutely nothing that was said or done throughout the weekend had triggered any kind of bad feelings.

I stood there smiling as I listened to this man's animated story, relishing his self-discovery of inner healing. He shared a few other things that had noticeably changed in his life since we had met and thanked me profusely for the time I had given him. As I left his store with my purchase, it occurred to me that I never did find out his reason for coming to see me in the first place. But that did not really matter now. I simply considered it among the serendipitous encounters of inner healing that can only be explained as divine appointments.

Faith, hope, and love

"And now these three remain: faith, hope and love. But the greatest of these is love." 1 Corinthians 13:13

Freedom for Bob came unexpectedly, suddenly. Not everyone stumbles upon a moment of inner healing that readily. Bob did not anticipate this surprise encounter with truth anymore than he could have been ready for the berating he received as a seven-year-old.

The latter had resulted in a part of him being stalled in a lie for half a century. In Bob's case, a distinct event caused dissociation and opened the door to the enemy's theme of invalidation. For another person, a series of events may lead up to a breaking point of dissociation, which was true for me in the bicycle incident I shared in the previous chapter. This was also the case for Melanie, who had weathered in childhood the deaths of several close family members in a relatively short space of time. But the instant she was told of her sister's suicide, part of her shut down in dissociation, the compounded losses being too great to bear any longer.

Regardless of the origin of dissociation, the enemy will seek to prey upon a person and attack him with doubt, despair, fear, and failure. These all stand diametrically opposed to God's intent that we live securely within the safe boundaries of faith, hope, and love. These three characteristics are core to one's being; yet of the three, scripture identifies love as the greatest. True to his purpose, the devil's scheme is to steal, kill, and destroy us at the core. By breaching the walls of faith, hope, and love, he will undermine an individual's ability to live life to the full. (See John 10:10) Fullness of life is meant to be experienced and lived out in the context of faith, hope, and love.

Faith vs. doubt

Of these three spiritual boundary walls – faith, hope, and love – faith is the one that protects people from doubt and disbelief. Faith is important to Jesus. *Very* important. Luke 18:8 records a sobering statement he once made: "When the Son of Man returns, will he find faith on the earth?" It is clear that faith is something Jesus will be seeking at his second coming. He will be looking for faith. Searching for it. On the hunt. And where will faith be found? In the hearts and lives of those in full submission to the authority of his Lordship, who are walking out their salvation by faith, not by sight. It will be discovered in those whose faith is defined both by knowledge of who Jesus Christ is and by experience of a personal relationship with him.

By contrast, doubt is the battering ram Satan uses against the wall of faith. Doubt is translated from the Greek New Testament word, *diakrino*. By definition, doubt "connotes a conflict with oneself, in the sense of hesitating, having misgivings, being divided in decision-making, or wavering between hope and fear." Acts 11:12 gives evidence of Peter's faith and willingness to obey God by going with men Cornelius had sent to him: "the Spirit told me to go with them, doubting (*diakrino*) nothing." In the next chapter, Acts 12:1-7, Peter is found to be imprisoned, awaiting his execution the next day. While he slept peacefully, chained between two guards, verse 5 tells us "the church was earnestly praying to God for him." After a miraculous escape and personal escort to safety by an angel, Peter found the place where those gathered were praying. A servant girl, Rhoda, went to answer his pounding at the door. When she told everyone it was Peter, those inside refused to believe her, and the poor girl was accused of being out of her mind! Peter's faith got him out of prison. The church's disbelief kept him locked outside, concluding it could only be his angel. When his persistent knocking finally convinced them to open the door, they were astonished at whom they found standing there: Peter himself, for whose life to be spared they had spent the night praying!

Satan assails faith by sewing doubt and disbelief into the mind. However, doubt cannot prevail against the superior mind of Christ. Romans 8 is an exposé of life through the Spirit. Verse 6 indicates that "the mind controlled by the Spirit is life and peace." How else could Peter have been sound asleep the night before he was to be killed? Doubt creates turmoil, even to the point of calling one's faith into question. This turmoil may be experienced in a variety of ways, including confusion, which is a common ploy of the enemy used to avoid truth. Rhoda was deemed crazy because she believed it was Peter outside the house. Once those inside were willing to open the door, all doubt was dispelled, along with all their confused reasoning about who might really be on the other side.

I have pictured in the spirit realm the superior mind of Christ as being overlaid upon my own human mind. The mind of Christ serves as a shield *of* faith, as well as a shield *for* faith, extinguishing every flaming dart of doubt targeted by the enemy against my faith. Ephesians 6:12 reminds me that "our struggle is not against flesh and blood, but against the rulers, against the authorities, and against the powers of this dark world and against the spiritual forces of evil in the heavenly realms." The only way I can stand firm against the devil in this matter is to stand *behind* the One who protects me. By *getting out of the way*, I enable Christ to do his work on my behalf.

Yielding to the impervious, superior mind of Christ allows me to be, as it were, "inside looking out" on the battle that is won by my Savior. When I first had this vision of Christ's superior mind over my own, it helped me to rest in the Lord rather than falsely trust in human abilities and futile efforts to resist the devil. I felt as though I was literally right behind the Lord, who was fiercely protecting me. He took all the pummeling hits of doubt, standing firmer with every blow, whereas each strike would have seriously wounded and weakened me. At the time, my faith boundaries were being stretched. After several days of this kind of battle, I felt doubt give up and back off. Since then, my faith has never been so sure, and I remain conscious of being in submission to the authority of Christ's Lordship over my mind as well as my faith.

"God, increase and strengthen my faith. Open my spiritual eyes to perceive the shield of faith you have placed about my mind and my life. Fight on my behalf. Disarm doubt. Humble the devil in the presence of your majesty and power. Free my mind of disbelief. May faith be clearly found in me, and may I impart faith to others. Amen."

Hope vs. despair

An overview of references to hope in the Bible helps us understand the importance of hope as another of the sections in the boundary wall of our spiritual lives. Scriptures reveal the tight connection between hope and God's unfailing love, the trustworthiness of his word, personal relationship with God, and eternity with him. If a person's life is deficient or void of these things – unconditional love, trustworthiness by others, intimacy with others, or a sense of future - he is left in a most despairing state of hopelessness. It is not uncommon for people who have lived through life-threatening circumstances to assert they are alive because they held onto a thread of hope that they would be spared. If hope is extinguished, life may hastily follow suit.

Proverbs 13:12 says, "Hope deferred makes the heart sick, but a longing fulfilled is a tree of life." The adversary of hope is despair. Demonic forces such as hopelessness, betrayal, abandonment, and disappointment fuel despair. For me personally, an accumulation of unfulfilled promises by my dad were recorded in the enemy's account book for later use. As shared in my own story in the previous chapter, little did I realize as a youth how this would affect in adulthood my relationship with and understanding of God. Because sabotage is a critical strategy of the enemy's warfare, he lies in wait for an opportune moment to attack. In my case, a circumstance arose when a project I believed was of the Lord, and in which I had heavily invested myself, was unexpectedly terminated. Even though my faith confirmed this could yet come to pass, I found myself wallowing in a dark despair that confirmed Proverbs 13:12: I literally felt sick in my heart. It was then that an internal check-up revealed the twelve-year-old, wounded part of myself who believed several lies that not only reinforced hopelessness but also incorrectly blamed God: "He always does things for others but not for me." "I can't trust him to keep his word." "I'll never be good enough for God." I found myself nearly crushed under the weight of despair. By allowing my relationship with God to be interpreted through these deceptive lenses, the boundary wall of hope was breached.

A step of faith is taken whenever a person seeks inner healing. Believing that God will help him, he embarks on the journey of having divine order restored in his life. As clutter is cleared, lies are confronted, and forgiveness is spoken, demonic attachments break off and strongholds come down. The emerging true person starts getting put back the way he was originally intended to be: united and whole. It disturbs the devil when the exercise of a person's faith results in renewal of the mind. He may then begin to attack hope. One way he does this is by attempting to intercept the plans God has for a person. Jeremiah 29:11 reveals that God's plan is "to prosper you and not to harm you, to give you hope and a future."

Despair breeds despondency. A person may become discouraged to the point of giving up hope. Even the hint of that to the devil is like blood to a shark. Both move in on their prey. Despite all the truth the Bible holds about hope, if a despairing person has never received revelatory truth to dispel hopelessness, it can overshadow and overcome a person, even to the point of death.

Eric's story

Eric was a thirteen-year-old when he responded to an invitation to accept Jesus as his Lord and Savior while attending a summer church camp. When the minister of his church made a follow-up call the next week to Eric's home, he quizzed Eric about the decision in front of his parents. Because of the awkwardness of being put on the spot, Eric clammed up and was unable to answer his questions. The minister looked at Eric's parents, then back at him and declared, "I guess you are not a Christian then," and excused himself from the house. Although Eric believed with all his heart when he went forward at church camp, the conclusion of the minister devastated him. Taking advantage of Eric's shallow spiritual roots, the enemy came along and began to enforce the lie that he was not a Christian. By fourteen, Eric had his first sexual experience. He began drinking and doing drugs before he left junior high school. He married his pregnant girlfriend at nineteen and began cheating on her before the baby was born. By the time he was in his early thirties, two decades of living for the devil had taken its toll. Wherever he turned, life looked hopeless and there were times he secretly contemplated suicide. When Eric was thirty-four, his wife began going to church. He did not hide his irritation the evening she invited a couple home with her, who came expecting to share a gospel message with Eric and ask him to accept Jesus. He tolerated their presentation and then asked them to leave without accepting their offer.

That night, Eric could not sleep. He got up and went into the living room where he had been several hours earlier with the unwelcome visitors. Grabbing the literature and New Testament that had been left on the coffee table, he walked to the kitchen intending to throw them away. But instead, he paused at the table and began thumbing through one of the brochures. Suddenly, he found himself back in the memory of the summer church camp.

He could hear the guitarist playing as kids quietly shuffled to the front in response to an invitation to accept Jesus. He sensed the same unavoidable tug on his heart of twenty-one years before that had drawn him forward with others. Eric buried his face in his hands. He called out to God to forgive him and accept him back. Now he was in the memory of the night the minister had visited. Eric sensed the Lord telling him the minister was wrong and to forgive him. Not sure what to do or say, Eric rushed to the bedroom to wake his wife. In that early morning hour, she helped him forgive the minister and, in a tender moment, expressed her own forgiveness of him. Life was not the same for Eric after that experience. From a position of restored hope, he began walking out a journey of rapid inner healing and transformation. With his heart made right with God, Eric's favorite verse became Isaiah 49:23, "Those who hope in me will not be disappointed."

Prayer Pause

"God, my hope is in you. I forgive those whom the devil has used to sabotage your call, your gifts, and your plan for my life. (Name those who may come to mind and forgive them for the specific things they have done.) Drive despair from my heart. I resist the devil and in Jesus' Name stand firm against all despair and hopelessness. Amen."

Love vs. fear and failure

"The greatest of these is love." Because love is the greatest boundary wall, it seems that the enemy bombards love at least twice as hard using the dual weapons of fear and failure. The Bible teaches, "There is no fear in love. But perfect love drives out fear, because fear has to do with punishment." (1 John 4:18) 1 Corinthians 13:8 reveals that "love never fails." 1 John 4:16

plainly states, "God is love." The antithesis of love is hate. Satan hates us. Having himself rejected God's love, he connives to see that as many as possible likewise reject God's love. Here again one can see the critical importance of the role of the human father and the devastation when he fails to love his children. Satan will gladly fill that void but only for destructive purposes. Even though God's Word reassures that "never will I (God) leave you; never will I forsake you" (Hebrews 13:5), if a person has not been loved by his father and has experienced his rejection and invalidation, it is hard to accept, much less display to others, the love of the heavenly Father.

Fear causes faith to fail and imagination to run wild. My wife and I were on a flight once where sheer winds forced the small passenger plane to pitch wildly. As we were flying over water, the cabin fell silent as the attendants sought to reassure passengers even as they prepared us for a possible catastrophe. You could sense the anxiety throughout the crowded plane. My wife slipped her hand into mine, and I hoped my mounting fears would not intensify her own. We quietly prayed and, in the unknown of that situation, whispered farewells to one another, honestly believing this could be the end. Although we were approaching our destination, we were little comforted knowing the landing would be preceded by a drop into mountainous terrain. I shut my eyes, trying to block out the dread I felt rising inside me. As the plane thrashed and plunged toward the earth, my mind raced with exaggerated and frightening thoughts. Perhaps this is how the disciples felt the night they were caught in a terrible squall. Matthew 8:23-27 gives this account of their experience:

> Without warning, a furious storm came up on the lake, so that the waves swept over the boat. But Jesus was sleeping. The disciples went and woke him, saying, "Lord, save us! We're going to drown!" He replied, "You of little faith, why are you so afraid?" Then he got

up and rebuked the wind and the waves, and it was completely calm. The men were amazed and asked, "What kind of man is this? Even the winds and the waves obey him!"

1 John 4:18 says "the one who fears is not made perfect in love." In the process of restoring divine order, God is perfecting us by his love. Fear and love are in opposition. When Jesus steps into the picture, his very presence exudes that perfect love that displaces all lies, threats, and fears of the devil. The love of the Lord is the greatest impediment to the schemes of the devil. The enemy knows that. So, he aims to cripple people with the double blow of fear and failure.

I used to not love myself. Because I disdained myself, neither could I love others as God would have me love them. This was partly due to a lie I believed about myself that I was ugly and, therefore, unlovable. While receiving ministry from others in an inner healing session, I remember the Lord stepping into the early childhood memory that held that lie. He showed me in a very personal way that I was beautiful to him and that was all that mattered. Any sense of worthlessness, fear, and failure evaporated. Then I heard echoing from my past the familiar children's song, "Jesus Loves Me, This I Know." I never believed the chorus, "Yes, Jesus loves me," until that moment. As I write, I can look at the wall immediately to my right and read the words of that song. They have hung there since that session as a constant reminder of the Lord's deep love for me. ME! And it is not merely because "The Bible tells me so." Yes, the Bible *does* tell me about Jesus' love. But it was not until he personally revealed his love to me at the source of my lie-based thinking that this particular truth from God's Word finally meant something real to me. Once Jesus spoke to my inner turbulence and dispelled the lie, I became completely calm on the inside.

The more I have developed intimacy with the Lord, the greater my love has become for myself and for others. Equally important has been my ever-increasing love for God. Jesus loved people without pretense, expectation, or condition. I imagine that when he stepped into the environment of the demon possessed, the infirmed, or the skeptical, the sheer magnitude of his love for all compelled some to seek his deliverance, healing, and renewal. No wonder that by a mere gesture, a touch, or a simple word, there were those who received his help and restoration. As people are drawn into the environment of inner healing, that is the same kind of love they deserve to encounter, which exposes them to the true love of God.

Prayer Pause

"God, I confess I have yielded to fear and failure. My heart's desire is to love you and be loved by you personally and intimately. In Jesus' Name I take authority over every barrier the enemy has set up in my mind and in my heart that keeps me from your love. Thank you for perfecting me in love. Thank you for your love that never fails. Amen."

Internal check-up

As you work through the following exercise, if you feel over-whelmed at any point, or unable to proceed, then stop. You may benefit by having a safe person with you who can help you process and pray about what you experience.

Find a quiet place to do this activity, where you will not be interrupted. Draw a circle in the middle of a piece of paper. Divide the circle into thirds. Write these three words, one in each third of the circle: Faith, Hope, and Love. Just outside the circle, write the corresponding opposite to each word: doubt (outside Faith), despair (outside Hope), fear and failure (outside Love). Your diagram may look something like this:

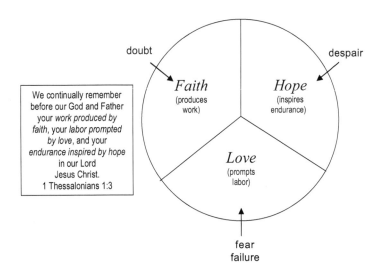

Prayer Pause

"God, as I engage in this exercise, I ask you to protect my mind and my heart from the evil one. Please reveal truth to me that will dispel any lies that I believe about myself. Restore and strengthen all boundaries of faith, hope, and love that the enemy has breached. Amen."

1. Underline the characteristic in the circle you most struggle with today: Faith, Hope, or Love.
2. State a lie you believe about yourself in relation to that core component. For example:

    Love: "I am not loveable."

Write this statement down on the same sheet of paper and then speak it out loud.

Note: It may take some trial and error to pinpoint the exact wording of a lie-based statement.

3. Record what kind of emotional responses this lie evokes. (e.g. sadness, fear, despair, rejection, etc.)

Note: Ranking a lie on a scale of 0-10, with 10 being high, may help you determine the intensity of emotional response linked to a lie. (See *Procedures: Documenting a Session: Lies* in the Appendix)

4. Ask the Holy Spirit to take you to the memory where you first believed this lie or statement was true. Get in touch with your emotions in the context of that memory.

5. Invite Jesus to reveal truth to you in that memory, however he chooses to do that. Quietly wait upon him. Record any insights or impressions you sense he has given you.

6. Speak forgiveness by name for anyone who offended or hurt you in that memory. Be specific in these expressions. You might simply begin, "Jesus, I forgive (name of person) for (state clearly what you are forgiving him or her for)." Do not forget to include forgiving yourself as needed. (See *Pointers: Forgiveness Prayer* in the Appendix.)

7. Return to the memory that held the lie. Restate the lie out loud. Rank it again using the 0-10 scale. If you still have a strong emotional response, it may be that the lie is rooted in another memory, or there are other related lies in that same memory that need to be dealt with. Repeat steps 2-5 as needed.

8. Pause to give thanks to the Lord.

Conclusion

Faith, hope, and love are powerful and intentional spiritual boundaries set in place to protect people from the evil one and help them maintain both relational and spiritual integrity. Whenever these are breached, the enemy may invade territory that he is not meant to occupy. The fragmentation of dissociation can contribute toward providing him habitation in the mind so that his debilitating themes may be carried out and his unholy strongholds set up. Part Three, Practical Application, explores ways to overcome dissociation, be free of deception, and restore your true person to wholeness.

Part Three
Practical Application

Trading Faces

Chapter 8

Mapping Dissociation
Three "Camps" of Dissociation

JOEL DESPERATELY TRIED TO COMPREHEND HIS DAD'S WORDS. "I'M LEAVING," dad said, looking down at his four-year-old son as they stood facing each other in the foyer. Then turning away, he walked out through the open door and disappeared into the darkness. Time seemed to stand still at that moment. Joel remembers hearing his dad's car start up and drive away. Other than that, his mind was blank, his emotions dead, his face expressionless. All of a sudden, the light in his eyes went out, and the wounded four-year-old whom Adult Joel had been talking about was now present. "Little" Joel stared vacantly over my shoulder at the wall behind me and whispered, "Nobody loves me."

Dissociation creates a type of historical programming that has roots in a particular event. For Joel, the incomprehensible notion that his dad was walking out on him scattered memory data in his mind that influenced this programming. A wounded four-year-old Joel stalled that night in the foyer in order to manage this painful reality. Gripped by the unknown of being raised as the only child of a solo mother, young Joel experienced a defining moment of dissociation. The encoding of the dominant lie in that memory, "Nobody loves me," came to be more specifically interpreted,

"Dad doesn't love me," later, "Mom doesn't love me," and eventually, "God doesn't love me." An alter identity formed that, ironically, protected Joel by preventing people from getting close enough to love him. Inside, Joel was desperately needing and wanting to be loved. Externally, his attitude and behavior only let people get so close, despite his charm, good looks, and capabilities. But there are several more sides of Joel that eventually would be created to help him manage well into adulthood.

The value of maps

I have had the privilege of traveling through thirty of our fifty United States. When my wife and I married, she did not know how to read a map. That was okay. I could. We set off by car on our honeymoon, traveling from Kansas to Florida. Even though we had a general route in mind, there were some fascinating and fun side trips that added to the spontaneity of our time together. On the way back, somewhere in the middle of Alabama, I became quite ill to the point we thought it wise to seek medical attention. A random doctor in a random town, suspecting strep throat, prescribed an antibiotic and wished us well. Feverish to the point of delirium, I handed the car keys to my bride and said, "You'll have to drive." I crawled into the back seat. The next thing I knew we were back in Kansas. Needless to say, my wife took a crash course on map reading!

Six years later, we found ourselves living on the other side of the world. New Zealand would be our home for the next ten years. Because of the nature of ministry I was involved in, there was hardly a road we did not travel in that South Pacific island nation. There were several driving challenges. Superhighways as we know them here in America were nonexistent. The main "highway" on the South Island's west coast was still gravel for much of its length. It was not uncommon to come upon a one-lane bridge where opposing drivers would eyeball each other the best they could, then someone would start across first. (There was even one such bridge that was also shared with the railroad!) I grew up on a farm and learned to tell direction by the sun and shadows. In the southern hemisphere, all the shadows are cast from north to south as the sun travels across the sky. To me, this always made east seem west and west seem east. I eventually got the hang of it. Perhaps the biggest challenge was getting used to driving on the opposite side of the road and from the right-hand side of the car. Even though so many things seemed to be different, New Zealand did have roadmaps – which even my wife could read!

Maps are important (even though many guys might dispute that!). They provide a lot of information about various routes to get to a destination, the types of roads that will be traveled on, the names of towns and points of interest, and a legend with symbols and keys that interpret where to find everything from scenic routes to rest areas. My United States atlas has a big, two-page spread of America showing the country's interstate system, principal highways, and general topography. Fortunately, its other pages are filled with maps of individual states with information about roads and towns and rivers and lakes and forests and parks and distances and many other things - all in great detail.

A map helps one chart a course from one destination to another. Mapping a person's dissociation is a critical component to reaching the destination of inner restoration. Chapter 6 diagrammed ways in which Satan's counterfeit "kingdom" is opposed to the true Kingdom of God. In a similar way, mapping dissociation reveals opposition within a person's dissociative system. By plotting the "lay of the land" within a person, it becomes easier to visualize the internal struggle for dominance. Mapping dissociation identifies the opposing sides in this battle and is an invaluable aid to strategically working toward wholeness. Bringing a person to this place of self-awareness increases the ability to achieve co-consciousness regarding historical causes of dissociation, his internal relationship with himself, his external behavior, and how these factors impact relational dis-order. Categorically mapping one's dissociation helps the true person emerge and become engaged in the self-monitoring of wounded parts and alter identities throughout the journey of healing and restoration.

A comment about documenting

Documenting a formal session of ministry will help facilitate the mapping of dissociation and serve as a tool to reaching the destination of wholeness. A sample outline can be found in the Appendix under *Procedures: Documenting a Session*. This outline may also prove helpful to individuals as they work out matters in their own healing journey, particularly the segments on pinpointing memories, lies, curses, and dissociation. It may also help an individual structure a personal journal that records his healing progress.

Mapping dissociation

Dissociation is mapped, or diagrammed, in three primary "camps" within an individual's dissociative system. Alter identities and wounded parts will be found in two dominant areas: God-focused or Self-focused and one subdominant area: Regulator. These may be thought of as a coin with the two sides being either God-focused or Self-focused and the Regulator represented by the thin edge.

1. **God-focused**. God-focused entities in a person are created to take care of the things of God by helping the person to focus on God or to represent him in some way.

God-focused alters may operate to protect wounded parts and help avoid pain. This area often includes the true person who loves God and is devoted to him.

Just because an alter is God-focused does not mean it is always or consistently God-centered. This is because dissociation is set up for a specific function such as to protect or control. For instance, there may be within a person's system a pharisaical alter that loves God and knows the Bible but functions in a restricted, religious legalism. While such an alter may not oppose God or the things of God, he may hinder the person, bringing a skewed representation of what it is to be genuinely God-focused. He may dislike, distrust, or criticize other alters, and even be in conflict with other God-focused alters.

2. **Self-focused**. These entities are generally established to take care of themselves and to mask pain. They will function to protect themselves and/or to control circumstances around them to avoid further woundedness. Self-focused alters within a person's dissociative system tend to be divisive.

Because self-focused alters are self-centered, they are often sin-centered. These are the alters that typically seek to relieve the pain of wounded parts by acting out through various types of selfish solutions, including addictions. These behaviors usually cause conflict and confusion for the true person or for God-focused entities. Self-focused alters often function out of deception and will promote the work of the enemy to steal, kill, and destroy. (John 10:10) Because of their sin-centered nature, these alters may be demonically influenced and linked to strongholds such as fear, anger, or despair.

3. **Regulator.** Between the two dominant camps at least one alter, a regulator, will typically be at work. Regulator alters are considered subdominant because they may have no personal attachment to any wounded parts or their trauma. Therefore, they may not play a direct role in protecting, controlling, or presenting as do other alters. Regulator alters are often the most difficult to identify because of their subliminal presence. They are characteristically neutral, devoid of feelings, and without personality. Despite their relative impartiality, they have a major responsibility within the dissociative system: mediating between the two dominant sides.

A regulator is often the most aware alter within a person's system. Regulators are usually more consistently active than individual God-focused or self-focused entities of a person. That is because they are always observing, filtering data, determining variables, making decisions, and acting on behalf of one or both sides of the system. A regulator may function as a type of gatekeeper to determine "who" may act at any given time or which "side" will get its way in a particular situation. Regulators may express fatigue because they are constantly receiving, processing, directing, and filing information.

Joel's story continues

Today, Joel is a corporate executive in his mid-forties. He exhibits a remarkable blend of people skills and business acumen. He is highly regarded by the CEO of the company, to whom he answers directly and from whom he has great trust. He has been instrumental in representing the company in ways that have brought success to many. Joel is both well liked and well paid, his affable personality equal to his professional confidence. People gravitate to his wife and him in both business and social settings. This is one man who gives every appearance of "having it all together."

Despite an evident tenderness toward God from an early age and even a sense of calling to ministry, Joel's framework of love and security was shattered when his dad walked out. Little Joel dissociated, taking with him all sorts of materials for the enemy to set up a demonic stronghold of fear: abandonment, rejection, anxiety, worry, apprehension, loneliness, and condemnation. Unexpectedly tossed outside the familiar and safe boundary of love, from that event onward, he battled daily with fear and failure. A corresponding alter system developed both to protect Joel and to control others in a way that would keep him from being further rejected.

Now, 41 years later, Joel sat across from a ministry partner and me, desperate to escape his personal prison of fear and find the lost trail of destiny that was abandoned in the foyer of his first home. As he navigated back into territory he had resisted returning to for nearly four decades, the map of his dissociation began to unfold. Several hours later, eleven distinct parts of Joel were identified and interacted with. Characteristically, these fell into one of the three "camps" mentioned above. Before diagramming Joel's dissociation, you will be introduced by name to various entities in his dissociative system. Each of these was named by Joel himself as he came to conscious self-awareness of each one. Alters will know which "camp" they are part of. If you are unable to tell, or the person is uncertain, simply ask the alter, who will know.

Little Joel

This is the wounded, four-year-old Joel who stalled the moment his dad walked out on his mother and him. Little Joel is honest, fun loving, and likes to make others happy. His curly, dark hair, dimples, and bright eyes have people doting on him all the time. He represents the time when things in Joel's life were innocent and the family was a complete unit. Little Joel loves people for who they are. (Note the contrasting statement made below by "Performance Joel," who loves people for what they can do for him.) Little Joel explained he had to "go away" when his dad left, because he could not be happy anymore. Despite the adoration he receives, Little Joel believes he is unloved.

Home Joel

Home Joel was set up to protect Little Joel, but the only way he knows how is to withdraw. When Home Joel steps into his house, he is a different person. Alone with his wife, he is inhibited and quiet. This part of Joel carries a lot of shame, rejection, fear, pain, insecurity, and worthlessness. This stems from his father's abandonment but also links to events in his life such as having premarital sex once he became engaged to his wife, a minister's daughter. Home Joel fears replication of such traits in his nearly grown children. Home Joel has little to give of himself once inside the safety of his house. His wife cannot understand his bouts with depression, chiding him to "snap out of it," which only triggers deeper woundedness and compounds his depression. Home Joel is secretly on an antidepressant, prescribed by a psychiatrist he sees when doing business in another state. Home Joel avoids interaction with people because of the pain they cause. This alter is virtually unknown outside his house. He is always in trouble with his wife because Joel is gone such long hours and never lifts a finger to help around the place. However, another alter, Worldly Joel is able to pacify her with gifts and other indulgences.

Missionary Joel

Missionary Joel knows that God loves him and has never left him but believes God wants to punish him. This alter emerged when Joel's true person gave his heart to the Lord at the age of eight. Missionary Joel feels he must work all the time to please God or Joel might die and go to hell. Missionary Joel is remorseful about other entities in the system that have "given up on God." Missionary Joel encourages Adult Joel to see his position in the marketplace as an opportunity to represent the Lord and find ways to serve others. He is frustrated about being less and less active at church. He troubles Joel with nagging reminders that to really please God he should be a fulltime missionary.

Boss Defender

Boss Defender has a tender heart toward his unchurched boss. He prays for him and, in partnership with Missionary Joel, does everything possible to show his boss what a "real Christian" is like. He is always building his boss up, because he loves this man for who he is. He is quick to defend his boss, cover for his inadequacies, and make things right when necessary so they both look good. He hopes and prays that his boss will one day come to know Jesus personally.

Negotiator Joel

Negotiator Joel is typical of a Regulator within a person's dissociative system. He describes himself as a "non-person" with neither feelings nor personality. Negotiator is like a radar scanner, constantly searching for, receiving, and processing information internally (within his own dissociative system) and externally (from others, from the situation he is facing, and from the environment). He is particularly alert in new situations and when meeting people for the first time. Negotiator has no allegiance to either the God-focused or the self-focused sides of Joel. However, he will operate as a spokesperson at times for either side, or determine which side will have its way, depending on the circumstances. His job is important because he sees to it that Joel is portrayed as intelligent, well informed, and decisive. All the same, Negotiator is *very tired* of his never-ending job.

Boss Blamer

This alter was set up to control and was established upon graduation from college to minimize the impact of Joel's self-doubt and fear of failure. No matter how hard Joel tries, the boss makes Joel feel like a failure. If it were not for Joel, his boss might not have a job, or so thinks Boss Blamer. He is angry with the boss, who does not affirm or recognize Joel as he feels he deserves. Behind closed doors and behind the boss's back, Boss Blamer criticizes the boss and faults him for company problems. Boss Blamer is irritated by Boss Defender's efforts to represent Jesus to the boss.

Business Joel

In the corporate world, Business Joel is self-assured, positive, and portrays a professional image in business circles. He is known for being decisive and making wise decisions that benefit the company. Business Joel has a charismatic personality and is always neatly groomed. Highly respected, Business Joel is sought after to sit on various boards and is committed to several community groups. Driven by perfectionism, Business Joel exhibits traits that are generationally linked to his father, who is a corporate executive in another state.

Church Joel

This is a presenting alter who only goes to church for the sake of appearance. He dutifully accompanies his family but finds himself sitting nearer and nearer the back pew. Church Joel knows all the religious lingo, the right things to do, and makes the effort to connect with people who might give him a business or social advantage. He used to play a key role in church leadership until he got off sides with the senior minister a few years ago. Church Joel tolerates church, but what he really wants is out.

Worldly Joel

Joel's mom struggled to make ends meet. One night, he overheard her telling someone on the phone she did not know how she would have enough money that month to feed the two of them. The fear of starving to death was the catalyst for Worldly Joe forming. This forced thirteen-year-old Joel out of the house to get a paper route, although his mother refused to let him use his earnings on household expenses. For the first time, Joel had spending money, and Worldly Joel showed him what money could do for him. This alter is vain and uses money to impress others. Worldly Joel is known in the business arena, both inside his community and beyond. Worldly Joel likes to foot the bill for others and lavish gifts on them so they will like and accept him, even though at times it extends his credit. This part of Joel is disgusted with Home Joel and wishes Church Joel would give up the whole church scene. He would especially like to put a stop to any money going into the offering plate every Sunday.

Cynical Joel

Cynical Joel is distrustful and sarcastic. He is easily triggered by frustrations at home, at work, and at church. Negotiator keeps Cynical in check so he does not readily show the anger that often seethes beneath the surface. This part feels he would be better off without Home Joel and Church Joel. He tolerates work but is dubious about how much longer Joel can keep up what, to Cynical Joel, is a facade.

Performance Joel

Performance Joel loves attention and has several talents deserving of recognition. As an experienced actor, he can perform his way out of anything, or at times, into anything. Performance Joel is a close companion to Business Joel and Worldly Joel. The three of them savor being celebrated at work, as well as in the world, where he seeks opportunities to act. This part of Joel loves people for what they can do for him. (Note the contrasting statement made above by "Little Joel," who loves people for who they are.)

Now that you have become familiar with these members of Joel's dissociative system and some of their characteristics, the following diagram shows which "camp" each belongs in:

God-focused	Regulator	Self-focused
Little Joel Missionary Joel Boss Defender	Negotiator Joel	Home Joel Boss Blamer Business Joel Church Joel Worldly Joel Cynnical Joel Performance Joel

As you can see, Joel's life is weighted in self-focused dissociation. Over time, Joel has increasingly yielded to this side of himself to mask unresolved pain. If a person's self-focused side is nurtured, he will become increasingly self-centered and view relationships, life, and work from the perspective of "What's in it for me?" As with a scale, the balance tips where there is greater weight placed. A goal of inner healing is not to "strike a balance" between God-focused and self-focused sides of a person. Rather, it is to help redeem both sides of a person and restore all the weight back in its rightful place so the true person can emerge and be strong.

Once dissociation is mapped in this way, the typical response of a person is relief. They finally have some answers to why they behave the way they do. They quickly become attuned to exactly where internal conflicts lie. They come to realize not only what they are dealing with but also with "whom" they are dealing. This level of self-awareness opens a door of hope most have never found before.

Another tool for mapping dissociation is a simple timeline that represents a continuum starting at birth. Checkmarks may be made at different ages on the timeline to indicate significant events that for various reasons contributed to dissociation. For example:

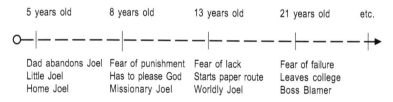

5 years old	8 years old	13 years old	21 years old	etc.
Dad abandons Joel	Fear of punishment	Fear of lack	Fear of failure	
Little Joel	Has to please God	Starts paper route	Leaves college	
Home Joel	Missionary Joel	Worldly Joel	Boss Blamer	

Traditional counseling, therapy, and psychiatry are unaware of this way of distinguishing and diagramming dissociation. Traditional approaches of treatment do not consider God as an answer and therefore would not distinguish dissociation in these three "camps." I minister to people under the premise that God is ultimately the *only* answer to their woundedness and pain. What traditional therapists identify as the "problem" (for example, an addiction), the person sees as his "solution." His "solution" to avoiding or numbing his pain may be an addiction to drugs, or alcohol, or pornography. Although these "solutions" may themselves be harmful, it seems more comforting to "medicate" with one of these rather than to revisit painful memories that hold equally painful emotions. Regrettably, addictions remain the "solution" for many because they are not aware that it is possible to receive complete freedom through Jesus Christ. Since the traditional approaches treat the person's "solution" as though it were the "problem," an individual may submit to medications, therapies, years of counseling, or all manner of treatments without receiving genuine healing. He may have a better quality of life. He may cope better under stress. He might function more productively under medication. But until the pain is healed by the love and power of God, neither professional therapies for changing behavior nor personal remedies for masking pain provide lasting cures. If anything, they contribute to the real problem of trusting in man for answers rather than God. That can even be the case with counselors who profess to be Christian.

In Chapter 3 you read Monty's story and got a similar glimpse of one way a psychiatrist often treats a person with depression: by prescribing medication to deal with a behavior. In both Monty's and Joel's cases, depression was the behavior that resulted in psychiatric care. But depression was not Joel's problem. Depression was Joel's solution for coping with his root problem of deeply buried pain and lie-based belief that nobody loved him. By mapping Joel's dissociation, it was discovered that depression was exclusive to Home Joel. We could then begin to search, with the help of that alter, for the source of pain that was being avoided and kept hidden by depression. This led to the memory you read about at the beginning of this chapter, which resulted in healing in that memory.

As subsequent sessions were held, we were able to work together to address other unique characteristics within Joel's dissociative system and the peculiar conflicts these created. In the process, several other entities were identified and mapped. Order began to be re-established both within himself and with others. Joel's healing journey continues, but he has found navigating life much easier with a map of his dissociation. With his mind being renewed and his soul being restored, the map has also served as a way to chart where his journey began and what kind of progress is being made toward the destination of wholeness.

Mapping exposes double-mindedness

Mapping dissociation helps illustrate double-mindedness, a concept that you read about in Chapter 2. When a person is of two minds, one "mind" may be God-focused, the other "mind" may be self-focused. The two are in opposition. Double-mindedness may throw a person into the dilemma of wondering which "mind" he will follow. Jesus taught in Luke 16:13, "No servant can serve two masters. Either he will hate the one and love the other, or he will be devoted to the one and despise the other." Double-mindedness also creates much conflict, turmoil, and confusion in the mind. Romans 8:6 reveals that "the mind of sinful man is death, but the mind controlled by the Spirit is life and peace."

Now I better understand why people thought to be Christian might simultaneously be engaged in some ungodly activities or conflicting lifestyles. Dissociation does not excuse them, but it provides a basis for understanding their double mindedness. Mapping dissociation helps expose the relational dis-order within a person that is behind illogical or clashing behaviors and their consequences. Not all mapping may be done as formally or as detailed as was done with Joel. However, understanding the three "camps" and their distinct focuses will help distinguish dissociation more clearly so that ministry may be more productive.

What happens in most cases is that the more the dissociation is fed, the more it becomes reinforced and the stronger it operates. The more comfortable a person becomes in his dissociation, the easier it is to default to operating out of relational dis-order. Part of Satan's scheme to steal, kill, and destroy is to influence self-focused entities to overshadow any God-focused entities. As the distance between the two "camps" increases, the more challenging the restoration process becomes. I will often ask an alter what percentage of the time it operates within an individual's dissociative system. Whenever an answer comes of over fifty percent of the time, that gives me a clue to the level of dominating activity. Of course, other alters may not agree with that alter's assessment, so after a little internal "committee meeting" or a quizzing of alters independently, there will probably come a more accurate picture of an alter's influence within the system. I have facilitated ministry to people where a dominating "camp" or a group of alters is genuinely operating 75-80% of the time. Such dominance reduces the activity of other alters, often weakens the God-focused side, and stifles the true person. When double-mindedness is exposed and mapped, it becomes more difficult for dominating alter activity to continue, particularly when inner healing is being pursued.

Spencer's story

I responded to a call from a distraught mother who had been referred to me by her pastor. She was concerned about her teenage son's depression and threats to commit suicide. She told me Spencer was a Christian, but then awkwardly explained that he struggled with gender confusion. Her son was seeing a local counselor in their community who felt she could be of no further help to Spencer and was preparing to recommend him to a psychiatrist. When the mother sought the advice of her pastor, they both concluded that this particular psychiatrist would likely affirm the boy's homosexuality and encourage him to embrace that lifestyle.

A brief interview with the mother gleaned some family history that helped me quickly ascertain the root of Spencer's pain as the abandonment of his father during his first year of life. Spencer was raised in a solo parent home, with each sibling of a different father. Therefore, his birth-father never had an active presence or role in his life. Spencer then got on the phone. A pleasant and articulate junior in high school, Spencer quickly made it clear to me that he was gay and quite comfortable with that, as was his counselor. He explained that neither he nor his counselor saw any reason for that to change, nor did he want to change. When he eventually returned the phone to his mother, I was surprised to learn from his mother that the local counselor he had been seeing claimed to be a Christian yet supported his lifestyle choice.

I have spent several years now ministering to Christians who sincerely want to be free of the "solution" of homosexuality. I know that what the culture accepts as a predisposition or identifies as an acceptable lifestyle actually operates out of dissociation and relational dis-order. In my brief conversation with Spencer, I spoke to two distinct alters that were easily mapped as being from two opposing camps. A God-focused side of Spencer was very sincere in his beliefs and had a gentle disposition. He told me he has been a Christian for several years but was not as active at church as he used to be. The self-focused side of Spencer I talked with identified himself as a homosexual. This alter was proud to be gay and explained he had become disillusioned with the church for not accepting people as they are. A lot of anger and rebellion were expressed by him in very defensive tones. The depression and suicidal tendencies never directly came up in my discussion with Spencer, although I concluded from the nature of what he disclosed that these were linked to the homosexual alter who was weary of being ridiculed and emotionally beaten by peers and others.

Before finishing my conversations with Spencer and his mother, I made sure they both understood the door was always open if either of them would like to contact me again. I hung up the phone feeling anguished for two reasons. First, I was reminded that a person must want inner healing for himself, not because someone else thinks he needs it. Second, knowing where Spencer's "solution" could lead, I paused to pray. Spencer's self-focused choices could possibly culminate in the extreme dissociative consequence of suicide, which he had already contemplated. Although I never got to meet with Spencer, I have met with and ministered to many who have been drawn to homosexuality as a way to ease the pain of woundedness in their lives. Each has grappled with compounded dissociation and other complex issues. These may have been averted had interventive inner healing been available to them earlier in life.

Carl's story continues

You will recall Carl's story from Chapter 6, the seven-year-old who stumbled upon pornography in the basement of his house. Many who have had their dissociation mapped during a session have struggled with sexual perversions, including an addiction to pornography. This example of double-mindedness is by no means limited to non-Christians or "backslidden" Christians. It is now running rampant among Christians who themselves thought they would never engage in such a thing. How does this happen? Until recent years, the possibility of getting caught purchasing pornography or visiting an adult video store served as a type of safety wall between a person's God-focused side and his self-focused side. The internet has effectively removed that wall. Many have unintentionally stumbled upon internet pornography while others take advantage of the ease and privacy of internet surfing. Either way, the availability of pornography through the internet has opened a wide gate that has exposed children and adults to extremes of unnatural perversion. For some, this has been a defining moment of dissociation that turns them onto the broad path of self-focused, often unnatural pursuits. For others, it reinforces the existing activity of self-focused alters who deliberately seek out pornography. Either way, dissociation is validated, as Carl's story expounds.

Time and again I have heard people's similar stories that describe their struggle with pornography either as an addiction or as a besetting sin. Each time, the story is linked to lies that cause conflict between a person's God-focused side and his self-focused side. In ministering to Carl, we were able to map his dissociation and isolate the alters that used pornography and masturbation as his "solution" for subduing the pain of shame and guilt which, in his case, were created by pornography in the first place. Perversion works through deception and distortion. When dealing with perversion issues, the most common lie is "This is okay as long as I don't get caught." Even when perverse experiences are shared with others, they typically stay hidden in secrecy and shame. Paul wrote in 2 Corinthians 4:2, "We have renounced secret and shameful ways; we do not use deception, nor do we distort the word of God." He goes on to speak of setting forth the truth plainly. When Carl was exposed to "truth set forth plainly," the common lie just stated above was squarely challenged. Truth also ferreted out other lies. As well, truth shed light into secret and shameful places of his mind that had never before been brought out into the open. As these places were mapped out, they could not be kept hidden. The web of dissociation began to be untangled as Carl renounced secret and shameful ways. With the dispelling of lies, corresponding perversion spirits no longer had a legitimate connection to Carl and simultaneously left.

As Carl's mind began to be renewed, transformation followed. Eventually, the map showed less dissociation as wounded parts were healed, and corresponding alters were brought back into their rightful place of intended standing within the true person. Carl did not need pornography or masturbation any more to ease his pain. He experienced redeemed strength, energy, and wholeness as his healing journey progressed, and his true person emerged. He was further restored in many areas and ways to resemble the original image God had intended for Carl all along. In one note of appreciation to us, Carl wrote, "I'm blown away by how healed I feel and am."

Summary

Once a person gets in touch with his dissociation, self-awareness opens a door to inner healing. By mapping dissociation, you can start identifying, for example, which entities are decidedly God-focused and how they can begin cooperating together to help facilitate healing. In recent years, "What Would Jesus Do" was a popular saying promoted through all kinds of Christian paraphernalia. Some might think that wearing a "WWJD" bracelet would serve as a simple safeguard to keep self-focused alters in check. But the fact of the matter is, self-focused alters do not care what Jesus would do! Their primary concern is taking care of themselves and doing whatever possible to ease pain or to protect from further wounding. Most alters eventually become willing to relinquish their role, position, or function so the true person may be restored. Most of them do not like their job anyway and will admit to being tired of it. But, because they have been established for a specific purpose, they perform their job even when it is hurtful or destructive. They will continue to do so unless given a valid reason to cease.

When someone outside a person is able to map his dissociation, the accountability becomes another factor that helps usher in healing. Satan does not like dissociation being mapped out in this way because it may lead to a person receiving deep inner healing and restoration of his soul. Mapping dissociation undermines the foundation of strongholds Satan has structured around a person. As fragmented entities of a person are introduced and mapped, each one can be individually ministered to and brought to wholeness within the person. Mapping dissociation is like constructing a superhighway of inner healing across the landscape of a person's life. The quicker one can get to lies, to memory destinations, and to the revelation of truth, the sooner the mind is renewed, the true person is restored, and the enemy loses influence over the person.

Trading Faces

Chapter 9

Restoring Order Within
Illumination of Truth

"KAYLIE IS STUPID," TRACY ANNOUNCED AS
A MATTER OF FACT. "IF IT WEREN'T FOR ME,
OTHERS WOULD SEE HOW STUPID SHE REALLY
IS." *This* alter was decidedly confident of her role. Tracy had
been part of Kaylie since she was three years old. At that age,
Kaylie was severely beaten with a switch, bare bottomed, as her
dad angrily cursed at her. She held no conscious recollection of
what stupid thing she had been accused of doing that incited his
wrath. But now, in her late twenties, Kaylie is coming to terms
with her dissociation. Among her fragmented parts is a wounded
three-year-old and this alter identity named Tracy, both linked to
the trauma of that violent beating. Tracy's job is to protect Kaylie
from appearing stupid. Tracy is a self-abuser. If Kaylie does
something that Tracy deems stupid, she will physically beat up on
Kaylie "to teach her a lesson" as her father had done years before.
This was Kaylie's second session of inner healing. Several
wounded parts and alters had been identified and mapped in the
first session. In today's session, we would meet several more,
Tracy being the most vocal among them.

The purpose of inner restoration is to put things back the way they were originally intended to be so a person may best reflect the image of his Creator. Two key elements in productive healing sessions are for a person to come highly motivated and well prepared. Although she was nervous as her first session began, Kaylie was determined to get help and had done everything recommended to prepare herself. In that session, Kaylie became self-aware of her dissociation and received some healing. This motivated her even more to keep working toward personal restoration, no matter how hard or long the process might seem. The second session was approached with that same resolve to take more forward steps on her journey toward wholeness. Because what happens between sessions may be as important as the sessions themselves, the intervening weeks had allowed Kaylie time to process, in a variety of ways, what she had first experienced. This was aided by a few simple assignments she had been given as an outcome of the healing she had already received. By applying these practical ways to engage in personal "internal ministry" – both to her wounded parts and her alters – she had been able to experience noticeable progress since our first session together. Working through these helped empower her outside the environment of the session and independent of her facilitator team. Kaylie had the added benefit of a viable support network, even if that was only two trusted friends.

Wonderfully made, uniquely restored

Each of us is created in the likeness of God and intended to represent him as a bearer of that image. The Psalmist writes "For you (God) created my inmost being; you knit me together in my mother's womb. I praise you because I am fearfully and wonderfully made." (Psalm 139:13-14) These words were written by David, who, according to Acts 13:22, was a "man after God's own heart." He knew both the simplicity of being a shepherd and the enormity of being a king. During his life, David suffered much conflict and loss, suffering and pain. There were seasons of hardship lived in exile, followed by jubilant restoration of position.

One of David's strengths was that he was willing both to confess and confront his weaknesses and wounds. Early in life, he had resolved that God was trustworthy and ever-present to help him in times of trouble. David made some poor choices and bad decisions along the way, but that did not mean life was over or God no longer cared about him. Despite his infamous adultery with Bathsheba, the murder of her husband, and the death of the child David and Bathsheba conceived out of wedlock, God did not give up on David. Neither did David ever give up on God.

Psalm 23, also penned by David, holds a key to inner healing in one of the most powerful, four-word phrases in the Old Testament: "He (the Lord) restores my soul." Inner healing is God's work. He is the one who puts the fractured soul back the way it was intended to be: whole and complete, renewed and restored. God is ever-present to meet a wounded person at his place of pain, to shine light into dark places, to dismiss lies with the truth, to drive out Satan and demolish his strongholds, and to fuse a person's mind, body, soul, and spirit to best represent his image and original intent. God does this in a way that is personal and as unique as the individual who comes seeking his help.

Seen from a spiritual perspective, healing of dissociation has three objectives:

1) renewing the mind,

2) restoring the soul, and

3) redeeming the loss.

Renewing the mind

"Do not conform any longer to the pattern of this world, but be transformed by the renewing of your mind. Then you will be able to test and approve what God's will is – his good, pleasing, and perfect will." (Romans 12:2) To renew carries with it the idea of making new again, to restore to freshness, perfection, or vigor. Extreme trauma fragments the mind of the true person, scatters information meant to stay together, and creates wounded parts and alters. Dissociation conforms the mind to patterns of double-mindedness and confusion. Transformation back to the original intent of single-mindedness is a process. In that process, God does not remove our memory, history, or humanity. But he does renew our perspective of ourselves and deals with the shame, fear, or guilt lodged in the memory of a trauma event. The duration of healing will depend upon the level of dissociation and the willingness of a person to receive healing. An important step toward mind renewal is coming to self-awareness and co-consciousness of one's dissociation. Another is trusting in the Lord, as the source of truth, to orchestrate the healing process. Part of the restoration to wholeness will include integrating wounded parts and alters and merging them back into one.

The quest of mind renewal is to restore single-mindedness, free of conflict and confusion. One of the best ways to renew the mind is to dwell on truth found in God's Word, the Bible. It is also important to know the one who reveals truth because he is the truth. Jesus says of himself, "I am the way, the truth, and the life." (John 14:6) He is the one who opens the mind so that the truth of the Bible can be understood. (See Luke 24:45) Jesus is also the one who dispels lies and ousts demons, freeing a person from their bondage. The Bible will give you many glimpses of the mind that is renewed, as illustrated in the following, sample verses:

It is steadfast and at peace: "You will keep in perfect peace him whose mind is steadfast, because he trusts in you (God)." (Isaiah 26:3)

It loves God wholly: "Love the Lord your God with all your heart and with all your soul and with all your mind and with all your strength." (Mark 12:30)

It is life and peace: "The mind of sinful man is death, but the mind controlled by the Spirit is life and peace." (Romans 8:6)

It is one with others: "All the believers were one in heart and mind." (Acts 4:32)

It is in agreement; in perfect unity within self and with others: "I appeal to you, brothers, in the name of our Lord Jesus Christ, that all of you agree with one another so that there may be no divisions among you and that you may be perfectly united in mind and thought." (1 Corinthians 1:10)

It is in one accord: "Be of one mind, live in peace. And the God of love and peace will be with you." (2 Corinthians 13:11)

It aids prayer: "Be clear minded and self-controlled so you can pray." (1 Peter 4:7)

It is transformed: "You were taught, with regard to your former way of life, to put off your old self, which is being corrupted by its deceitful desires; to be made new in the attitude of your minds; and to put on the new self, created to be like God in true righteousness and holiness." (Ephesians 4:22-24)

As the mind comes into renewal, the soul comes into restoration.

Restoring the soul

Restoration means "to put back into consciousness or health; recovery of health and strength; to put back into original form." It is interesting that the word restoration emphasizes, "to put back into consciousness." Dissociation scatters information and data. Much of this goes into hiding in the subconscious because of the experience of trauma. Dissociation impedes the proper working of the intellect, will, and emotions of a person. I reiterate the importance of self-awareness and co-consciousness in the healing process. As dissociation is exposed, memories, emotions, thoughts, data, and other information are brought forward into the conscious mind. When the Lord brings healing, there is recovery of health and strength which has been diminished or lost due to dissociation. Whereas dissociation hinders spiritual maturity, healing accelerates maturity and restores the loss of spiritual gifts as well as other abilities. With a return to wholeness, a person is "put back into original form": the image and likeness of God and the power to represent him with singleness of mind. The following steps toward restoration may serve as guidelines in helping a person rediscover his true self as a whole person.

As these steps are read, uncomfortable thoughts or emotions may be stirred up. If so, pay attention to these. Perhaps write them down. You may want to share your findings with a person you consider safe and who can help you process your feelings. Responding to and praying about them – rather than pushing them away – may motivate healing.

1. *Determine the level of dissociation.* For example, a person may simply have dissociative states of splintered memory data without having alter identities. Or, he may have a highly functioning dissociative system. (See *Pointers: Dissociation Assessment* in the Appendix)

2. *Put dissociation on a more normal footing with plausible explanations.* Dissociation is a usual occurrence in life and need not be thought of as something rare, bizarre, or frightening. It is a natural function of the mind to "check out" when terrible things happen. The mind is designed to aid survival, so it is only doing its job. Everyone experiences some degree of dissociation, at least in its mildest forms (e.g. normal daydreaming as a brief, mental escape), and most will encounter some level of uninvited trauma.

   Generally, people are oblivious to their dissociation. Many people sense there is something not quite right within them but have no clue that wounded parts or alter identities may be responsible for some of their life responses. Until they get clarity as to what may be wrong, they continue an internal struggle with little hope of getting better. However, most will relate to their dissociation once it is explained, and they can identify it within themselves. Self-awareness actually brings hope and empowers them to begin taking responsibility for their dissociation in a way that leads to healing and wholeness.

3. *Listen and watch for signs of dissociation.* (See *Pointers: Dissociation Assessment* in the Appendix) As an example, dissociated people consistently report how tired they are. The level of trauma, degree of mental activity, range of dissociation, and number of alters in the system will all contribute to the measure of weariness they

feel. There is a lot of mental and physical energy expended to manage dissociation. Many also report the frequency of headaches. During one particular session, a recipient was under a great deal of mental stress as her dissociation was being unveiled, and painful memories were visited. She suddenly realized her head was pounding and begged for an aspirin. Nearly two hours later, after some resolution and healing, she no longer had a headache and had forgotten about her request for an aspirin, which we had failed to get for her. Benefits of healing and integration reported by recipients include increased energy, less fatigue, and fewer headaches.

4. *In the process of healing, everything is significant.* People often preface a thought, memory, or disclosure with the phrase, "I don't know if this is important or not, but ..." This is often the most important matter the Lord wants to address! Follow that thought as it may lead to a significant memory or somehow be a key to inner healing.

5. *Lead a person to discover his dissociation.* Avoid unnecessarily drawing it to his attention, telling him he is dissociated, or that he has alters. Self-discovery enhances self-awareness. Self-awareness is essential to the healing process. Coming into co-consciousness of one's dissociation is typically met with relief as it provides a legitimate explanation for a history of confusion and conflict. One man exclaimed, "But I didn't want to be dissociated!" yet was grateful that there were people who not only understood what he was going through but also able to help him. Increased awareness of personal dissociation often leads to recognition of dissociation in others.

6. *Acknowledge and affirm a person's dissociation, wounded parts, and alter identities.* Acknowledge the

hurts, the tiredness, and the fears. Recognize the wounded parts and the alter identities. Respect their names and affirm their functions. Affirmation does not mean agreement. Alters have specific roles to play and are highly invested in protecting the wounded parts of the person they represent. As guardians of the wounded parts of a person, anger is perhaps the most common defense of an alter. Work with the parts and alters that are willing and cooperative.

7. *Be patient and deal responsibly with dissociated people.* Wounded parts are hurt, fearful, and in pain. Alters are protectors. They will not respond to people they deem unsafe. If pushed, they will resist and even become uncooperative. Both wounded parts and alters will respond well to you if they are called by their preferred names, so find out what those names are and use them. Wounded parts are often the name of the true person at that age (e.g. seven-year-old John) whereas alters may have a different human name (Dan, not John), function name (Angry John), or some other distinct way to be identified (e.g. a type of animal). Acknowledging their existence, calling them by name, affirming their purpose, seeking their help and cooperation, and keeping them informed are all ways to assure alters that you mean no harm. An alter holds valuable information helpful to reaching the place of pain so that a wounded part may accept truth and receive healing.

8. *Map the dissociation.* As more dissociation is discovered, mapping assists you in keeping track of all parts and alters and whether they are God-focused, self-focused, or regulators. (See Chapter 8, *Mapping Dissociation*)

9. *Reassure the parts and alters by recognizing them as part of the person.* They are not demons. They cannot be cast out. They cannot be killed. They cannot be "fired" or in any other way "terminated." One man suggested of a troublesome alter he had, "Can't we just shoot him and get it over with?" This triggered both terror and opposition on the part of an already somewhat uncooperative alter. I calmly explained to him that an alter cannot be terminated because it is part of him and that no one is going to die. I asked the man to seek the forgiveness of his alter for wishing him dead. After some lengthy dialogue that persuaded the alter he was not going to be killed, we were able to continue the session. In another case, a wounded part of a person was offended because her needs had not been considered when a temporary roommate moved into the efficiency apartment. Once some forgiveness was spoken between the true person and the wounded part and there was some reconciliation, tensions between the person and the roommate subsided.

10. *Focus on the whole, not the part.* Keep in mind the objective to bring the individual into singleness of mind and wholeness. Therefore, any interaction with wounded parts or alter identities should have that purpose in mind. Inordinate amounts of time can be spent interacting with alters without gaining access to wounded parts who are in need of healing. As expediently as possible, respectfully get past an alter to bring healing in the memory that holds the fragmented data and pain.

11. *Seek alter cooperation.* The nearer you get to the place of pain, the more resistance you can expect. Never force a person to go somewhere they are unwilling or unprepared to go. However, if you have set safe boundaries and

have earned his trust, a person and his dissociative system will be more likely to cooperate with you in ways that will lead to an opportunity for healing. Reluctance to visit a memory or feel the pain may be challenged with a comment like, "I don't think I am ready to go there." I may offer a sympathetic response such as, "I realize that is a very painful place to go." (Acknowledgement) To prevent you from accessing certain memories, protective alters may try to convince you, "He will not be able to stand the pain," or "He will die if you go there." I may recognize the aid they have already given by saying, "You have been a big help so far in approaching this painful place." (Affirmation) The apprehension of returning unaccompanied to that place may be eased by offering, "How about if we go there together?" (Reassurance)

I find consistently that, if gently persuaded, a person is willing to visit a trauma memory if they know they do not have to go there "alone." Therefore, the groundwork of genuine acceptance, safety, and trust that has led to this point will have established a rapport whereby there will be willingness, even though there may be reluctance. Every time "we have gone there together" has resulted in some measure of healing.

12. *Let the whole person know you are working in "everyone's" best interest.* Always keep in mind that you are dealing with one person who has one mind that happens to be fragmented in dissociation. Other parts and alters in the system will become aware of who you are and that you can be trusted. Observing or participating in the restoration of the true person often encourages other entities in the system to reveal themselves and cooperate. The focus is not to be on healing alters, but healing the

individual in his place of woundedness in order to bring him into wholeness.

13. *Be alert for the enemy's attempts to derail healing.* The devil knows that the outcome of ministering to people in their dissociation is to bring them to a place of restored divine order and the original image of God they are meant to bear. Identifying the original place of deception and inviting God to speak truth means that lies are dismissed and corresponding demonic attachments released. Knowing this, those who facilitate inner healing must be attentive to the enemy's desperate attempts to foil restoration, for instance, through confusion and mockery, fear and failure. By calling these ploys to the attention of the person receiving healing, both the recipient and his facilitators can be watchful for these obstructions and together be on guard against them.

14. *Wounded parts and alters are not "lost" if the true person has made a personal commitment to follow Jesus Christ as Lord and Savior.* However, you may encounter parts and alters that know who Jesus is, but lack conscious knowledge that they are part of the saved whole of the person. A younger, wounded part may have gone into subconscious hiding before the true person accepted Jesus. An alter may similarly be devoid of personal understanding of salvation. Neither one may consciously realize they are in relationship with Jesus. You cannot "save" parts of the mind; you renew the mind and bring parts and alters to a place of experiential connection with Jesus and, therefore, under submission to the authority of his Lordship.

The process of educating and introducing dissociated entities to Jesus is sometimes similar to evangelizing a person who is outside of a personal relationship with him. However, the result is not a redemptive conversion but a psychological awakening of those parts of the mind that do not know that a personal relationship with Christ exists. A part or alter is often more than willing to be open to embrace Christ when there is genuine realization that he has been duped or used by Satan. There is usually even more eagerness when he realizes it is Jesus who has taken the pain away and turned the tables on lies that were believed to be truths. Willingness may also be motivated when there is co-consciousness of God-focused entities, knowledge that the true person is a follower of Jesus, or there has been an experiential encounter with Jesus that resulted in healing. When an entity comprehends that his abilities are restricted and he is limiting the true person from achieving wholeness, there will often be willingness to accept and acknowledge the Lordship of Jesus. In all steps toward restoration, always follow the leading of the Holy Spirit at this important juncture of mind renewal.

15. *Take your time.* This is the recipient's healing, not yours. Do all that you are led to do in a session and stop. People need time to process and do some personal work toward wholeness. Schedule ongoing sessions according to the recipient's needs. We often hold a follow-up session two to four weeks after the initial session. Some recipients may be scheduled regularly, others on an as-needed basis. It is not uncommon to have a recipient, who has journeyed a distance through healing, to phone months or even years later, having come to a place where he needs some more help to move forward.

16. *Integration is a process, not an event.* Integration is generally defined as "joining separate alter identities back

together into one whole person" and is the healing goal of many therapists. However, from a spiritual perspective, integration is not the objective of healing but rather a result of renewal of the mind and restoration of the soul. Integration is that step of identifying and bringing together entities within a person into familiarity and cooperation that will lead toward merging as one, all under the authority of the Lordship of Jesus Christ. Integration is never to be forced or manipulated. When directed by the Holy Spirit, integration will occur personally and in God's timing.

People often express fear or misgiving that an alter will no longer be available to help them once merged and wonder if their life will fall apart or part of their mind will cease to function. Integration is about bringing things back together, not keeping them divided as has been the case in dissociation. When the mind is renewed, and the soul is restored, what has been fragmented due to dissociation becomes whole. When integration occurs, the mind functions even more productively, a person's life begins to come together, and redemption of loss is experienced.

Redeeming the loss

There is a tendency for things to get lost when they become separated. We have all lost a button, a piece of paper, keys, or some object because it got loose from our hand, was not put back where it belonged, or for some other reason disappeared. When a person is fragmented by dissociation, things that are meant to be together are now scattered in other parts of the mind, hidden with wounded parts, or concealed by alters. One ministry recipient tells of having misplaced her checkbook. Her solution was to dialogue with her dissociation, saying, "Okay, *one* of you knows where I set this down." Instantly she was reminded because one of her alters knew exactly where it was!

With restoration of the soul comes redemption of loss. Dissociated people report the loss of many things – memory, emotions, abilities, time, confidence, and relationships to name a few. Aspects of their lives seem lost, scattered, out of order, or have simply disappeared. A common complaint of dissociated people is how exhausted they feel all the time. Until they enter into self-awareness of their dissociation, they are not conscious of the amount of energy that is consumed to maintain dissociation. Because dissociation dominantly functions at the subconscious level, alters do not necessarily sleep on the same schedule as the true person. There is enough evidence from working with dissociated people that at times what were thought to be dreams may instead be activity attributed to wounded parts or alters. For example, the thoughts of a self-focused alter who manages an addiction to pornography may be the culprit behind what is thought to be perverted dreams. When a person reports, "I don't feel as though I slept last night," even though he did, it may be that his physical body and conscious mind were at rest, but his subconscious mind was alert, and his dissociative entities were active.

Another ministry recipient, when awakened from a disturbing dream, will now dialogue with his dissociation to determine who is responsible for the dream. He also seizes the opportunity to pray and ask the Lord to give some insight that may lead to healing. He has discovered that when defenses are down while he is sleeping, wounded parts may be looking to have needs fulfilled or alters may be seeking expression in some way. This can at times be connected to demonic influences. Because demons exist in a spiritual realm, they never sleep. The tandem working of dissociation and demons in the subconscious mind may be consciously interpreted as fitful sleep, nightmares, visitations, communications, or other kinds of nocturnal disruptions.

It can require much mental effort to keep a memory hidden, to live with multiple entities in a dissociative system, and to function out of relational separation. It may also be demanding physically. People who boast of needing only three or four hours of sleep at night could possibly be under the control of alters. For example, Jake was known as a workaholic builder with a reputation for high-quality construction. This fed his approval addiction that was managed primarily by an alter named Regis. Regis, who relentlessly drove Jake to perform and produce, did not seem to need much sleep. As Jake received healing that ended his need for approval, Regis no longer had a reason to keep pushing Jake and eventually merged. Jake now found himself soundly sleeping for eight to ten hours at night. Yes, there were adjustments Jake needed to make to his work schedule, business, and family life. He lost none of his building skills or management capabilities. But without an alter taskmaster, who had also kept people at a distance, other relationships started coming into healing and restoration as well.

As another example, Vienna was gaining weight uncontrollably, to the alarm of both herself and her husband. She always ate sensibly at home and when they went out together. What he did not know and she did not consciously realize was that stressful triggers at work were provoking her to constantly consume sugary snacks throughout the day and overindulge at lunchtime in the staff cafeteria. Her husband did not know that was happening and neither did Vienna because a subconscious, wounded part was being pacified by food. When fears of rejection and lies of invalidation were dispelled, her eating habits balanced, and the excess weight began to drop off.

As the mind is renewed and dissociation is healed, both mental and physical energy are freed up. Fresh vitality and strength become available for more productive and healthy living. When the power of a lie is stopped, any demonic attachment connected to that lie also ends. Corresponding alter activity ceases. Mental and physical health is redeemed. Behaviors, attitudes, habits, even addictions that supported the lie will end. The consequent redemption of both mind and body contributes to the increase of energy and activity in both. Clouds of confusion dissipate, allowing clearer thinking. Physical maladies symptomatic of a person's former lie-based thinking and behaving will fade away. Does that mean all of a person's mental, physical, and demonic problems instantly disappear? No. But those directly linked to a specific lie, trauma memory, wounded part, and alter identity will no longer have a basis for remaining active once there is healing in that area.

As the mind comes to a greater measure of renewal, as the soul is restored in relation to that area of healing, redemption will follow. If there is still evidence of similar behaviors, there are likely still areas of woundedness that need to be addressed. Operating out of a position of wholeness better enables a person to pursue restoration in areas of his life where there is still brokenness. Having escaped from lies, the empowerment of truth intrinsically motivates a person to let light expose other areas of darkness. Just as renewal and restoration are a process, so is redemption.

Patty arrived at her first session anxious and downcast. She shamefully disclosed childhood experiences of incest and constant exposure to pornography. This young mother of two found that faith in her husband was being eroded by her distrust of men and her belief that they were all hopeless perverts. Conflicted about her own self-worth and sexuality, lie after lie after lie came tumbling out of her. Patty was helped to face her woundedness in a succession of disturbing and hurtful memories. Many expressions of forgiveness were spoken toward her offenders, as well as over herself, as these memories were visited. A combination of her desperation for healing, her resolve that God would help her, her willingness to trust (the very thing she found hardest to do), and her readiness to forgive made this a particularly comprehensive session of renewal, restoration, and redemption. The Lord began revealing truth after truth after truth that resulted in a dramatic transformation of her mind and beliefs about herself, men in general, and especially her husband. The anger displaced toward her husband was dramatically replaced with a deep sense of love, acceptance, and forgiveness.

As though blinders came off of Patty's eyes, she could see perhaps for the first time the working of the enemy to destroy her life and her marriage. A valid anger was expressed toward the enemy of her soul when she realized Satan had lied to both her and her husband. A bold authority came over her to resist the devil. We all sensed the fleeing of demons when lies they had held onto systematically vanished. Damage to a knee several years prior had prevented Patty from running, something she had always loved doing. As led by the Lord, my female ministry partner laid her hands on the knee and prayed. God supernaturally and instantaneously redeemed the loss of strength and healed her knee completely. Patty's heightened sensitivity to the Lord's power opened her up to receive a fresh outpouring of God's Spirit. It was all pretty remarkable! Afterward, my ministry partner and I both commented on how Patty literally appeared to glow as she left the room.

In a follow-up session the next month, Patty reported several things. Others, especially her husband, had noticed positive changes in her. She had resumed running and was able to share testimony of how God had healed her knee and given back her love of running. Patty recognized in herself a stronger sense of spiritual authority, citing her prayers as having become bolder and more targeted. She attributed her confidence to resist the enemy to the redemptive experience of her first session. Now that she had tasted the marvels of healing, she was eager to confront a few more issues, lies, and fears that had surfaced in the intervening weeks. Patty came to her second session with a clearer mind and took an even more active role in addressing issues she faced. As this session drew to a close, Patty exclaimed, "I feel so clean!" Two and a half years later, my family was invited to a dinner party that included Patty's family. Still glowing, she enthusiastically shared things the Lord had been doing in her life and family, changes they had made, and joys they shared. Not everyone who comes seeking healing may have a similar, seemingly rapid, initial experience as Patty. But for those who likewise desire healing and are willing to trust in God's ways and timing, their stories can be among those that successfully result in renewal of the mind, restoration of the soul, and redemption of loss.

Forgiveness

Being freed of limitations of dissociation, a person's relational boundaries are likely to extend. As a dissociated person, Patty was imbalanced in herself. Consequently, relationship with God and with others was unstable as well. As her internal equilibrium was redeemed, healing of external relationships followed. Unforgiveness had held Patty in bondage to her abusers. Sincere expressions of forgiveness, spoken at the experiential memory level, helped break the power of unforgiveness and oppression. Many who have walked through healing and forgiveness discover that people who formerly wounded them are no longer able to trigger or hurt them. This is often because forgiveness has finally become a settled issue, not as words of the mouth or as an act of the will, but in the depths of both the mind and the heart. This was certainly the case with Bob, whose story in Chapter 7 is but one of many where forgiveness contributed to the redemption of broken relationships as part of the healing journey.

The power of forgiveness

In recent years it has been popular to teach that forgiveness is an act of the will. Like many, Jen had been instructed to pray along these lines: "As an act of my will I forgive (name of person) for (offense of that person)." For Jen, that person was Bruce. Yet every time Jen encountered Bruce on the campus of the college they attended, saw his picture, heard his voice on the other end of the phone, thought of him, or even caught mention of his name, she would immediately tense up on the inside. Any reminder of this man she had consciously forgiven made her feel anything but peace. In fact, she felt quite the opposite. Fear would grip her, and she would find herself scanning for an escape route – either physically or mentally. Despite her determination to forgive "seventy times seven," this repeated act of her will did not seem compatible with the emotions she suppressed. Adding to the fears triggered by Bruce was a growing sense of guilt that, although she had repeatedly spoken forgiveness as she had been taught, she sensed no freedom from his inescapable influence. She was now confused about what forgiveness was supposed to feel like. She had heard others utter similar prayers, and they seemed to be fine. At least that was how they appeared.

As the session unfolded, Jen was reluctant to think about Bruce. "Besides, I've forgiven him," she asserted, hoping to avoid a painful encounter and desperately wanting to believe her words made it so. Urged to get in touch with her feelings at the mention of Bruce's name, Jen began following the trail of lies and fears strewn along her memory pathway. She finally stopped at the recollection of the first time Bruce had fondled her behind the junior high school. "It's my fault I didn't stop him," and "I'm dirty," were pinpointed as the two lies linked to that encounter which had been tucked away in her subconscious. Fear, shame, guilt, and confusion mingled with the pleasure and excitement of what was happening in that memory. As a result of the experience, thirteen-year-old Jen stalled in dissociation. Three years later, Bruce robbed Jen of her virginity. "My life is ruined," she concluded. "No one will ever want me now." Hatred and anger reached the boiling point in the pot of destructive feelings now stirred up as she thought of and talked about Bruce.

Perhaps it was Jen's true person who had forgiven Bruce "as an act of my will." Maybe it was an alter. It is possible they had expressed this together. Regardless, they were both politely asked to "step aside" so that wounded thirteen-year-old Jen could have her say. In the original memory, Jen realized she had dissociated on all three relational levels. She had disappointed God, she had compromised herself, and she had distanced herself from others – even Bruce, around whom she thereafter wore a facade. Thirteen-year-old Jen dropped her head in shame and started to weep. As the lies came crashing down upon her, this wounded part was asked if she would be willing to forgive Bruce. As a thirteen-year-old, Jen had no idea what to say or do but was agreeable to let us coach her. Once she became familiar with the language of forgiveness, Jen was able to express herself before God as she visited various memories. With the clutter of unforgiveness removed, she was then in a position to receive truth about herself and be set free from the bondage of lies she had believed.

The example of forgiveness

Many people are dissociated because of the abuse they have suffered at the hands of another. For example, when an adult violates the boundaries of innocence and abuses a child, he has no idea what the outcome of that trespass may be. The injustices against Jesus Christ in the brutal events leading up to and including his crucifixion are beyond human comprehension. As he surveyed his accusers and abusers while hanging nailed to a cross, he spoke to God and said, "Father, forgive them, for they do not know what they are doing." (Luke 23:34) As you are brought to a place of forgiving your offenders, remember the example of the Lord. Allow him to go with you to the place of pain and, together, express forgiveness for those who have wounded you.

The language of forgiveness

Forgiveness is appropriately expressed by the part of the person who was offended while in the memory where the offense occurred. By tapping into the pain of the memory, it is often timely and appropriate for the ministry recipient to verbalize sincere forgiveness for what any person in that memory has done to wound him. This can be as powerfully liberating as revelation of truth that dispels lies. It is often in this context that a person may find the freedom and peace that is rightfully anticipated when forgiveness is spoken. The following guidelines and sample prayers for use by facilitators were applied with Jen. And they will work for you as well. (See *Pointers: Forgiveness Prayer* in the Appendix)

1. While in the memory, have the person name each offender, being specific about what needs to be forgiven.

2. You may prompt the recipient to repeat after you the first time or two.

3. Refer to your session notes to help remind the person of offenses that were identified.

4. Check to see if there is anything else that comes to mind that needs to be expressed in the context of forgiveness.

5. Make notes of the recipient's expressions of forgiveness in the right margin of your session notes. This provides an important record of those expressions.

(See *Procedures: Documenting a Session* in the Appendix)

Sample prayers of forgiveness

God,

1. I forgive (name of the offender) for (specify the offense/s) and for causing me to feel (describe emotional and/or physical pain).

2. Forgive me for anything I have done to hurt (name of offender/s or of other/s; you may specify anything you have done to him/her).

3. I forgive myself for (specify what you need to forgive yourself for).

4. I ask you to forgive (name of offender; your name) and to bless/help (same name).

I am free in Jesus' Name! (State this as a declaration of truth.)

Amen

Once the forgiveness valve is opened, it is not uncommon for a torrent of statements to flood out of a person. Jen's forgiveness inventory became surprisingly long as she moved from memory to memory and found there were more individuals than just Bruce who had deeply hurt her. She even realized how she had hurt herself. If her true person or an alter attempted to interject interpretation of a memory, justify an offender's behavior, or otherwise disrupt the flow, they were respectfully asked to allow the wounded part of Jen to continue without interruption. After some time, Jen could not think of one more statement to make. The mental exercise she had just been through was exhausting. Sinking back into her chair, she said, "I feel as though a huge weight has been lifted off me." Unlike Patty, Jen had a steeper road to travel on her continued journey of inner restoration. However, she was able to report at the next session that an intervening encounter with Bruce did not trigger any ill feeling. Quite the opposite, she found she felt sorry for him and was able to look upon him for the first time with compassion as a person who was also wounded.

Documenting a session

Note-taking by a facilitator during a formal ministry session records encounters with a dissociated person's woundedness, dissociative system (wounded parts and alter identities), demonic influences, and other factors impacting the recipient's life. In an individual's personal history timeline, trauma events are a point of reference for woundedness and dissociation whereas a healing experience is a benchmark for restoration and wholeness. Documenting a formal session of ministry is profitable for a variety of reasons. As a facilitator records throughout the session, consecutive notes help manage the flow of the session and later provide relevant information to create a summary for the recipient's benefit. Highlights written down by a ministry facilitator on behalf of the recipient include:

Pertinent historical information,

Destructive themes linked to the schemes and strongholds of the enemy,

Summary of dominant memories,

Lie-based statements,

Encounters with the demonic,

Interacting with and mapping dissociation,

Addressing forgiveness,

Personal prayer and ministry for the recipient, and

Assignments.

A detailed, sample summary outline can be found in the Appendix at the back of the book under *Procedures: Documenting a Session.*

Summary

Isolation: The work of the enemy is to isolate a person for unholy purposes, making him a target for trauma that could result in dissociation and demonization.

Dissociation: The true person dissociates (separates) within himself to deal with the pain of trauma. Wounded parts, hidden in the subconscious mind, hold the pain and trauma memory data. Alter identities may form to protect the person from being re-traumatized.

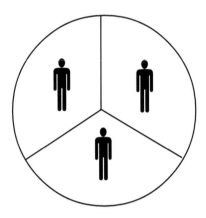

Self-awareness: As a person's dissociation is exposed, he becomes self-aware of his other parts and alters, their history, function, and purpose. This can be unnerving at first for the various parts and alters, who are unaccustomed to co-consciously operating around and with one another.

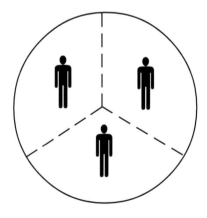

Integration: As a dissociated person comes into self-awareness and co-consciousness, existing barriers begin to diminish or be removed. As dissociated entities receive truth and healing, they can begin to cooperate and may eventually merge back into rightful place within the true person.

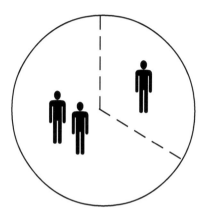

Restoration: The goal of ministry to dissociation is for the mind to be renewed, the soul to be restored, and loss to be redeemed. When dissociated parts that have been separated unite, their strengths are joined, and the true person operates from a position of greater wholeness, peace, and original intent.

"I am the way, the truth, and the life. You will know the truth and the truth will set you free."

The words of Jesus, as recorded in John 8:32 and John 14:6.

Chapter 10

Power Over Dissociation

Keys to Unlock Your Personal Prison

WHEN THE HAMMER STRUCK THE CLAY POT, SHARDS EXPLODED IN EVERY DIRECTION. A few minutes before, Sandi had finished recording everything she could think of onto the pot. In big letters around the rim, "DESPAIR" was boldly written. Elsewhere around the pot many smaller words were randomly printed: hopelessness, withdrawal, doubt, desperation, fear, mockery, shame, loneliness, and others. Sandi turned the pot slowly in her hand, reading aloud all the various expressions that represented the despair she had known most of her life. When she finished, Sandi solemnly announced, "I'm ready." The three of us walked together out to the back terrace. Each of us placed a hand on the pot, gripping it at the rim, and prayed an end to despair in this woman's life. Sandi turned the pot upside down on the concrete, and I ceremoniously handed her the hammer.

There is something powerful about demonstrative experiences linked to inner healing. For Sandi, despair had been built into her life from an early age, amplified by the internal conflicts of dissociation. Many memories had been visited, lies confronted, and forgiveness expressed over our four sessions together. She had now journeyed to this place of healing where she was able to identify despair as a theme that had been replicated in nearly every area of her life. As we prayed for guidance, the Lord impressed upon us to have Sandi symbolically break the mold of despair by destroying a clay pot. Right then we stopped to hunt for a pot and find a permanent marker. We soon regrouped so Sandi could write down everything that had been linked to despair in her life. For her, it was not enough to have a few broken shards to mark the end of despair. We all took turns pulverizing the clay fragments into dust so not even a hint of one of those words remained!

Over the years, I have engaged in numerous types of demonstrations as guided by the Holy Spirit. The smashing of a clay pot was a unique directive for Sandi and something we have never been impressed to do again. Such experiences are not formulas for healing but on-the-spot promptings of the Holy Spirit. What I always enjoy about such occasions is how the Lord ministers so personally to an individual, yet there is usually something we all get to participate in together.

Demonstrations and declarations that restore order

Dissociation keeps an individual divided and intercepts the true person from emerging. As the dissociative system is rehearsed and developed, increasing energy is directed toward maintaining the system and away from releasing the true person. Often, the scale tips toward self-focused endeavors that keep a person distanced from legitimate relationships and intimacy. Conventional approaches to helping dissociated people include focusing on an individual's behavior, addiction, attitude, or whatever is perceived as his "problem." If a behavior is all that is addressed or modified without understanding that this is in fact a person's solution to salving his pain, the dissociative system may compensate by seeking other ways to cope. The system will typically resist someone from outside trying to alleviate or eliminate a "solution" imbedded in dissociation. Alters are not only protective of hidden, wounded parts but also defensive of their purpose. In whatever way they are positioned to protect, they will persist in their habit unless given reason to change. The goal of inner healing is not to stop a behavior but to have truth revealed. As a person is led to a place where Jesus can remove the pain and bring genuine healing, the behavioral "solution" will no longer be needed. But the path to that place and what is encountered there may be as unique as the individual who is receiving healing.

Demonstrations

Demonstrations often happen spontaneously and are usually simple. Once we were led to set a woman in front of a mirror to interact with her dissociation. This helped her see the changes in her face when she would switch between dissociative entities. For her, it also helped her connect with her dissociation in ways that led to deeper healing. Another time, a recipient knew he was uncomfortably tied to a relationship but could not figure out what it was that bound him to it so negatively. We were directed to simply tie a knot in a length of string and for the man to hold either end. As he visited memories and wrestled with various lies, it suddenly dawned on him that the knot represented unforgiveness. As soon as he responsibly dealt with that, he was able to untie the knot and drop the string.

Physical touch can be a powerful form of demonstration in the healing process. There is wisdom in the advice of those who ban any kind of physical contact with another person during ministry, particularly of the opposite sex or when sexuality issues are involved. However, there may be suitable exceptions when physical touch is appropriate although discretion must always be exercised any time physical touch is considered. Always ask permission first and never touch a person in an inappropriate way or in a place that makes them feel uncomfortable. For instance, I personally never touch a person even on the shoulder or head to pray for him without his consent. Corporately, there are times during a session we have all agreed to hold hands together to pray. Any touch used during ministry should be under the supervision of a ministry partner so nothing may be misconstrued or misinterpreted.

When ministering to a person's dissociation, there will be encounters with wounded parts who are stalled in childhood. These parts may show themselves at the point of pain and be greatly distressed. This is a moment when sensitivity to the leading of the Holy Spirit is critical. Depending upon the circumstance that caused the dissociation, to touch the person voluntarily may either exacerbate or alleviate his fear.

Mitchell had leapt back to a pivotal childhood memory of being abandoned by his parents and left at a children's home with total strangers. As he watched them turn their backs and walk away, two adults physically restrained Mitchell from chasing after them. Because he was so hysterical, they locked him alone in an empty room for several hours until he calmed down. My ministry partner and I observed Mitchell abreact in the memory and listened to the gut-wrenching cries of this child who was overwhelmed with terror. I felt prompted to ask "Little Mitchell" if I could sit by him and put my arm around him. He nodded "yes" through his uncontrollable sobs. The moment I did so, I could feel his body relax slightly, even though it continued to shudder. I gently reassured him but mostly sat quietly with my arm draped across his shoulders. Several minutes passed before Mitchell settled down and became still. When he was ready to interact, I withdrew my arm but continued to sit next to Mitchell rather than returning to my usual seat opposite the recipient. Somehow the physical proximity was still important, even as the embrace of his shoulders had been. What this frightened "child" needed most was someone to help him make sense of the abandonment and to speak to the lies he believed about himself. That Spirit-led moment of physical connection helped prepare the way for Little Mitchell to be receptive to what the Lord wanted to do next to bring healing. Whereas it was not necessary to have contact with Adult Mitchell in this way, it was a central element in helping Little Mitchell relax, trust, and receive healing. (See *Procedures: Prepared Facilitator* in the Appendix for more implications and cautions regarding physical contact with recipients, in particular when dealing with sexual issues.)

There are often strong spiritual metaphors in demonstrations. While we ministered to Clark, he was impressed that God's people are to be as altars of worship. For Clark, the application became very personal and also held spiritual significance at this juncture of his healing journey. We stepped out to the rock garden and had Clark pick out thirteen smooth river stones. He brought these back in and scattered them on a mat in the middle of the floor. Each stone represented a wounded part or an alter identity that had been mapped in Clark's dissociative system. Clark picked up one stone at a time and symbolically either forgave self-focused entities in turn or expressed thanks for ways parts and alters had helped him survive. Each representative stone was then stacked into an "altar." Clark anointed this liberally with oil, which turned the stones from a dull grey to a glistening black. For him, this signified the personal transformation of his dissociation being brought back together and a return to wholeness as an altar of worship unto God. We spent time praying together over this insight he received and the symbolism that it represented. It was a powerfully demonstrative experience we shared together and particularly significant to Clark, whom we learned is skilled as a stone mason. This miniature altar remained a focal point for the remainder of the session and then was bagged up for Clark to take with him. Such demonstrative applications teach and instruct us. They give us visual and tactile reminders of healing. Like the smashing of the clay pot by Sandi, the building of a symbolic altar has been a once-only exercise prompted by the Holy Spirit and tailored to the individual.

You will recall from Chapter 6 that authority has a voice. Declarations and demonstrations, exercised in tandem, are a potent force in capsizing the enemy, setting captives free, and restoring order. Love, whether verbalized or displayed, is a persuasive expression, particularly to those who may be unfamiliar with genuine love. Romans 5:8 tells us, "But God demonstrated his own love for us in this: While we were yet sinners, Christ died for us." The Apostle Paul explained to his audience in Corinth, "My message and my preaching were not with wise and persuasive words, but with a demonstration of the Spirit's power, so that your faith might not rest on men's wisdom, but on God's power." (1 Corinthians 2:4-5) Words and wonders are not what heal a person, but they are a connecting point. They are simply tools in the hand of the living God, who is the real healer and the only one who can renew the mind and bring the true person to completeness.

Declarations

A declaration is "a proclamation, assertion, or formal announcement, typically done in a public setting and supporting a ground or side taken on a particular subject." Jesus was accustomed to making bold declarations. These were often controversial because they were truth, and they were life. Once, in front of a mixed crowd and despite protest, he ordered the stone to be taken away from the tomb of a man who had been dead for three days. You may be familiar with the story of Lazarus, found in John 11. He declared to Lazarus' sister, Martha, that if she believed, she would see the glory of God. Once the stone was removed, he looked to heaven and audibly prayed to God so that those standing around who heard might believe God sent him. Next, he announced the dead man's resurrection with a loud voice, "Lazarus, come out!" (verse 43) Finally, he ordered that the man's grave clothes be removed and he be let go.

Taking authority over dissociation may also include declarations of truth and life that help overcome the dilemma of relational disorder and mental fragmentation. In truth, it is only God who can heal dissociation. Therefore, one way his ability to do so can be acknowledged is by proclaiming God's power to renew the mind, restore the soul, and redeem what is lost. Using scripture as a platform for prayer is powerful and effective. For example, with the text of Ephesians 6:10-20 as a guide, figuratively donning together the full armor of God helps set spiritual boundaries for ministry. Speaking scripture over wounded parts and alter identities is a legitimate declaration that brings truth, hope, and healing. Using Jesus' precedent with Lazarus, you may call for the true person to "come out" and for him to be unwrapped and "let go!" As ministry proceeds from a spiritual perspective, sensitivity to the Holy Spirit will guide facilitators to relevant scriptures, prayers, renunciations, declarations, and demonstrations that will be both personal and meaningful to the ministry recipient. Declarations of forgiveness are extraordinarily liberating. Forgiveness is one of the keys to inner healing, which will be elaborated upon elsewhere in this chapter.

We are very verbal in our ministry sessions and encourage declarations to be audible. As much as possible, we engage the recipient in these as part of developing his own repertoire of inner healing language and resources. There are, of course, times for silence, reflection, and waiting. The voice we most desire to hear is the Lord's. When he meets people at their point of pain and reveals truth, however he may do that, it is an experience that will not be forgotten. Irrespective of what has happened to a person to cause dissociation or to reinforce relational dis-order, there is encouragement and hope in this declaration of truth from Romans 8:1-2: "There is now no condemnation for those who are in Christ Jesus, because through Christ Jesus the law of the Spirit set me free from the law of sin and death." Jesus does not deal with us according to what we deserve but according to what we need. He neither condemns nor judges. He loves and forgives. He redeems and restores. That is good news.

The following statements were the result of ministry to a woman we met with several years ago. As the Lord revealed truth about each lie, offense, pain, or hurt as it was dealt with, she responded by recording the insights in the context of being a target. This became both a demonstrative and a declarative tool for her that she has been able to share with others.

Although this list was developed by and for a particular individual, you may be able to use it in your own personal inner healing journey. Slowly repeat each phrase, "testing" it to see if there is a ring of "truth" to the statement. Sometimes, the negative part of a phrase may hit a nerve, possibly touching a wounded part within. At other times, the positive part of a phrase may resonate with a yearning in the heart that finds hope through expression. If you identify strongly with a particular phrase, repeat it, and invite the Lord to work with it as he wishes.

Prayer Pause

"God, I commit to you the part of this phrase that stirs me within. Reveal to me the source of this stirring. If there is a memory that holds woundedness, I am willing to explore that with your help, knowing that you are ready and able to heal. Reveal truth in the manner of your choosing. Bring healing and restoration, I pray. Amen."

"I am no longer ...

    ... a target of abuse but a target of protection."
    ... a target of cursing but a target of blessing."
    ... a target of evil but a target of godliness."
    ... a target of lies but a target of the truth."
    ... a target of rebellion but a target of obedience."
    ... a target of pain but a target of peace."
    ... a target of rejection but a target of acceptance."
    ... a target of weakness but a target of strength."
    ... a target of bondage but a target of deliverance."
    ... a target of shame but a target of honor."
    ... a target of guilt but a target of pardon."
    ... a target of hatred but a target of love."
    ... a target of condemnation but a target of mercy."
    ... a target of perversion but a target of purity."
    ... a target of opposition but a target of affirmation."
    ... a target of corruption but a target of innocence."
    ... a target of weakness but a target of power."
    ... a target of cruelty but a target of compassion."
    ... a target of accusation but a target of forgiveness."
    ... a target of fear but a target of courage."
    ... a target of death but a target of life."

Renunciations

Renunciations are a form of declaration that announce "refusal to continue following or participating in" something. These need to be stated authentically and in submission to the authority of the Lordship of Jesus Christ. Therefore, it may be beneficial to pronounce declarations as well as perform demonstrations in the company of others of stronger faith and spiritual maturity. Examples of simple but effective statements of renunciation include:

"I renounce the power and effects of dissociation over my life and relationships."

"I renounce the power of lies and all lie-based thinking."

"I renounce the power of the enemy, Satan, over my life and relationships."

"I renounce the power of demonic themes and strongholds."

"I renounce the power held by others over me."

"I renounce the power that painful memories have held over me and all corresponding attitudes, behaviors, habits, and patterns." (Note: Memories do not change but the perception of the memory can.)

(See *Pointers: Renunciation of Curses* in the Appendix)

Prayer

Prayer is a fundamental declaration that leads to restoration. Many do not realize that prayer has as much to do with listening to God as it does with talking to him. In the environment of inner healing sessions, a learning-by-doing approach to prayer is offered both for and with the recipient. This includes the "pre-prayer-ation" of facilitators in advance of the session. Many simply lack a vocabulary for making inner healing prayer declarations, for praying forgiveness, or for dialoguing with God. Throughout the session, a recipient is often coached in what to pray and then allowed personal expression to come forth. It is then not uncommon to sit quietly, to listen, and to wait on the Lord. It is surprising how quickly a reply may come. It might even astonish a recipient to sense something that is clearly from the Lord. His reply may come as an impression, a thought, a phrase, a picture, a feeling, a Bible verse, a song, a memory, or some other expression. This kind of exchange does not have to be in the context of a formal session. Recently, I was in a conversation with a young adult who was explaining that he had gotten pulled off center in his relationship with God. I suggested we pause the conversation and that he simply ask the Lord when this happened. So he did. I then said, "Let's just be quiet and see what he may have to show you about this." The young man replied, "Oh, we don't have to do that because he has already reminded me of something that happened back in high school." It was one of those serendipitous moments that instantly opened a way for him to prayerfully speak forgiveness and then receive some revelation of truth about the repressed situation that had been surprisingly thrust into his conscious mind. It mattered to neither of us that we were in a public place at the time.

1 Peter 4:7 instructs us to "be clear-minded and self-controlled so that you can pray." Many people's minds are not clear because of the conflict of dissociation. They live in a clouded, confused state that debilitates self-control and hinders their ability to pray. We often find that people struggle with their personal prayer life or Bible reading because they are double-minded, not clear-minded. They live in dissociative dissonance because they are not operating out of the clarity and peace of single-mindedness. Earlier, 1 Peter 2:11 urges us "to abstain from sinful desires, which war against your soul." Dissociated people engage in mental combat upon the battlefield of the mind. While it is commendable

to cease giving in to the passions of the flesh, that may be easier said than done when wounded parts and alter identities are at odds, caught up in self-preservation, or exercising corrupt solutions. The self-restraint of abstinence is not victory. Victory comes when the Lord fights on your behalf, defeats opposing forces of darkness, and heals double-mindedness. One reason Satan wants to hinder prayer activity and thwart Bible comprehension is because they are offensive to him. Ephesians 6:17-20 emphasizes that application of the Word of God, prayer in the Spirit, prayer for others, prayer for self, and prayer for the fearless declaration of the gospel of Jesus Christ are all highly offensive to the devil. When dissociated people are released into prayer and schooled in how to get out of God's way, he can step in and do his work on their behalf. In the process, the mind is renewed, the soul is restored, and the true person emerges in wholeness and strength.

Keys to unlock your personal prison

Dissociation stalls a person in a place of woundedness, debilitates a person through personal fragmentation, and alienates a person because of relational dis-order. There are numerous keys to unlocking dissociation that result in freedom, unity, and wholeness. Knowledge of dissociation, personal self-awareness, and willingness to receive healing are all important factors. The following keys are clustered by topic and are by no means exhaustive.

1. *Realize you are not alone.* While each person is unique, many falsely believe, "I am the only one like this, who has this issue, who thinks this way, who does this thing, who has this problem," and the like. The sense of aloneness may be attributed to never having shared deep hurts and fears with

another person. It may also be due to no self-awareness of dissociation.

2. *Get help.* Many will not stop long enough to heal. They may think about it, talk about it, postpone it, avoid it, or ignore it. But unless they pursue help, they will not receive it. There are many ways you may personally connect with and minister to your own dissociation that will lead to healing. However, because dissociation is a relational dis-order, full restoration is not likely unless the healing process also includes others. Dissociation distances and alienates, which heightens the difficulty of going to others for help. People are often afraid to go to those they know – a friend, a family member, or a pastor, much less a stranger such as a counselor – for fear of being rejected. The need to protect wounded parts, fear of judgment and condemnation, lack of trust, fear of betrayal, and other factors reinforce the tendency for dissociation to keep a person separated from the very ones who might help bring healing, including God.

3. *Go to the place of pain.* Alters distance you from painful memories to protect wounded parts from being re-traumatized. However, it is the wounded part who needs truth from Jesus in order to be healed. Therefore, you may need to either work with or get past an alter in order to minister to a wounded part. Once back in a trauma memory, a dissociated wounded part returns to the "now" of an event; the trauma is experienced again as though it were currently happening. Because God is ever-present, while in the "now" of a memory, invite Jesus to reveal truth however he may choose. While there, express forgiveness toward anyone who has hurt you. Allow healing to come at this experiential memory level. (See *Pointers: Forgiveness Prayer* in the Appendix)

4. *Call forth and draw out the true person* you were actually born to be. There is only one true you. Seek to interact with and be that single person or you will constantly contend with alters in negotiation, dialogue, or argument. It makes life easier and brings healing more quickly when you are dealing with the one true person and calling him to wholeness and singleness. Consistently calling forth the true person brings you into greater self-awareness and co-consciousness, which expedites healing.

5. *Break all unholy soul ties* to anyone with whom there have been ungodly, unnatural, illegitimate, perverse, demonic, sexual, corrupt, and fraternal (e.g. where freemasonry or fraternity vows have been made) relations that have opposed the things of God. (See *Pointers: Renunciation of Soul Tie Curses* in the Appendix).

6. *Weigh the benefits of therapy options.* Understand that therapy, medicine, self-effort, and support groups will only help you cope with your dissociation. We have ministered to many people who have come to us after years of counseling yet are still far from genuine healing. Maybe they have been propped up, aided, encouraged, or medicated in some way but have never been given real hope of recovery. They have come to believe "this is as good as it gets" and live in a state of tolerable improvement. Inner restoration from a spiritual perspective is often missing from a person's healing journey. There is a huge need for people to find valid and comprehensive help when they turn to others.

I personally believe that only God can ultimately help a person overcome his dissociation and be truly healed in Jesus' Name. I encourage working together with others who have resources I cannot offer. But most conventional approaches never address healing in the context of dissociation, much less in ways that consider God as the answer. If dissociation is identified, it is viewed as a mental illness, not as a relational dis-order with spiritual implications. It is not by human wisdom or strength that dissociation and relational separation are overcome. When people encounter the truth, forgiveness, and hope that Jesus offers at the place of pain, they experience healing in a way never known before.

7. *Settle in your mind who Jesus Christ is.* Depending upon the age and circumstance of dissociation, there may be hidden parts or functioning alters that have no knowledge of God or awareness of Jesus. Some people in their dissociation may have accepted Jesus as a "solution" to their pain but have no personal relationship with him. Others may become reactionary, even volatile, at the name of Jesus. Whether it is consciously accepted by all in the dissociative system or not, this truth stands: Jesus Christ is the son of the living God. He alone can authentically heal you, forgive your sins, restore your soul, and redeem your life to wholeness. By accepting Jesus Christ as your personal Lord and Savior, you will be saved from all the destructive works of the devil and positioned for eternal life with God.

If you do not have a personal relationship with Jesus Christ, the following prayer is for you. It is important that your true person pray this prayer, on behalf of and as spokesperson, for all your wounded parts and alter identities. Pray this prayer out loud. Share your commitment with another person, and find a Bible-believing, life-giving church to join. Being part of the Body of Christ is an important aspect of inner healing and overcoming the relational dis-order of dissociation.

Prayer Pause

"God, I present all of me to you and ask that you accept me as I am. All of me believes and declares that Jesus Christ is the Son of God. All of me put my trust in your salvation and the hope of eternal life with you. Jesus, you alone can save all of me from my sins. Please forgive all of me for sinning against you, against others, and against myself. You alone can renew my mind to wholeness, restore my soul, and redeem my life from the conflicts of dissociation. Please heal all of me. I commit all of me to you, Jesus, and humbly surrender all of me to the authority of your Lordship. Come into my life and reign over all of me as Savior and Lord. I pray this in Jesus' Name. Amen."

8. *Acknowledge the horror of abuse and who is responsible for it* but realize that it is not God who has abused you. God does not instigate evil. Abuse is inflicted by another person acting out of unnatural motives, possibly out of his own pain and dissociation. Pain and suffering are the consequence of sinful choices of broken people, even when worked against the innocent. People are often quick to blame God even though neither they nor he are the cause of the abuse or some other trauma. Many ask, "Why did God allow this to happen?" and blame God for their suffering. The more appropriate questions to ask may be "Why did (name of abuser) let this happen?" or "Why did my parents let this happen (i.e. not protect me)?" or "Why did the drunk driver (who killed my family) let this happen?"

Satan, disguised as a snake, deceived the woman in the Garden of Eden. Satan still wears many disguises because his nature is to lie, and his goal is destruction. He has no regard for anyone, whether blameless or guilty, infant or adult, wealthy or poor; all are subject to his deceptions. Conversely, it is God's nature to love unconditionally, to give generously, to redeem wholly, and to renew completely. Because of fear or shame or both, a person – or at least a wounded part of him – will attempt to hide from God. But when a person receives truth that is illumined by God, any veil that has kept God hidden is removed. Romans 11:33 declares the mystery of God in this way: "Oh, the depth of the riches of the wisdom and knowledge of God! How unsearchable his judgments and his ways beyond tracing out!" God is not holding out on us. But if we hold out on him, our healing is denied.

9. *Journal your journey.* Keep a notebook to record memories, dreams, ideas, thoughts, feelings, pains, fears, and impressions that may be linked to dissociation. Getting these out on paper is a tangible means of processing that helps clear clutter and makes a way for truth to be revealed. Documenting helps to identify patterns, habits, behaviors, and attitudes that may be linked to dissociation. Journaling may also help distinguish the various identities in an individual's alter system. Making notes may facilitate heightened self-awareness and co-consciousness. Journal entries may also provide helpful information when shared with ministry facilitators in a formal healing session. A chronicle of inner healing records points of reference in the process of being made whole.

10. *Read the Bible and pray.* I encourage people to read God's Word out loud. "Faith comes by hearing the message, and the message is heard through the word of Christ." (Romans 10:17) Declaring God's Word by reading it audibly builds faith and lends itself to the spiritual application of healing. It also engages more stimuli gates than just the eyes so more of the person is alerted to and impacted by helpful insights. Similarly with prayer, I urge people to pray aloud. Praying

specifically for your wounded parts and alters helps pave the way for truth to be revealed and received. In both disciplines, it is important for the communication to be two-way. Therefore, incorporate silence, listening, and waiting to heighten sensitivity to what the Lord may reveal to you that will result in healing. Include insights in your personal journal.

11. *Be persistent.* A dissociated person lives much of life repeatedly defecting to "the other side" and being a traitor to God-focused entities, the true person, or to others. As a person comes into spiritual and relational healing of his dissociation, the enemy will go all out to intercept that from happening. With every "hill" won in battle, the enemy has to retreat and regroup for fear he will lose his hold on a person. Healing is a process, not an event. But in the process, there will be episodes and benchmarks of renewal and restoration that motivate you to press forward. You do not want to plant a victory flag prematurely, nor do you want to give up the fight when there may be only one hill left in the battle to claim. In the end it is not your fight but God's fight, and the result is in God's hands.

12. *Release all debts related to others because of unforgiveness* and break the power they may hold over you. Forgiveness is essential in order to deal with past hurts, restore relational order, and heal dissociation. Many remain stuck in the pain of the past because they have not forgiven those who robbed, violated, or abused them. Often veils of denial must be removed in order for a wounded part of a person to express forgiveness. Denial may be by choice, it may be in the form of an amnesic memory block, or it may be otherwise linked to the fragmentation of dissociation.

The Bible reveals dozens of benefits based on forgiveness, including healing and redemption. Psalm 103:1-6 say, "Praise the Lord, O my soul; all my inmost being, praise his holy name. Praise the Lord, O my soul, and forget not all his benefits – who forgives all your sins and heals all your diseases, who redeems your life from the pit and crowns you with love and compassion, who satisfies your desires with good things so that your youth is renewed like the eagle's. The Lord works righteousness and justice for all the oppressed." The benefits of the blessings of God cannot come to your life if there is unforgiveness. Jesus included in his teaching on prayer, "For if you forgive men when they sin against you, your heavenly Father will also forgive you. But if you do not forgive men their sins, your Father will not forgive your sins." (Matthew 6:14-15)

Many fall into the trap of retribution, even if that is limited to mental overtures that are never carried out against an offender. Romans 12:19-21 advises, "Do not take revenge, my friends, but leave room for God's wrath, for it is written: 'It is mine to avenge; I will repay,' says the Lord. On the contrary: 'If your enemy is hungry, feed him; if he is thirsty, give him something to drink. In doing this, you will heap burning coals on his head.' Do not be overcome by evil, but overcome evil with good." One reason people remain stalled in dissociation is because they have not allowed forgiveness to resolve the offense committed against them.

You cannot be healed of hidden pain unless you face what happened and forgive those who hurt you. It is important at the memory level, for example, to acknowledge the genuine evil done against you in the past by someone who abused you. Even though you may have been rejected, invalidated, or ashamed, if you do not forgive, you will be unable to fully resolve former woundedness. Forgiveness sets you free and helps you press forward toward personal wholeness. (See

Pointers: Forgiveness Prayer and *Pointers: Renunciation of Soul Tie Curses* in the Appendix.)

When is this over?

There have been those occasions in ministry sessions where it looked as though "nothing" happened. From a human perspective, the hours together seemed frustrating, unproductive, or somewhat disappointing. In my own personal journey of inner healing there have been occasional setbacks. Or, as one issue got resolved, it seemed that another rose right behind it with a vengeance. At times I have thought, "Will this never end?!" and simply wanted to give up. Everyone will have times of regression in life's journey, for whatever reason. All of these circumstances could be mistaken as failure. But a setback does not negate what the Lord has done so far, nor does it stop him from completing what has begun. And what appears to be "nothing" may be more significant than what is perceived at the time.

During Raewyn's first two sessions, there had been rapid healing and several demonstrative experiences. We had begun mapping her dissociation, and she had responsibly interacted and dialogued with her system between sessions. But the third session was laborious. The hours seemed to crawl past. I felt relieved when it was over, wondering what, if anything, had really been accomplished. Several days later, I received a very upbeat phone call from Raewyn. She expressed her gratitude for the ways the session had helped bring much clarity to her thinking, even though it had culminated with a big question that did not have an accompanying answer. She attributed being able to pinpoint that important question to accountability with her facilitators, something she realized she could not have accomplished on her own. She had already begun her quest for the answer and felt better equipped to do so after all she had learned during the recent and prior sessions.

In all three sessions we had forewarned Raewyn that the enemy would attempt to discredit her experience or interfere with her journey in some way. She explained that this is exactly what happened right after the third session. Before she had driven off the property, the enemy tried to attack her with the familiarity of depression. Raewyn had left so highly motivated that she had no problem immediately standing up to and overcoming the depression, something she did not previously feel she could have done. From our perspective as facilitators, the session had seemed weak and unfruitful. From the recipient's viewpoint, it had been tremendously beneficial! Our phone conversation reminded me that a ministry session is not about me or for me; it is about God's timing and his way of bringing wholeness to those who seek it from him. Often God's work is done beyond the parameters of a formal session. Helping recipients to understand that builds rightful anticipation of God's ever presence to heal. It also keeps recipients from becoming dependent upon their facilitators and formal sessions for healing.

Summary

There are a number of tools that may be implemented to overcome dissociation and restore order in a person's life. When led by the Holy Spirit, demonstrations are a tangible reference point of healing. Declarations, renunciations, and prayers are also powerful as they help draw boundary lines in the spirit realm when made with authority and as statements of truth. The first two keys to overcoming dissociation are to realize that you are not alone and to accept that you need help. The next chapter offers practical advice on how to dialogue with dissociation in ways that lead to wholeness.

Trading Faces

Chapter 11

Dialoguing with Dissociation

Working Together, Restoring the Soul

THOMAS SIGHED. "GOD IS A TOUGH TASKMASTER," HE THOUGHT TO HIMSELF. At thirty-eight years of age, Thomas responded well to his perception of God as a disciplinarian. He lived a regimented life, always alert to keeping issues of sin, self, and the flesh at bay. However, despite years of self-control, he was weary of the perpetual battle which kept him conflicted, frustrated, and ashamed. His unmet need for validation as a child screamed for attention and affirmation. If so much as a thought crossed his mind that echoed that need, his self-righteous side managed to suppress it immediately. Did Thomas know God loves him? Absolutely. Did Thomas love God? Without a doubt. Was God proud of Thomas? ... Prolonged silence was his answer. Thomas had resigned himself to the belief that he would always have this "thing" that plagued him, and the best he could do was to keep resisting, as he had done for the last twenty-one years. This "thing," he came to discover, was a deeply wounded part of himself.

As we talked and mapped out Thomas's dissociation, two distinct identities were found to be at odds with one another:

Logical Thomas	Tommy
• God-focused	• Self-focused
• Has much knowledge of God	• Wounded four-year-old part
• Views God as taskmaster	• Seeks validation and veneration
• Responds to God's discipline	• Hopeless; beyond getting help
• Self-righteous	• Shamed and invalidated by father
• Believes he is stuck with Tommy	• Sees no point in living

Thomas explained that he had been fighting himself since he became a Christian at age seventeen. Logical Thomas likened his dilemma to that which Paul speaks of in Romans 7 when he describes struggling with sin. "When I want to do good, evil is right there with me," lamented Logical Thomas, quoting the twenty-first verse. Logical Thomas thought God should just "kill this thing" that plagued him.

As we dialogued, Thomas became aware that this "thing" was actually a wounded part of himself that had been repeatedly shamed and invalidated by his father. Logical Thomas was reluctant to go to the place where this "thing" was in his subconscious mind, reasoning that it was too risky. I offered to go with Logical Thomas to that place and suggested we invite Jesus to accompany us as well. Whom Logical Thomas met there was not a "thing" at all but a younger part of himself he identified as Tommy, his childhood name. He suddenly found himself in a memory of his father wagging his finger in Tommy's face and being told, "You ought to be ashamed of yourself."

At my request, Logical Thomas agreed to silently observe so I could interact with Tommy. Tommy cowered nervously and wanted to hide himself. "I am bad," and "Jesus doesn't want me" were two lies he held in that stalled memory. Tommy suddenly had a real sense of Jesus' nearness, which unnerved him. But Tommy accepted my offer to pray to see if there was something Jesus wanted to reveal to him about his situation. Tommy then reported he could see Jesus' arms wide open toward him and that Jesus was beckoning him. Tommy gingerly moved toward Jesus, who embraced Tommy once they were close enough together. He described Jesus' embrace as firm and gentle, and in his arms the desperation was quieted. Tommy said he felt peaceful and unafraid.

While in that memory, I coached Tommy in forgiveness. He forgave his father for always punishing him in anger, for making him feel that he was always in the way, and for never apologizing to Tommy. Tommy forgave Logical Thomas for punishing him by keeping Jesus away and for thinking he was a thing to get rid of and not a real part of Thomas. This whole time, Logical Thomas had been silent. He then spoke, apologizing to Tommy for shutting him out, for always trying to compensate for him, and for wanting him killed off. He then asked Jesus to forgive him for being self-righteous and for invalidating Tommy like his father had done. Suddenly, Logical Thomas sensed the same pure acceptance from Jesus that he had seen the Lord give to Tommy. Next, both Tommy and Logical Thomas felt Jesus embracing them together. Logical Thomas said, "This feels wholesome."

Momentarily, I suggested we visit the lies Tommy held. In reply to "I am bad," Tommy retorted, "Jesus says I am good." When "Jesus doesn't want me" was restated, Tommy replied, "Jesus *wants* me!" Thomas then sensed something going on inside of himself. He perceived reconciliation going on and said, "We're not enemies here – we are one." Thomas felt the darkness recede that for many years had been so familiar. He remarked, "God looks less like my father now." With a sense of oneness in himself, he could feel the Lord's presence very near and somehow knew Jesus had been there all along.

As Thomas and I reflected on what had just happened, I explained to him that when one believer receives healing, the whole Body of Christ is strengthened and made more complete. I also helped him understand that when an experiential revelation of Jesus Christ comes as personally as it had to Logical Thomas and Tommy, no one could take that from him. Our dialogue that day ended with Thomas knowing something significant had changed in his life.

Why dialogue with dissociation?

Dissociation is a relational dis-order that keeps a person divided within himself and separated from others. Typically, wounded parts of a person are hidden away in the subconscious and alter identities are formed to protect those parts from further hurt. Dissociation is commonly at work to keep the conscious mind, or others outside the person, from getting too close to younger, wounded parts. The main goal of dialoguing with entities within an individual's dissociative system should never be for the fascination of interacting with a person's dissociation. The goal is to discourse in a way that leads to inner healing and mind renewal. By learning to dialogue, you will be able to determine which entities are alters and which are wounded parts. Dialoguing will help identify whether these entities are God-focused, self-focused, or regulators. Dialoguing may also identify any demonic presence that could be impeding restoration. Most importantly, dialoguing will help mend relational brokenness and redeem the true person to wholeness.

Dialoguing with dissociation is an essential part of a person's healing journey. Most of a person's conversations, conflicts, and battles are on the inside in his mind. Dialoguing brings these outside the person and among those who can safely help the true person emerge. But dialoguing with dissociation is not as simple as picking up a phone and dialing someone with whom you would like to speak. First of all, a person's dissociative system has no directory of names, much less numbers to call. Their "addresses" are unmarked "streets" in the subconscious mind that are often barricaded off or have the access guarded in some way. Alters are not always cooperative; in fact, they may be quite the opposite unless you have earned their trust. Wounded parts of a person will be stalled in the time of the memory where they were formed. Corresponding alters will function in present time but also be linked to the memory time of the wounded parts they protect. They may at times say, "You can't go there" when you seek to access a memory, or "You can't speak to him" if you want to dialogue with a wounded part. Other factors add to the mystery (and the frustration at times) of steering through the maze of a person's dissociation that leads toward the outcome of healing.

Signs of dissociation are "everywhere." I am astonished at the increasing numbers of movies, books, programs, articles, and other resources that identify or capitalize on dissociation without ever identifying it as such. On the whole, dialoguing with dissociation has been limited to "professionals" who treat it as a mental disorder. In the case of complex dissociation, I feel the assistance of qualified therapists can be advantageous, even necessary. However, dissociation is a common phenomenon rooted in relational dis-order that separates a person within himself, as well as from others. The average person can be equipped to identify the kind of dissociation that is openly being presented all about us. He can then responsibly interact with his own dissociation or that of others for the purpose of inner healing. I can offer you no set formulas to follow, but I share the following insights and principles gleaned from my years of experience studying dissociation and interacting with those who are dissociated.

Observing dissociation

Rule number one is to never tell a person he or she is dissociated. Some feel very uncomfortable with the idea they are dissociated because they equate that with being crazy. By promoting self discovery, people accept more readily that they are relationally separated, and they generally want to discover what is at the root. It is not necessary in every case to expose a person's dissociation. I have conducted entire ministry sessions where dissociated entities have been interacted with and healing has occurred, yet the word dissociation has never been uttered. But for the most part, tapping into, naming, and mapping a person's dissociation accelerates the healing process.

Observation is a helpful tool when dialoguing with dissociation. There are a number of recognizable signs that a person may be dissociated and is switching between entities. One common indicator is the perceptible shifting of the eyes, usually in a side-to-side quivering motion that is rapid or jerky. This is usually a clue that parts or alters that are not presenting are "inside looking out" and sizing up who you are or what you may want. The reason for the rapid eye shifting could be that several entities are vying for a peek. Keep in mind that dissociation is in place to protect a person. Entities may be assessing if you are safe, trustworthy, or accepting. They may be trying to determine if you are judgmental, antagonistic, or threatening in some way. As an example, when engaging a total stranger in conversation, I sometimes observe this phenomenon, such as at a customer service counter in a store. Maybe the previous customer was upset and had tapped into the person's woundedness. Maybe there is something about my approach to them that subconsciously triggers fear. For whatever reason – whether in daily conversation or in a ministry session – the person I am talking to will be totally unaware that their eyes are doing this.

More exaggerated shifts between entities may include sudden changes in posture, facial expression, or voice. When you are dialoguing with a wounded part who is stalled at a certain age, anticipate the characteristics of the person at that age. A young child part, for example, will use a childlike vocabulary. His face, mannerisms, and voice will suddenly take on the character of the person at that young age. You may find the fifty-year-old across from you suddenly speaking and behaving exactly like a five-year-old. A protecting alter may abruptly show signs that his defenses are up. Maybe he becomes rigid, crosses his arms, leans forward, or takes some other self-protective stance that is a clue you are dialoguing with that alter.

One woman we worked with wore her hair down but had an alter that wore her hair up. Every time she would switch to that alter, she would take a moment to rearrange her hairdo before talking. When the true person would speak, the hair would be put back down. This ritual continued throughout the session, and the woman was completely oblivious that she was doing this. One man had a distinct posture for several of his alters. One would sit straight up in the chair, another would slouch, a third would only present when his legs were crossed, one would lean over on the right arm of the chair, and another would shift his weight to the left arm of the chair. When I would ask to speak to a different alter he would say, "Hold on," readjust his posture, then instantly begin communicating as that alter.

Other examples throughout this book have been given to help you identify switches. These include changes in name, age, body language, attire, handwriting, personality, or attitude, each consistent with a particular entity. Voice changes are a common clue that a switch has occurred. These may even be picked up in telephone conversation with a person should a switch occur while he is talking. Listen for distinct vocabulary, phrases, accents, or tone of voice. A self-focused alter may curse. A God-focused alter would never think to do such a thing. One man spoke several foreign languages fluently. A younger, wounded part only knew English and had no conscious awareness that other languages were known by his adult self.

Be alert to phrases people use that hint at dissociation: "A part of me feels …," "One side of me thinks … but another side of me thinks …," "I am so confused," "I have conversations that carry on in my head," "I feel at times as though I am two different people," "I act one way here but another way there," "I talk with myself," and other similar expressions may give you clues about dissociation. (See *Pointers: Dissociation Assessment* in the Appendix) I will often seek confirmation of what I am hearing. For example, I may bodily shift my weight to the right and extend my right hand outward and repeat back something like, "So part of you feels aroused whenever you look at pornography," then mirror that posture by a deliberate shift to the left and say, "But then another part of you feels disgusted and ashamed every time you look at pornography." "That is exactly what is going on," may be the response. This will also help you distinguish God-focused and self-focused sides of a person. I may then be able to probe a bit deeper and ask, "When the self-focused part of you is looking at pornography, where does the God-focused part go that is disgusted by pornography?" This may startle the person at first, but then he will tell you where that God-focused part goes.

Not all switches are distinct or readily identified. If you suspect a change has taken place but are uncertain, ask either, "Who am I speaking to?" or "Am I now speaking to (name of entity)?" Question-and-answer is an important part of dialoguing with dissociation to help identify, map, and interact productively with those in a person's dissociative system. This is not an exact science, and no single entity may have all the information. For instance, wounded parts may have only portions of memory data that have been scattered due to the circumstances under which they were formed. Not all alters may be telling you the truth, either deliberately or unintentionally. One woman was asked if she had followed through on her commitment to be in church weekly. She hung her head and admitted she had not gone the previous Sunday. Later in the session, an alter told us all about the exciting service she had attended the previous weekend. The first alter suddenly popped up with the self-realization, "I *did* go to church last Sunday!" Obviously that alter was not consciously present at the service but co-consciously gleaned the information from the second alter.

Self-discovery and self-awareness go hand in hand. Once a person discovers his dissociation, he is then positioned to face the relational dis-order in his life. Self-awareness is necessary to the healing process. Once that occurs, it becomes easier to unfold the map of a person's dissociation and plot the course toward wholeness.

Gaining cooperation
Earn trust

"I have to wear masks," Penny admitted. "I don't know how to survive without them." As I observed Penny wringing her hands, I was becoming even more familiar with the masks of dissociation she so comfortably wore. It was obvious that her alters were well established and that her wounded parts were well protected by them. So I asked, "Can you tell me what your name is?" "I'm The Costume Department," she replied, "I decide who will wear what mask." As I dialogued further, it became apparent that The Costume Department was Penny's regulator alter who helped facilitate what entities would speak, when they would speak, and how they would present themselves. And even though Penny was only in her twenties, The Costume Department was already weary of her job. We had arrived at this place of openness in our conversations with Penny because we had developed a relationship that she knew was safe and confidential. In the process, we had built a rapport with entities in her system that had learned we could be trusted.

In the quest for inner healing, the conscious mind may want to go to the place of pain, but the subconscious mind may be unwilling to go there. Alters may be skeptical or cautious about facilitators, and rightly so. As guardians of wounded parts, their primary job is to protect the person from getting hurt. They need to know that you are a safe person. They may have no idea who you are or why they are sitting across from you. They may be reluctant to be present because they have been "forced" to come by "whoever it is" that set up the appointment for a session. We are sometimes "warned" by an alter that we have one or two chances with him "and that is it" – he will no longer cooperate after that. We occasionally have some kind of threat made. One woman arrived at her first session so nervous that she warned us she might throw up at any moment. As we typically do, we spent the first thirty minutes or so engaging her in casual conversation to get acquainted and put her at ease. "Everyone" relaxed. Not only did she have some tremendous breakthroughs that day, she never once threw up. These are examples of how alters will immediately work to establish their boundaries with you or to set up their familiar barriers to maintain distance and keep the person safe.

Sensitivity needs to be exercised when accessing wounded parts of a person. Often this is a child part that has been deeply buried in the subconscious. I will first ask, "Do you know who I am?" "No" is a common response. So I will explain, "My name is Quinn and this is (name of ministry partner). We are friends of (name of his true self)." Then I may say something like, "He brought you with him today so we could talk together and see if we can help you feel better. Would that be okay with you?" This part may still have no conscious clue who I am or even who his adult true self is. But by dialoguing for a few moments to establish safety and trust, the part will normally cooperate. Usually you are able to dialogue with a wounded part because an alter has first trusted you and has "given you permission" to talk with this part. At other times, an alter may talk on behalf of the part if it is still unsure of your trustworthiness. I am an educator and have taught a variety of ages in both churches and schools. I may use my experiences to help find connecting points with a wounded part. For instance, "I used to teach children your age. You may enjoy playing with dolls" (or whatever may be an appropriate comment). Or, "When I was your age my sisters and I liked to play at the park. Is that something you enjoy doing?" or "What is your favorite thing to play on at the park?" Each situation will be different. Learn to trust the promptings of the Holy Spirit to guide you in the quest to earn trust and to dialogue effectively.

Identify the name

Alter identities are not a person's problem. Alters are a part of the mind's protective mechanism set up to hide, mask, or avoid pain, especially to protect the mind from going to the place of pain associated with the cause of dissociation. Once accessed, alters are well aware of their origin and purpose. They will have distinct names or ways to be identified. Everyone prefers to be called by name, and this is true of alter identities and wounded parts. Remember that wounded parts are usually the same name of the true person (e.g. Penny) at the age when they stalled in dissociation (e.g. seven-year-old Penny), whereas alters will have a completely different human name (e.g. Lana), a nickname (Dolly), a function name (Depressed Penny), or a non-human name or identifier (e.g.

The Costume Department, or possibly the name of an animal, object, or some other thing). Therefore, aim to learn the name of the alter by simply asking, "What name do you prefer to be called?" They know their names and will tell you. Then be sure to use that name.

Identify the function

Because alters have functions, it is important to identify what those are. Once the function of an alter is known, he needs to be acknowledged and affirmed in his role, whether you personally agree or disagree with what the alter does for the person. Generally, it is pointless to try to reason or argue with an alter or attempt to tell him what to do. He already knows what he is supposed to do. In fact, you may need to "agree to disagree" with an alter while finding common ground for working together to help the person. Pinpointing the function of an alter will also aid in mapping a person's dissociation.

Show respect

It is never my place as a facilitator to judge or condemn the recipient, or any wounded part or alter identity within his system. I will do everything possible to avoid bringing greater fear or shame upon a person or any entity within him. If I come across as threatening in any way, "no one" may be willing to cooperate or dialogue with me. In fact, alters may become fiercely protective and uncooperative if they feel attacked or pressured. Corresponding wounded parts will also sense this and may back off, run, or hide.

When dialoguing with a person's dissociation, apply the "Golden Rule" of doing to others as you would have them do to you. Avoid speaking about or referring to alters in the presence of the true person as though they do not exist or are unable to hear you. Demanding puts them on the defensive. Use language with alters such as, "I would be grateful if you would ... ," or "Would you be willing to ... ." Once accessed, some alters may feel obligated to participate, which is not always necessary or helpful. Allow them an opportunity to rest by saying, for example, "You have my permission to take a break while I speak to (another alter; a wounded part; the true person)." Thank the alters for their contributions and help.

Practical dialoguing tips

The following list includes a variety of tips to enhance dialoguing with a person's dissociation. This list is neither sequential nor exhaustive but is simply a compilation of practical ideas, reminders, resources, and guidelines.

1. Jesus is the true healer and the source of truth. Keep the focus of inner healing on what Jesus is doing to renew the mind and restore the person to wholeness.

2. Seek to identify and engage the true person. As early as possible, draw out the true person who has been fragmented by trauma and pain. The true person may be overshadowed by dissociative entities yet needs to "stay present" as much as possible. Aim to empower the true person to become the spokesperson for the system. Pray specifically for the true person. As the true person receives healing, it will become easier for him to walk through some "self-healing" experiences on his own.

3. Dissociated entities may not be conscious of one another until the person is brought to a place of self-awareness and co-consciousness. Understand that just because a part or alter gives you information or receives healing, no other entity may

be aware that this has happened. Capitalize on co-consciousness to increase awareness, participation, and cooperation. Aim to "bring everyone along" at all times and include all known parts whenever possible. For example, one woman pictured her system as board members who met around a large table to communicate and make decisions. For her, this was a helpful scenario to aid dialoguing that led to integration and restoration.

4. Get acquainted with a person's wounded parts and alters. Map the dissociation to aid dialogue from the outside as well as to encourage internal dialogue within the person's system. The map will change and develop as the person receives healing, identities merge, or new identities are identified. (See Chapter 8, *Mapping Dissociation*)

5. Seek to determine when or where alters or parts communicate with others. For example, "home" alters may only talk at home and be unaccustomed to dialoguing outside that context. Some alters only interact with or react to certain people; say that person is mother. To engage one of these alters, you may have to create a context that will help them open up. For instance, "If your mother walked into the room right now and sat down beside you, what would you say to her?" Realize that those closest to the dissociated person may be his or her biggest trigger.

6. As the true person and/or God-focused entities are strengthened, a sense of accountability within the system will aid restoration. Encourage the true person and God-focused entities to help mentor other parts and alters toward healing and wholeness.

7. Wounded parts of a person are stalled in a memory and limited to the time frame surrounding that memory. Corresponding alters, set up to protect wounded parts, are not stalled in the

context of the memory and therefore can function both in the memory and in the present.

8. Ask alters if they would be willing to help you get to the place of woundedness. This will be more likely to happen if they determine you are safe and can be trusted. By offering to "go along" with them to that place, they will have less reservation than if they think they have to go alone or that the wounded part will be exposed without their protection.

9. If the Lord does not reveal truth in a particular memory, it could be that the wounded part in that memory may not be ready to accept what the Lord wants to say or do. Or, it could be that a different memory will provide the context where healing may occur.

10. Ask the same question of each part or alter in turn to gauge the impact of a lie-based statement or to understand each one's viewpoint on a matter. Record individual responses and impressions next to each entity's name. This insightful and helpful exercise can also aid in the mapping of dissociation.

11. Similarly, you may find out what percentage of the time a particular alter believes it is active. See if other entities are in agreement. This will help you determine the perceived influence of various entities within the dissociative system.

12. Generally, parts or alters will not refuse prayer if you offer to pray for them. A recipient also can be encouraged to pray for his parts and alters.

13. Dialogue is not always verbal. As already noted, pick up on communication clues such as body language, facial expression, or tone of voice to distinguish between entities. If you are uncertain about whom you are talking with or "miss the switch," ask to confirm which alter or part is presenting.

14. Be aware that the enemy, Satan, will attempt to interfere with the healing process. Do not go looking for demons or presume they are there. The Lord will reveal these as needed. He will also guide you in how to deal with the demonic.

15. Log the dialogue. Keep a journal of the interaction with a person's dissociation. (See *Procedures: Documenting a Session* in the Appendix)

16. Sometimes when working with dissociation funny things happen. Even alters can have a sense of humor, so laugh with the dissociation but never at it.

Integration

Whereas dissociation results in disorder, integration helps restore order and put things back the way they were originally intended to be. Integration is often used to describe two different aspects of the restoration process. One aspect is that of parts and alters coming to co-conscious self-awareness. As this happens, entities learn to dialogue, cooperate, and share their memories and information with one another. The other aspect of integration is that of actual merging, or fusion, of separated entities back to wholeness within the true person. Some fear that when the latter happens, a piece of them will die, become passive, or simply disappear. When merging occurs, all memories, history, talents, and gifts are preserved. Certain behaviors, attitudes, habits, or patterns peculiar to the dissociation or that were functions of alters will either cease or change.

Healing is a process that takes time. Merging is a part of the process that happens in God's timing and in his way. A facilitator should never attempt to force or otherwise seek to coerce merging prematurely. Each person's experience with integration, merging, and restoration will be unique to the individual. I have observed in others and experienced in myself the tangible sensation of internally uniting. Attempts to describe what this is like include a sense that entities are being "zipped back together," "folded back in," or "snapped back into place." Regardless of what is going on or how it is experienced, most make some statement to summarize the completeness they feel in that area.

As integration and merging take place, the true person begins to operate from a position of greater strength, soundness of mind, and wholeness. Sometimes people begin sleeping better or longer. Headaches cease. Mental conflicts abate. People often give evidence that spiritual gifts that have been blocked or hindered are suddenly operating. Satan's goal is to keep a person fragmented and relationally separated. God will bring glory to himself when a person's dissociated entities are united, his mind is renewed, and his soul is restored. One person realized, "I had a mind of my own before I was dissociated." He was determined to "get his mind back" and no longer have it be a battleground for dissociative conflict or demonic influence.

Just because you receive healing in an area or you experience integration or merging does not mean all your problems go away. Dissociation, as a relational dis-order, impacts others from whom you are separated. As the "real" you emerges in wholeness, some people may still want you or expect you to be the "old" you. The whole process of dialoguing and integrating starts to be taken outside yourself as healing begins to include others, or exclude them as the case may be. The goal of inner healing is not merging. The goal is to present your redeemed self to God, renewed in singleness of mind, and restored in the original image and likeness you were created to bear.

Prayer Pause

"God, you designed me for association and relationship with you and with others. Please remove all barriers that exist within my mind so that I may be restored to wholeness and peace. Demolish all walls that have gone up that separate me from others, including you. Help me forgive those who have hurt me. Help me forgive myself. And Lord, please forgive me for all I have done to hurt others. I choose today to love all of me, including all fragmented parts and alters. Heal me this day and restore your perfect order within myself, with others, and with you. May your original intent for my life be realized fully as I put my trust in you. I speak all this in the Name of Jesus and in the power of the one true God. Amen!"

Chapter 12

Making Contact

Practical Application
for Ministry Facilitators

WEBSTER LOOKED WARILY AT MY MINISTRY
PARTNER. "DO YOU KNOW WHO HE IS?" I
ASKED. Without taking his eyes off of him, Webster shook his
head menacingly. "No." The man co-facilitating the session was
fairly new to the inner healing prayer ministry team. He tried not
to show his astonishment. He had known Webster for nearly a
year and a half and had seen him regularly at church and at other
times. But this streetwise alter did not have a clue who he was.
His body tensed, and he suddenly started scanning the room for
an exit.

We had been hearing about this side of Webster, whom he
had described as "gangsta," using some of the following adjectives:
distant, defensive, rebellious, angry, independent, tough, hard, and
a troublemaker. He even talked about his preference for attire,
sordid interests, and gang activity. I had suggested that, instead
of Webster telling us *about* this side of him, if this side was allowed
to speak for himself, what would he say? All of a sudden, there
was a shift that resulted in both the suspicion of my ministry partner
and an instinct to flight. Although agitated, this alter was willing to

speak with me while keeping an eye on my ministry partner. This alter wanted to be called Gerard and divulged very personal details of a chaotic and abusive upbringing. Consequently, Gerard held to some deeply rooted lies and fears that punctuated a primary function of dissociation: to aid survival and to protect a person from being hurt again. He believed he was all alone and there was no one to protect him, that he was a mess-up and a troublemaker. Gerard formed and eventually became a thug. How else could Webster possibly survive, especially without him?

One of the goals of dialoguing with dissociation is to directly engage parts and alters in a responsible way that will lead to healing. In most cases, common dissociation is *provoked* into presenting. For example, something may spontaneously trigger an alter to protect, to control, or to present in a given situation. But in the safe and protected environment of an inner healing session, the dissociation can be *invited* forward. An alter is already functioning anyway, but may typically show up when least expected, possibly taking the individual and others by surprise. When Gerard abruptly appeared, it was not by provocation but by invitation. It is often the case that an alter has never been invited to show himself in this way. Rather, circumstance has compelled him to function.

Webster had been dialoguing with me about Gerard, although did not know him by name. Because Webster had been telling me about Gerard, Gerard had some idea who I was. However, Gerard-the-alter did not know the other man with me (even though Webster did), had never been to church (although Webster was a regular), was unfamiliar with the room he was in, and survival instinct had kicked in. I reassured Gerard and thanked him for being willing to speak with me directly. I introduced myself, then my ministry partner, to him. I explained that Webster had brought him along today and that, instead of just hearing about Gerard, we wanted to let him speak for himself and help us understand who he is and how he helps Webster. Gerard relaxed slightly but stayed perched on the edge of his seat. Soon we began to hear his side of the story.

Qualification and character

I am a degreed and ordained pastor who has studied counseling academically. I am not a licensed therapist or professional psychiatrist. I do not diagnose people with psychological disorders such as Multiple Personality or Dissociative Identity Disorder. However, I effectively help people connect with their dissociation and the "relational dis-order" that separates them within themselves, from others, and from God.

People frequently want to know exactly how I start talking with a person in order to distinguish his wounded parts and alter identities. Whether in a formal ministry session or an impromptu encounter, I believe a number of factors have enabled me to "make contact." These include:

Training

- I have availed myself to years of ongoing study, personal training, and application in the areas of inner healing, dissociation, and deliverance ministry. Some of this has been "on-the-job training" experienced both as a recipient and as a facilitator.

- I have researched these subjects from both Christian and secular perspectives. I have grown accustomed to perusing books, publications, articles, programs, and other resources through inner healing lenses to glean insights that better equip me to minister as well as to teach others.

Experience

- Experience builds confidence. I have logged thousands of hours working directly with dissociated people ranging in actual age from 5 to 77 years. No two sessions are alike because no two people are the same. There is great variety of personal history, unique backgrounds, and expressions of dissociation. It is one thing to read about dissociation. It is quite another to encounter it. For me, the "classroom of experience" has been one of my best teachers in practically understanding and ministering to dissociation.

- I am a firm believer in peer accountability. For example, an inner healing mentor and I get together for an annual "internal check-up" with one another, typically near the beginning of each year. This also allows us to learn from each other and grow together. Over time, the mutual vulnerability has deepened our trust in and respect for one another. Because my mentor and I live in different states, local relationships and accountability are integral to my ministry experience and add to credibility.

Preparation

- There seems to be a correlation between the consistent exercise of both prayer and fasting and the effectiveness of ministry. I willingly serve others out of the overflow of these disciplines as well as other personal preparation. I encourage my ministry team members, as well as ministry recipients, to prepare personally by exercising prayer and, if they are able, fasting. In addition, a core of committed intercessors provides prayer covering for the inner healing prayer ministry. I could never overemphasize the significance and power of prayer.

- An environment that is conducive for ministry is private, peaceful, and safe. As a ministry facilitator, I am integral to that atmosphere. The "environment of who I am" helps me to minister in both scheduled sessions and unplanned situations. In the Appendix of this book are pointers on preparing the facilitator and recipient as well as the physical environment for formal ministry.

Submission

- Submission to Christ's authority is clearly stated as a session begins by sincerely praying together, "God, we humbly submit to the authority of the Lordship of Jesus Christ." This positions my ministry partner, the recipient, and me in our rightful place in relation to the Lord. It also serves to remind all of us that this is the Lord's work, not man's. We merely facilitate what he wants done as we represent him to the best of our ability.

- Submission to one another out of reverence for Christ establishes spiritual boundaries that acknowledge the Lord's presence and invite cooperation with him. Inner healing is not something "I do for you." Rather, it is something God does among us that helps restore and redeem the Body of Christ.

Boundaries

- The spiritual boundaries that are set communicate to the enemy (Satan) and his minions that we understand our authority and are not afraid to use it! Once submission to Jesus Christ is clearly expressed, I briefly address the enemy and tell him that he is not allowed to interfere with, intercept, hinder, block, or stop what the true Lord Jesus Christ will do throughout the session and is already doing among us. I avoid and discourage dialoguing with demons. The Biblical precedent is to speak *to* demons rather than *with* them.

- I typically speak upfront specifically to spirits of fear and shame, confusion and mockery because of their prevalence. I let the enemy know that he has no right to manifest in any way unless given permission to do so by the true Lord Jesus Christ and only for his intended purpose. This does not mean that the enemy will not try! However, in my experience, setting such boundaries in advance seems to debilitate the enemy. Should there be a demonic manifestation, it is addressed firmly and authoritatively. The focus is always kept on Jesus and our trust is in him to guide us at such times.

Sensitivity

- First, there must be sensitivity to the Holy Spirit. Ministering inner healing boils down to two basic components: praying and then getting out of the way of what God wants to do! I absolutely trust in the leading of God's Spirit. My personal spiritual gift-mix includes discernment and faith. I expect these to be called upon by the Spirit in order to contribute to the healing process. Your spiritual gifts will similarly be instrumental as you submit them to the leading of the Holy Spirit.

- Second, there must be sensitivity to the ministry recipient. People often arrive anxious and fearful about what might happen. They may come wondering, "Will I be accepted?" and, "Will they be able to help me?" Gentleness and compassion help put people at ease. One extremely nervous person arrived with his own five-gallon bucket, certain he would throw up. In all my years I have only had one person so apprehensive that she did not keep her appointment. She later apologized. We rescheduled and had a fruitful experience.

Protection

- The ministry recipient must know he is safe. As a session gets underway, I will state, "One of the commitments my ministry partner and I make is to protect you and keep you safe." This reassurance also contributes to the setting of spiritual boundaries.

- Assure the recipient of confidentiality. I have ministered to family members, close friends, and total strangers. No matter what the relationship, I commit to protecting their disclosures even in impromptu ministry opportunities. People regularly confide to me, "I've *never* told this to *anyone* before ... ." They would not risk such vulnerability if they felt unprotected. I consciously thank people for trusting me.

Authenticity

- I am grateful to those who have compassionately walked with me as I have "worked out my deliverance with fear and trembling." (Philippians 2:12) I have dealt with dissociation in myself so am familiar with others' pain and bewilderment. I am no stranger to demonization and demonic expulsion. I know what counseling and support groups are all about. I can testify to the power of God to renew, restore, and redeem, yet admit that I am still a "work in progress."

- Wounded people find it hard to trust. Sensitivity, humility, gentleness, patience, and respect are characteristics that genuinely convey trustworthiness to others. Therefore, these must be genuine. If you propose to facilitate healing in others, I recommend that you receive healing yourself. The credibility of your own healing journey will increase compassion for others, communicate integrity, and go a long way in making contact that leads to deep inner healing.

Compassion

- Many seeking healing have been shamed into silence, betrayed, or taken advantage of by those they sought help from. I reassure a recipient by telling him, "I am not here to condemn you or judge you for what has happened in your life. God's Word says 'there is now no condemnation for those who are in Christ Jesus.' (Romans 8:1) Jesus is not present among us to condemn you, but to love on you and set you free."

- Genuinely love the person. Let him know he has value and worth to Jesus and to you. "Love must be sincere." (Romans 12:9) Let the Christ-in-you express that love to him in Jesus' Name.

Observation

- Observation involves watching and listening for clues and cues of dissociation. A person may say "we" or "us" when referring to himself, make contradictory statements, or exhibit noticeable switches in demeanor, attitude, countenance, voice, and posture. Other evidence may be changes in name, age, body language, attire, handwriting, personality, or attitude, each consistent with a particular entity. (See Chapter 11 section, "Observing dissociation")

- Dissociation seems to be "everywhere." As you become oriented to identify dissociation it becomes easier to recognize just how common it is, such as in magazines, movies, and other mass media. One of my favorite examples is Disney's "The Kid" where adult Russ Duritz meets his 8-year-old self, Rusty. The movie reveals the trauma event that caused dissociation, corresponding lie-based thinking, the alter identity, dialogue with dissociation, healing, merging, and more. Although not presented from a spiritual perspective, most aspects of common dissociation are evident and can be identified in this family-friendly story.

Journaling

- As a session begins, I advise the recipient that notes will be taken and explain the types of things being recorded: general information, memories, lie-based statements, dissociation, and demonic influences. Documenting provides reference points when, for example, keeping track of alters or going back to express forgiveness.
- Journaling provides a tangible record of a session. It chronicles what was experienced, confirms what God has done, and provides information for a recipient summary should one be provided. (See Appendix: "Documenting a Session")

Taking the initiative

Some are hesitant to initiate a dialogue with a person's dissociation. As I have pointed out, it seems easier to talk *about* dissociation than to speak *with* dissociated parts and alters. Therefore, casually but conversationally explaining dissociation can put it on a more normal footing and help people understand what it is about. The following exercises will help you move from talking about to dialoguing with dissociation.

I can relate

Most people will experience dissociation to some degree. A non-threatening way to help someone relate to this is by asking three simple questions:

1. "Do you ever daydream?"
2. "Do you ever experience 'highway hypnosis' while driving?" (That is, you can't remember a short segment of travel.)
3. "Do you ever 'zone out' during a dull conversation?"

Invariably, people will relate to one or all three of these. They typically respond with laughter, an "of course," or "all the time!" In other words, they can identify with these common experiences.

Then I tell them, "These are all examples of dissociation in its mildest form – brief mental escapes or momentary relief from the mundane. Almost everyone dissociates in this way."

"But, if a person experiences extreme stress or trauma, in his mind he may separate himself from the pain. It is a normal function of the mind to separate, or dissociate, in this way in order to survive whatever is going on."

Explaining dissociation this way is disarming and relevant. It quickly moves a person from something they can personally identify with (e.g. daydreaming) to regarding dissociation as quite common, even necessary, in order to endure intense physical or emotional pain.

Getting into their head

What I call "the head" diagram (below) simply and clearly illustrates dissociation. Its effectiveness of use is not dependent upon artistic inclination. However, with a little practice, you will be able to draw this adequately enough to make your point. I simply begin drawing out "the head," casually explaining the components of the picture as I go.

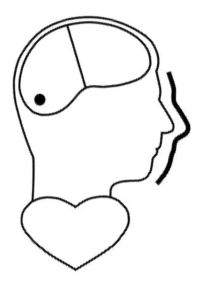

I recently met with a couple at a coffee shop who wanted to learn more about the ministry. I sketched the profile of a head on a napkin. As I began to draw the brain, I said, "I know the brain isn't really kidney-shaped, but we're going to let this represent the mind." I add a line to divide it in half "to separate the conscious mind from the subconscious mind." I may designate these simply as "c" and "sc" in my sketch. "This line that separates the mind (which I emphasize by drawing over it several times) represents the barriers that keep dissociation hidden away in the subconscious, separated from the conscious mind."

"When a person experiences trauma – let's say a 5-year-old child is being severely beaten for the first time by her mother – the mind searches for a way to deal with the pain of that event and to aid survival."

I draw in a large dark dot in the farthest recess of the subconscious mind. "Often, a wounded part of the person stalls at that moment. This part will hold fragmented memory data associated with that event." I write in "Wounded Part" and draw an arrow to the dot in the subconscious mind.

I continue. "Lie-based thinking may be attached to that wounded part in that memory. For example, 'It was my fault,' 'I am bad,' 'My life is ruined,' 'No one will love me now,' or something of that nature. Logically, the conscious mind knows this is not true, but this wounded part of the person functions out of that false belief system."

Next, I outline a "mask" parallel to the profile of the face. "If the trauma is severe enough, an alternate identity, or 'alter,' may correspondingly form. A job of the alter is to protect the person from returning to the place of pain and being re-traumatized." I write in "Alter" and draw an arrow to the "mask."

I usually expound, "While the primary job of an alter identity is to protect, an alter may also function to control relationships or circumstances in order to keep the person from being hurt again. Or, there may be alters that present themselves in specific situations. For example, there may be a 'home' alter or a 'church' alter or a 'work' alter that operates in relation to each distinct environment."

Tapping the point of my pen back and forth between the wounded part, mind, and alter identity, I suggest, "This may help you understand why some people seem conflicted: they have become separated within themselves. When a person dissociates in this way – the word dissociate simply means 'to separate' –

they also tend to become separated from others, including God, which creates a spiritual dilemma."

Seeking feedback, I ask either, "Does this make sense to you?" or, "Can you identify with this in any way?" Then I await a response. Typically, this *is* making sense and the person *does* identify with the diagram.

The whole time, I am deliberately conversational and matter-of-fact as I interact with the drawing and monitor the person's reactions. I interject comments about how this is a normal response of the mind. I convey dissociation as something common, something most people deal with in some way (either in themselves or in others), and something that does not necessarily label a person as psychiatrically disordered, mentally ill, or "crazy." Common dissociation is not unusual or something to fear. Communicating about it in these terms makes sense.

But I want to move beyond comprehension to anticipation of healing. Finally, I draw in a large heart below the head and say, "This represents the 'True Person.'" I write this in the heart, saying that there is only one true person who happens to be a bit fragmented. I may point to the "mask" and explain, "Alters are merely 'counterfeit images' of the true person who are in place to protect and to aid survival."

I like to tell people that my favorite, four-word phrase in the Old Testament is found in Psalm 23:3 which, referring to the Lord, records, "He restores my soul." God puts things back the way they were originally intended to be: whole and complete. He not only restores the soul, but also renews the mind to singleness and redeems losses incurred by dissociation.

People are comforted when I tell them, "Inner healing calls forth the true person in wholeness, healing, and peace." Culminating this exercise with such an expression of hope encourages many to want that for themselves.

Summary of the Diagram

1. Draw the outline of "the head."
2. Draw a kidney-shaped "brain" that represents the mind. Add a line to divide it in two.
3. Label the "conscious" and "subconscious" mind.
4. Add a large dot deep in the subconscious mind.
5. Label the dot "Wounded Part." Draw an arrow from the words to the dot.
6. Outline a "mask" parallel to the face.
7. Label the mask "Alter." Draw an arrow to the mask.
8. Draw a large heart below the head. Label the heart "True Person."

Practice

1. Team up with your spouse, a friend, a colleague, or a ministry partner. On pieces of paper, each of you takes a turn drawing "the head" diagram, explaining the components as you draw. The emphasis is not upon drawing aptitude, but rather gaining confidence with the illustration.
2. Be casual, matter-of-fact, and informal as you interact with the diagram. Take your time. Offer explanations and make relevant comments as you go. Aim to keep the conversation as simple and understandable as possible.
3. Seek feedback by asking, "Does this make sense to you?" or, "Can you identify with this in any way?" Wait for a response.

Cutting up

Chapter Two presents "A picture of dissociation" to explain how the enemy works to destroy the original image a person is meant to bear. It also illustrates how dissociation creates separation, misalignment, confusion, and relational discord.

Practice

1. With a partner, practice demonstrating "A picture of dissociation." Use either the picture above, a photo of your own, a person on the cover of a magazine, or some other image of a face.

2. Review the section in Chapter Two of "A picture of dissociation." Then, in a conversational way, explain such components as:

   • how Satan targets innocence;

   • how and when Satan begins "slicing away" at a person;

   • how the original image becomes misaligned;

   • how Satan keeps a person in a state of "con-fusion."

Moving from generals to specifics

From Chapter 8, "Mapping Dissociation," recall that wounded parts and alters will be primarily either God-focused or self-focused. Learning to differentiate generally between these two "sides" will help you as wounded parts and alters begin to emerge and be identified more specifically as distinct to one side or the other.

Say we are working with Jenna. I may draw a line down the middle of a piece of paper with headings that say "God-focused" on one side, "self-focused" on the other. I invite Jenna to talk *about* her "God-focused side," drawing her out by asking simple questions that help identify characteristics, habits, attitudes, strengths, when this side is most active, and the like. I do similarly for the "self-focused side."

Jenna's lists look something like this:

God-focused	Self-focused
Believes God is the answer to all her problems	Is weak; expects failure; fears disobedience to God
Happy-go-lucky; likeable	Withdrawn; not out-going
A successful businesswoman	Depressed; won't leave house
Obedient to God	Says, "I can't help but be disobedient – why try?"
God says I am his friend	Says, "I am not worthy to be God's friend."
Says, "God can use me as I am."	Says, "My failures impede my witness."
Logical truth; has rational belief	Illogical; lives in fear
Has mistakenly thought self-focused side is a demon	Feels hopeless, confused
Is pushed down and silenced by self-focused side	Does not want to be here today

My goal is to move Jenna from talking *about* her dissociation to *identifying* her dissociation. For example, starting with the God-focused side, I verify what I have been hearing *about*. I say, "Thank you for sharing this about your God-focused side. Now, if you were to wrap your mind around these specific thoughts and attributes and allow this side to speak for herself, what would she say? I don't want you to speak *for* her; I want to give her permission to speak for herself."

Jenna may have difficulty doing this at first. Keep reassuring her. You may urge, "If this side of you were given a name, what would she be called?"

Jenna replies, pointing to the God-focused side of the paper, "This is Godly Jenna."

"Is this what *you* want to be called? Godly Jenna?" I am deliberately shifting the conversation away from Jenna so I may begin speaking directly to her dissociation. I am searching for confirmation that I have made contact. She may respond, "Yes, I am Godly Jenna," or she may announce another name she prefers to be called.

Now I want to affirm and reassure her. "Godly Jenna, 'Adult Jenna' has been telling us about you," thereby distinguishing this alter from the adult who has brought Godly Jenna with her today. "Let me share some things she has told us about you." I review the list with her. "Do you feel what is recorded here accurately describes you?"

Godly Jenna adds that she also loves to worship. She explains that this is when she feels closest to God.

"Thank you for sharing that, Godly Jenna." I write her preferred name above the "God-focused" side of the paper, then add that she loves to worship.

I make sure Godly Jenna knows who I am and introduce her to my ministry partner. We may dialogue with Godly Jenna for a little while to put her at ease. I will thank her for speaking with us and invite her continued participation in the session. All the while, I continually reassure Godly Jenna and affirm her place within Jenna. But there is more to discover.

"You will see on the paper that there is another side that Adult Jenna has told us about. Godly Jenna, would you be willing to step aside for a moment so we may also get acquainted with that side of Jenna?"

Having gained the cooperation of both Adult Jenna and Godly Jenna, I will proceed in a similar fashion to begin drawing out and dialoguing with Jenna's self-focused side. Essentially, this is the process that was used ultimately to engage Gerard, who appears in the story that opens this chapter.

Contact points

A prospective ministry recipient may initiate a request for inner healing via a conversation, phone call, e-mail, letter, or an introduction that results in a request for ministry. I will "interview" a potential ministry recipient to discern his understanding of and readiness to receive inner healing. Providing a formal application for ministry may eventuate in an appointment for a session that will be co-facilitated by two trained ministry facilitators.

Contact might also occur unpredictably in someone's home or office, in coffee shops and restaurants, or while walking or traveling together. Whether ministry is pre-arranged or happens unexpectedly, the following insights have been instrumental in productive dialogues that lead to healing and restoration.

Reflect what you see and hear

Be alert to commonly used phrases that hint at dissociation such as, "A part of me feels ..." or "One side of me thinks ..." or "Sometimes I feel like two different people."

To confirm what I am hearing, I may bodily shift my weight to the left, extend my left hand outward, then paraphrase a response indicative of the person's self-focused side. "So part of you feels angry whenever you are disrespected." I mirror that posture by a deliberate shift to the right and infer from what he has shared about his God-focused side, "But then another part of you feels embarrassed and ashamed every time you have an angry outburst."

A response such as, "That is exactly how it feels," verifies I have understood correctly.

Listening will help both you and the recipient to differentiate God-focused and self-focused sides. I may then be able to probe a bit deeper and ask, "When your self-focused side is provoked to anger, where does your God-focused side go during the outburst?" This question may startle the person at first, but usually he will be able to tell you where his God-focused side goes.

Hayden sat across from us in a ministry session and described a debilitating internal conflict. I intently listened and occasionally jotted a few words on my pad to keep track of his comments. My ministry partner was recording more detailed notes. Soon I was reflecting on what I had both observed and heard.

"Hayden, on the one hand (said as I shift my weight in my chair to the right, my hands moving that same direction), I hear you say that you have a religious standard to live up to and feel you have to be perfect. On the other hand (now shifting myself to the left, hands following), you're telling me you may risk dangerous behavior and don't really care what others think."

Hayden nods his confirmation.

"So, it sounds like one side of you (as I shift back to the right, perhaps slightly more exaggerated) truly does care what others think and is easily offended by Christians who appear to have a double-standard. (Now shifting the opposite direction, I might cross my right leg over the left for emphasis.) But another side of you will throw caution to the wind and has become really good at keeping certain activities hidden from other Christians."

Hayden concurs, but appears perplexed.

I quickly scan my notes to pick up on things he has revealed as we were mapping. "Does it seem to you that a God-focused side of yourself (said as I bend to the right) may be holding you to a rigid structure of rules while a self-focused side (now bending to the left) is rebelling against all the religious expectations?"

In the process of drawing out Hayden's dissociation, my deliberate posture shifts and purposeful reflection helped him recognize his own double-mindedness. Often, it is in my echo of what he has just disclosed that a recipient comprehends the mixed messages he has given. I may repeat his exact words then ask, "Can you hear the contradiction in what you have just told me?"

Talk to, not about, the dissociation

No one likes a tattler, especially if you are the one about whom something is being told. In essence, this is what is going on when a person talks *about* the characteristics or behaviors of one of his dissociative entities. A drawback of conventional support groups is that wounded people, who do not know they are dissociated, come together and tell *about* what their dissociation has been up to since the last meeting. Whatever alter may be doing the addictive behavior may not outwardly participate at the meeting. He may be peeved knowing he is being talked about. If that alter has no commitment to the purpose of the support group, he could continue his behavior outside that group, much to the dismay of the individual and the puzzlement of fellow support group members – who might also have alters acting furtively outside of the meetings.

It is important to move the person from talking *about* his dissociation to talking directly *with* the dissociation. Having made initial contact and engaged in some dialogue and mapping, I will probe deeper. From what has been exposed so far, perhaps in memories visited, feelings recorded, or other information, I will summarize characteristics I am detecting. After sharing my synopsis, I often ask, "If you could wrap your mind around these thoughts and allow them to speak for themselves, what would they say?" At this point, I am *inviting* the dissociation to speak for itself.

Keep reassuring both the person and the entity whom these thoughts represent. You will generally encounter an alter before you will meet the part he is protecting. He may be reluctant or untrusting. He may be accustomed to using only an internal voice, never speaking outside the person. It helps the recipient when he hears one of his alters speak for himself. Your role is to make contact respectfully, to acknowledge and affirm what is happening, and to encourage this self-discovery.

Getting acquainted

Ask the alter his name. Often this is immediately shared, usually to the astonishment of the recipient. I had agreed to meet Ron at his job site. He soon confessed a troubling personal desire that was both out of character and out of control. As I listened and reflected with Ron, we got to a point where I asked, "What does this side you are telling me about like to be called?" "Ricky" *instantly* identified himself, much to Ron's surprise! (I will admit, at the time I was a bit surprised, too!) Quite outside the framework of a formal ministry session, contact was made.

At other times, a name may need to be drawn out if there seems to be uncertainty. While making observations during a formal session, I may recognize certain characteristics, defined functions, and particular behaviors that lead me to ask something like, "You've expressed a lot of anger. How would you feel if I call you 'Angry Ron' for now so we can distinguish you from the rest of Ron?" If the part is not comfortable or happy with that, this may get him to reveal a preferred name, whether a human name ("Ricky"), a function name ("Furious Ron"), or something else depictive of the dissociation ("Volcano"). Once the alter is identified, speak to him by his name.

I will familiarize myself with this alter to build rapport and trust. I will also coach Ron and Ricky in getting to know and consciously dialogue with one another. Ron, who is a Christian, will discover that Ricky is an "unredeemed" alter who does not personally embrace relationship with Jesus. This is a common disparity in a person's dissociative structure, particularly if the separation occurred before the person committed his life to Christ. The Chapter 9 section on "Restoring the soul" elaborates on this phenomenon.

I do not presume that just because a part or alter is presenting that others within the system are co-conscious, that is, mutually aware of one another. As it becomes appropriate, I will introduce other alters and parts to one another.

Integration occurs when alters and parts come into co-conscious self-awareness of one another. As this happens, entities learn to dialogue, cooperate, and to share their memories and information with each other. They find out what it means within the dissociative system to "love your neighbor as yourself." (Matthew 19:19b) "Love your enemies and pray for those who persecute you" (Matthew 5:44) takes on new meaning if entities are polarized or at odds with one another. God-focused entities frequently become instrumental in helping to redeem self-focused entities. It is ultimately God's work and his timing that will merge back to oneness what dissociation has separated.

While strides in healing may occur in a structured setting, advances can also be made independent of a facilitator. After all, Jesus is the healer and he is ever-present to help. In the process of facilitating ministry, I endeavor to equip people to work some of this out on their own. For example, once Ron and Ricky acknowledged one another, they agreed to some simple "assignments" to continue jointly mapping and dialoguing. As Ron discovered, if a person is willing and acquires some skills, he can receive measures of healing between facilitated sessions. This also prevents a recipient from becoming dependent upon a ministry facilitator.

Willing to vs. want to

I have found it extremely beneficial to differentiate "want to" from "willing to" and use language accordingly. For example, a wounded part may not want to forgive her offender. I acknowledge that by saying, "I understand you don't *want to* forgive him for what he did. However, would you be *willing to* forgive him for (specify the offense)?" The part may need to think about that. She might say, "Yes, I am willing," or "I can't do that *yet*." If a part or alter is not ready to do something at that time, do not push. Nevertheless, I find an entity will almost always respond willingly whether that means agreeing to forgive, dialoging with another part, going to a painful memory, or doing whatever might be asked of her.

Be respectful

Protect a person's dignity, whether in private or in public. One time, I was at a restaurant with a friend. The nature of our table conversation tapped into his dissociation. We happened to be seated in a corner of the room. At one point in the dialogue, I suggested he and I swap seats at the table. This simple change placed me with my back to the corner and put him in the position of having his back to the dining area, which minimized his sense of self-consciousness. He was not distracted by activity or people around him and, except for me sitting across from him, only had the wall to look at behind me. With a pen and a couple of napkins we were able to map two distinct alters conflicted in double-mindedness. I put him at ease and gauged his readiness to take another step in this surprising path onto which we had stumbled.

Before parting company, I agreed with his request that we sit in his car to pray together – something he did not feel comfortable doing inside the restaurant. This became a holy moment of divine intervention and healing that would not have occurred without the conversation that had just taken place. Two days later I received this confirming e-mail from him:

"I had an awesome time and am beginning to dialogue within myself about some matters that were revealed the other night. Some exciting things are happening. I will keep you posted as I delve deeper. Thanks for your help and prayer."

Protect yourself

I stress here the importance of never putting yourself or a ministry recipient in a compromising situation. Formal sessions are done with a co-facilitator who is there for accountability and assistance. I will rarely engage a person in his dissociation one-on-one if that means we are alone. In the account I just shared, I was with a long-standing friend, surrounded by people in a public restaurant. Even moving to a vehicle just to pray had a safety factor in that the car's interior was fully visible from both the restaurant and the parking lot as others passed by. I will never meet alone with a woman. Period. There are too many risks working behind closed doors without accountability – both for you and for the person receiving ministry. Should you experience a spontaneous or unexpected conversation with a person's dissociation, you must quickly ascertain if the circumstance is conducive to a moment of ministry or if it is best to stop and arrange an inner healing session. An outcome for my friend whom I talked with at the restaurant was formal ministry that led to healing and restoration.

Don't act shocked

Try not to act shocked if something shocking is said or done. I may announce my resilience by stating in advance there is probably nothing one can say or do that will shock me. You can be sure there are dissociated parts or demonically influenced alters who will test that boundary! They may be gauging your acceptance "no matter what" or seeing if they might run you off as they have done others who have tried to draw close.

Encourage wounded parts and alters to express themselves honestly. A believer may be shocked and embarrassed not only to hear himself cussing *out loud*, but also to have no apparent control over this. Chances are, there has been mental conflict with profanity going on in his head before an alter was ever invited to be candid and vocal.

People may harbor suppressed anger toward God but have never dared verbalize that for fear of *really* making God mad or of being shamed in front of another believer. I reassure them that this is a safe place to express their true feelings and I will not condemn or judge them. Together, we can take this to the Lord. Anger with God is always rooted somewhere else. By confessing this anger, that root may be discovered.

The journey's end

"Submit yourselves, then, to God. Resist the devil and he will flee from you. Come near to God and he will come near to you." (James 4:7-8) These verses reveal four practical actions for navigating the journey of inner healing:

1. submitting to God – yielding to Christ's authority and Lordship;
2. resisting the devil – taking a stand against Satan's schemes;
3. coming near to God – approaching God together and trusting his leading;
4. God coming near to you – receiving his love and healing.

The goal of inner healing is three-fold. These outcomes reveal God's plan and purpose for the person seeking healing:

1. renewing the mind to singleness, free of conflict and confusion;
2. restoring the soul, putting things back the way they were originally intended to be;
3. redeeming losses incurred by dissociation, including memory, emotions, abilities, time, confidence, and relationships, to name a few.

God is ever-present to meet a wounded person at his place of pain, to shine light into dark places, to exchange lies for the truth, and to drive out Satan and demolish his strongholds. He heals a person's mind, body, soul, and spirit. He does all this in a way that is personal and as unique as the individual who comes seeking his help.

Forgiveness

Forgiveness is a vital component of inner healing. Many who come for healing have been wrongfully accused, abandoned, abused, or in other ways deeply hurt – sometimes by the very ones who should have protected or helped them. Offenses may be buried with wounded parts or guarded by alters. It is important that the entity who was offended be the one engaged to express forgiveness. For this to happen, that part or alter must be identified and willing to forgive. Do not allow one part to speak forgiveness on behalf of another if that entity is not ready or willing to forgive. Otherwise, the offense remains unresolved and troublesome.

Prayer and Praise

1 Peter 4:7 instructs us to "be clear-minded and self-controlled so that you can pray." Many people's minds are not clear because of the conflict of dissociation. They live in a confused state that debilitates self-control and hinders their ability to pray. Some struggle with their personal prayer life or Bible reading because they are double-minded, not clear-minded. As a dissociated person receives inner healing, his mind begins to clear. From a place of restoration, he can effectively pray. As measures of healing are experienced, it is appropriate to pause to thank God and praise him for what he has done!

Prayer Pause

"God, you designed me for relationship with you and with others. Remove all barriers that have gone up within my mind that separate me from others, including you. Please renew my mind, restore my soul, and redeem my life from the conflicts of dissociation. Help me forgive those who have hurt me. And Lord, please forgive me for ways I have hurt others. I receive your love for all of me, including all fragmented parts and alters. Heal me this day and restore your perfect order within me, with others, and with you. May your original intent for my life be fully realized as I put my trust in you.

I speak all this in the Name of Jesus. Amen!"

Chapter 13

Designed for
Association

Restoring Relational Order

BARBARA SAT IN STUNNED DISBELIEF AS
PEOPLE THROUGHOUT THE AUDITORIUM ANGRILY
LEFT THEIR SEATS AND STOMPED OUT. With tears
welling up, she turned to her husband and quietly whispered, "I
have to get out of here but don't want to talk with anyone." Slipping
out a side door and skirting the tumult in the foyer, Barbara vowed
to herself that she would never return. Having grown up in the
church, in all of her years she had never seen those meant to be
the spiritual leaders of the congregation handle something so
callously. In the days that followed, gossip and rumors coursed
through the little community, presumptions were made, and
judgments declared. Never had she experienced anything that so
clearly divided a group of people who one day were co-laborers,
the next day adversaries.

Regrettably, many of you reading this book will have your
own "church split" story. Barbara explained that she was in shock
as she watched her church family dissociate right in front of her
eyes. To escape the trauma of the spiritual abuse being suffered,

people fled to distance themselves from the hurt of what took place in that devastating meeting. Many, like Barbara, vowed "never to go there again" as their way of protecting themselves from further harm. Some went to other churches. Some never went back to church at all. One disillusioned faction decided to start its own church. Now, several years later, Barbara was ready to face her unresolved anger and unforgiveness toward those who had wounded her and whom she felt had also hurt many in the community.

Restoring relational order

Dissociation, as a relational dis-order, not only divides people within themselves but also separates them from others. Consequently, spouses, family members, friends, business associates, churches, and communities can be impacted by one person's dissociation.

When people hear the word church, the majority think of a building, a day of the week (Sunday), and activities that happen in that building on that day. The word church, in the original language of the New Testament, is actually a relational term that simply means people called together as an assembly, or congregation. In the first century, they networked interdependently, supported and helped one another, and served others. The church grew exponentially as spheres of relational influence expanded throughout a community or region. Centuries passed before there were formal buildings for worship as we know today. When emphasis began to be placed on "the house of the Lord," those who translated the Bible into Latin inserted a word, our English equivalent being "church," to refer to a building rather than to people. One way Scripture describes the church is to identify it in relational terms as "the Body of Christ" with the Lord as the head of that body. (See Ephesians 5:23) Paul gives us a glimpse in 1 Corinthians 1:10 of the ideal for relational order in the church when he writes, "I appeal to you, brothers, in the name of our Lord Jesus Christ, that all of you *agree with one another* so that there may be no divisions among you and that you may *be perfectly united in mind and thought.*" (*Emphasis mine.*) The church is a group of people designed for association with one another because they are designed for association with God.

A person fragmented in dissociation is internally separated. Barriers that exist between his conscious and subconscious mind can cause confusion and conflict. Until those obstructions are removed and he is brought to a place of co-consciousness leading to healing, he will remain divided and therefore relationally separated from others, including God. The individual who is dissociated is a microcosm of the church. Neither the individual nor the church started out divided. Both started out whole, but eventually fractured because of abuses, trauma, shame, fear, unforgiveness, and other reasons. The multiplicity of church denominations is evidence of relational separation within the Body of Christ. Over time, walls have gone up. Theological positions have thrown congregations or whole denominations into conflict and confusion. Doctrinal views have caused some to end up in either God-focused or self-focused camps. Churches have distanced themselves from one another to protect themselves and to aid survival.

In the city of 69,000 where I live there are over fifty-five churches representing nearly thirty denominations. There are additionally at least fifteen parachurch ministries. It is a unique community because there is more intentional activity here to bring churches together as a catalyst for spiritual transformation than in any other place I have known. Even so, many churches remain uncommunicative and uncooperative. Historical divisions and polarized positions keep barrier walls firmly in place. This situation is not unique to this city. Consequently, there appears to be little evidence anywhere of co-conscious collaboration among churches generally, much less among denominations, to show singleness of mind and purpose. In those instances where I do find churches teaming up for common purposes, there are healthy signs of integration as churches and ministry organizations find common ground to do together what cannot be achieved in isolation. Another depiction of the church found in scripture is that of a bride. (See Revelation 19:7; 21:2, 9) God is not sending his Son back for a dissociated, divided Bride, but one that is seen to be radiant, "without stain or wrinkle or any other blemish, but holy and blameless." (See Ephesians 5:27) The true church is not meant to be divided and weak anymore than is one's true person. The original intent for both is to be united and strong.

Dissociated individuals can have difficulty relating in a church and finding acceptance or genuine help. One disheartened female recipient lamented, "The church as a whole stinks. People sing and smile but don't want to get dirty and care. They say they are praying for you but don't bother to call if they haven't seen you for months. When I confided in those whom I thought would help me, I was given a pretty speech and sent on my way. Aren't pastors, of all people, the ones who are supposed to see the signs of need and help? That's the church for you." Another recipient came to realize she had an alter who would only attend church and go to her adult Sunday School class when she had a need. By her own admission, she would go there to "dump" her problems on people and make them feel guilty. Once she received the help she demanded, she would not show up again for weeks until her woundedness was triggered by another crisis that arose in her personal life or family. She only sought relational connection with this group at her convenience and to aid her own survival.

Both of these women were well-presented, capable individuals who gave no outward appearance of need. But both of them had relational dis-order in their lives due to dissociation. Both of them sought help from their churches. But because churches themselves may function dissociated, they often do not know how to respond to people such as these two who do not fit their mold or who threaten their well-defined boundaries. It is easier to shun people like them, shut them out completely, or in other ways maintain a distance from their complicated issues. As a result, both women had to search outside the church for help. As they came into inner healing, healthy relationships began to form not only at church but also in their families and with others. The genuine healing and relational order being restored to individuals is a model of what is available to the church. But not every person or every church wants to be healed. Not all know that healing is possible or where it can be found. Consequently, they continue to be disconnected within themselves and from others, including God. They remain fragmented in their dissociation.

God is at work, restoring relational order. When a light gets switched on in a dark place, everyone winces and turns from its brilliance until they gradually adjust to its intensity. In a similar way, when the light of Jesus Christ penetrates our dissociated lives and disconnected relationships, the initial reaction is to turn away. However, by moving toward his light rather than away from it, truth will be illumined and relationships once separated can be restored. Association – the opposite of dissociation – speaks to the uniting of hearts and minds and wills by the power of God. His ability to restore relationships transcends man's efforts to do so. Restoration is intended to be experienced in the context of community and relationship. God, the master of association, connects people with himself, with others, and within themselves. Our cultural inclination, reflected even in the church, is to uphold independence and honor individualism. By contrast, God calls for an interdependence that helps people, individually and collectively, to bear his image and to best represent the Lord and his church. People are designed for community and relationship;

it is in this context they will be genuinely healed, renewed, and restored – personally and interpersonally.

A work in progress

Inner healing is a process. If you stop the process, you stop the progress. I marvel that God wants to associate with me and is willing to use me as his representative to help bring inner healing to others. How grateful I am to the Lord for the hope he gives, the insight and wisdom he provides, the authority of his Lordship, and his revelation of truth that sets people free from deception and dissociation. I personally testify to the power of God to transform my own life from what it was to what it is becoming. I am a work in progress who, by God's help and power, is being restored to more wholly reflect his image and likeness. As that happens in me and in you, the entire Body of Christ is strengthened and God is glorified.

"May the God who gives endurance and encouragement give you a spirit of unity among yourselves as you follow Christ Jesus, so that with one heart and mouth you may glorify the God and Father of our Lord Jesus Christ." Romans 15:5-6

Prayer Pause

"God, help me to comprehend the bigger picture of what you are doing to restore order in the Body of Christ. Unite us so we may follow Jesus and glorify you. Distance us from our fears, from shame, and from the deceptions of the enemy. Heal us so we may be one and together reflect the image you have created us to bear. Amen"

Appendix

Pointers
Procedures
Précis
Post Script

Trading Faces

Pointers

Frequently Asked Questions
About Dissociation

1. What does the word dissociation mean?

   To dissociate means "to separate from union; to disunite." Dissociation is "the act of dissociating, or state of being dissociated (separated, separate, disunited)." Dissociation is a preferred defense mechanism and common solution of the mind to protect a person experiencing trauma and to aid survival.

2. What causes a person to dissociate?

   Common dissociation is typically caused by extreme stress brought on by such things as trauma, abuse, tragedy, terror, neglect, abandonment, and rejection.

3. What happens when a person dissociates?

   The mind functions by association. During trauma, data may get separated and stored in a dissociated state. A wounded part of the person may "go into hiding" in the subconscious mind where the pain of the trauma and other memory data is stored. A separate alter identity may form to protect, if possible, that wounded part from being re-traumatized.

4. What could happen if a person is incapable of functioning in his dissociation?

   Extreme outcomes of dissociation include insanity, suicide, and desertion of significant relationships or responsibilities.

5. How do you distinguish a wounded part of a person from an alter identity?

A wounded part holds the pain of the event and other trauma memory data. This part will often have the same name as the true person at the age of the trauma event. An alter is an encapsulated and separate identity that forms in dissociation which holds its own memories, thoughts, feelings, attributes, and characteristics. An alter is set up primarily to protect a person from being re-traumatized. An alter identity will typically have a distinct name different from that of the true person.

6. What is an example of how an alter identity functions?

An alter may support its primary role of protection by controlling or presenting. Presenting alters will have distinct functions that correspond with life areas where they are called upon to perform, for example, at work, at home, or at church.

7. Are dissociated entities (wounded parts and alters) demons?

No. Wounded parts and alter identities are real entities of the one true person. While it is possible that entities may become demonically influenced, they are not themselves demons. Therefore, entities cannot be cast out, exorcised, or in other ways terminated.

8. What triggers a person's dissociation?

A sight, sound, smell, touch, taste, or other memory connection may stimulate recollection of trauma. To guard a wounded part from being re-traumatized, these same "triggers" may activate a protecting alter identity.

9. Where do other entities go when a person switches and an alter is presenting?

They may rest, recede, or hide in the subconscious mind. They may be blocked by amnesic barriers in the mind. They may simply be incapable of functioning when an alter is presenting.

10. What happens to a wounded part of a person once healing takes place?

It is integrated back into the true person, restoring mental and physical strength, emotions, spiritual gifts, and natural abilities. Alter identities will also integrate. When lies are dispelled, any demonic attachments connected to a lie are simultaneously removed.

11. Can a dissociated person really be healed?

Yes. A return to healing, wholeness, and singleness of mind is a process that takes time. Integration is a result of mind renewal and restoration of the soul. True healing is ultimately only possible with God's help.

Forgiveness Prayer

Forgiveness is appropriately expressed by the part of the person who was offended while in the memory where the offense occurred. By tapping into the pain of the memory it is often timely and appropriate for the ministry recipient to verbalize sincere forgiveness for what any person in that memory has done to wound him. This can be as powerfully liberating as revelation of truth that dispels lies. It is often in this context that a person may find the freedom and peace that is rightfully anticipated when forgiveness is spoken. Although the following guidelines and sample prayers were created to help ministry facilitators, they may also be applied by individuals.

1. While in the memory, have the person name each offender, being specific about what needs to be forgiven.

2. You may prompt the recipient to repeat after you the first time or two.

3. Refer to your session notes to help remind the person of offenses that were identified.

4. Check to see if there is anything else that comes to mind that needs to be expressed in the context of forgiveness.

5. Make notes of the recipient's expressions of forgiveness in the right margin of your session notes. This provides an important record of those expressions.

   (See *Procedures: Documenting a Session* in the Appendix)

Sample prayers of forgiveness

God,

1. I forgive (name of the offender) for (specify the offense/s) and for causing me to feel (describe emotional and/or physical pain).

2. Forgive me for anything I have done to hurt (name of offender/s or of other/s; you may specify anything you have done to him/her).

3. I forgive myself for (specify what you need to forgive yourself for).

4. I ask you to forgive (name of offender; your name) and to bless/help (same name).

I am free in Jesus' Name! (State this as a declaration of truth.)

Amen

Curses

Everything in the demonic realm is a counterfeit of the truth of God. The enemy's realm is diametrically opposed to the realm of the Holy Spirit and is built on deceit leading to destruction (see John 10:10). God's Kingdom operates by true authority. Satan's counterfeit kingdom works by imitating authority. Jesus demonstrates that authority is exercised through the mouth (see Luke 4). Words will either be expressed under the true authority of the Lordship of Jesus Christ to bless, or under the imitated authority of the enemy to curse.

To bless literally means, "to make or pronounce holy." A blessing is pronounced to release and redeem. To curse means, "to send injury or evil upon; to damn." A curse is pronounced to rob and restrain. Curses may be spoken, inherited, or transferred. Their effects are merely works of the devil, which Jesus came to destroy (see 1 John 3:8).

The Bible lists at least sixty curses people may come under. Curses open the door to demonic influence and activity both into and through people's lives. Curses are real, and the power of a curse is demonic. However, the superior power of God and the Word of God will break every one. Curses fall into four basic categories: Generational Curse, Word Curse, Self-Curse, and Soul Tie Curse. If you believe you are under the bondage of a curse, to the best of your ability identify what you believe that curse may be and which one of the four categories you believe it may fall under. Use one of the "Renunciation of Curses" in this section to break its power.

Generational curse

A generational curse is a form of involuntary inheritance through the bloodline of lineage and ancestral sin. Ill effects such as poverty, barrenness, chronic or hereditary infirmity, addiction, mental illness, failure, and hindrances to spiritual growth often distinguish this type of curse.

Word curse

A word curse is a declaration that is targeted and effective, putting a person in bondage under that curse, under the power of the one who pronounced the curse, and under the power of the devil. A word curse may be deliberate, as in a premeditated occult curse sometimes associated with ritual ceremony or witchcraft. A word curse may be spoken rashly ("You'll never amount to anything.") or even profanely ("Go to hell."). Whether intentionally or carelessly declared, the stage is set for a life lived in corresponding bondage to that curse.

Self-curse

A self-curse can be spoken against oneself by reinforcing the power of another's curse ("I'll never amount to anything"), by self-pronouncement ("I am so stupid."), or by profane declaration ("Well, I'll be damned."). Boasting can even be a form of a self-curse, exalting oneself through pride and arrogance.

Soul tie curse

A soul tie curse is one acquired through an unholy, unnatural, or ungodly relationship that brings a corresponding transference of demonic influence from one person to another. This may happen through a range of relational connections including generational inheritance, illegitimate sexual union, poronography, occult activity, abuse, and trauma.

Renunciation of curses

To renounce means "to announce, declare, or proclaim one's abandonment of the ownership of; to give up, abandon, or resign; to refuse further to follow or obey the authority of." To renounce a curse means to declare your rejection of that curse, in Jesus' Name, and to no longer be under its power. To help facilitate your ability to do that, the following renunciations are included. The first one – Renunciation of Generational Curses – incorporates a confession of Jesus Christ and a statement of dedication to him. It is recommended that renunciations be declared out loud and in the hearing of another person.

Renunciation of generational curses

I confess that Jesus is the Christ, the Son of the Living God. I am a child of God, redeemed by the blood of his Son, my Savior, Jesus Christ the Lord. His shed blood has paid the price for all of my sins. By the power of his resurrection, death has no hold over me, and I embrace the hope of eternal life with him. By covenant right of relationship with my Lord, Jesus Christ, I take authority over the enemy, Satan, and the harm he has sought to do directly to me, through my ancestry, and through others.

In the name of Jesus Christ and by the power of his blood, I here and now renounce and reject all sins, word curses, unnatural soul ties, involuntary inheritances, and demonic influences that have come upon me from my ancestors and from any other person whatsoever from working in me or through me. In the name of Jesus, I ask that all generational sins of my forefathers through the bloodlines of both my father and my mother be revoked and forgiven. I forgive all others, as I want God to forgive me. I ask that all ancestral and other sins and their effects, and all demonic influences and their workings, be canceled now in Jesus' Name from the beginning of time, to the end of time, to the present. They will not be visited upon my children or my children's children.

I renounce any and every way in which Satan and his forces illegitimately claim ownership over any and all parts of me. By the superior power of God and in the name of Jesus Christ, I separate and remove the power of Satan upon me, over me, in me, and through me. I declare that all of Satan's schemes, assignments, and intents to destroy my life are terminated now by the blood of Jesus and by the authority of Jesus' Name.

In him I have full redemption and the forgiveness of sins. I am eternally surrendered and dedicated to Jesus Christ as my only Lord and Master. Jesus Christ is Lord over every part of me, all aspects of my being, and with all that is within me I bless and praise his holy Name.

All this I do in the power, in the authority, and in the Name of Jesus Christ.

(See Psalm 103; Galatians 2:20; Ephesians 1:7; 2:4-7; Colossians 1:13; 3:13)

Renunciation of word curses and self-curses

I renounce in Jesus' Name all curses spoken against me that are from the enemy. I break their power by the blood of Jesus Christ, and I declare, in his Name, freedom from all word curses and self-curses.

I renounce in Jesus' Name and revoke as null and void any and all word curses spoken over me by others and all curses I have pronounced upon myself. I reject their influences and declare them ineffective in my life.

Father, bridle my tongue so that I may only speak blessings and not curses. Breathe your very breath on my words so that they may be empowered by you to bless others, to declare truth, and to speak words of life. Convict me immediately of any word curses I speak so that I can repent. I resist in Jesus' Name all word curses spoken against me. In accordance with the Word of God, I bless those who curse me and pray for those who persecute me.

(See Matthew 5:44; Romans 12:14)

Renunciation of soul tie curses

In the Name of Jesus Christ and by his blood, I break all soul tie curses and all soul tie attachments that are unholy, ungodly, unnatural, illegitimate, perverse, and demonic. I renounce the soul tie curse of any and all illegitimate sexual relationships or one-flesh bonds experienced in the physical body, or through pornography, fantasy, or perverse dreams.

I renounce, declaring null and void, all unnatural soul ties between me and (name of person) and between (same person's name) and me. Forgive me, Lord, for ever initiating unnatural soul ties. I receive your forgiveness, God, even as I forgive those who have sinned against me. I receive freedom from all soul tie curses from the beginning of time, to the end of time, to the present.

Father, I ask that only wholesome, holy, and godly soul ties connect me with others and others with me. Grant me your wisdom and protection in forming relationships. May I live in relational purity and in ways that bring honor and glory to your Name. May I represent you to others in ways that bless them and draw them closer to you.

(See Matthew 6:12; Galatians 5:1)

Dissociation Assessment

The following statements may help assess dissociation in an individual. It is recommended that the assessment be interacted with several times over the course of a week, in various settings (e.g. at home, at work, alone, with others around, etc.), at different times of day, or when in a noticeably different mood. If dissociation is present, protracted and varied interaction with these statements allows more opportunity for wounded parts or alter identities to respond.

Each time this is read through, an initial response is to be given by placing a checkmark in the box preceding the statement. Avoid "analyzing" each statement. If in another reading you have changed your mind or disagree with a statement previously checked, do not change your previous marking of the assessment.

It is recommended to read each statement aloud and then respond before moving on to the next statement.

I experience:

☐ Feelings of "having things together on the outside" yet "falling apart on the inside."

☐ Sleep disturbances (75% or more of the time) including insomnia, sleepwalking, traumatic nightmares, and/or night terrors.

☐ Recurrent, intrusive, traumatic imagery and/or thoughts.

☐ Frequent headaches.

☐ Blanking out, staring into space, or losing track of time.

☐ A tendency to react to my environment with either exaggerated or inhibited behaviors.

☐ Thoughts in my mind that cause arousal.

☐ Acting one way in a given situation (e.g. with a certain person, group of people, or environment) but a different or opposite way in another situation.

☐ Impulsiveness.

☐ Frequent loss of train of thought in conversation, a "wandering mind," or breaks in concentration while listening.

I experience:

☐ Very selective memories of childhood experiences.

☐ "Arguments" or "conversations" that carry on *inside* my head. (Versus conversations *outside* your head, such as an external voice or an inanimate object talking.)

☐ Being accused of lying when I know that I am telling the truth.

☐ Intermittent depression.

☐ Periods of explosive anger.

☐ Extreme mood swings, often with little or no warning or for no discernable reason. (If yes, do you find this bewildering?)

☐ Inability to feel or express some or most emotions.

☐ Unusual fear and consistent anxiety disproportionate to the present situation.

☐ Bruises, scratches, injuries, or pain I cannot explain by any current experience.

☐ Talking out loud to myself when I am alone.

☐ Inability to comprehend what I am reading in the Bible.

☐ Saying "we" or "us" instead of "I" or "me" when referring to myself.

I experience:

- ☐ Periodic but intense extremes in my eating habits. (Either indulgence or denial.)

- ☐ Anxiety, anger, or difficulty associated with prayer, worship, and/or Bible reading.

- ☐ A desire for alcohol, drugs, or sex despite an aversion to them.

- ☐ Driving a car but having no recollection of some or all of the trip.

- ☐ Confusion because of fluctuation of intellectual ability, skills or creativity. (For example, you feel very capable in one area but at other times experience difficulty in doing what was previously easy.)

- ☐ Self-inflicted pain.

- ☐ Being absorbed in fantasy to the point that it seems real.

- ☐ Occasional confusion about what "just happened" or whether an incident occurred a few hours, days, or weeks ago.

- ☐ Acquiring or losing possessions about which I have no knowledge. (You may wonder, "Where did this come from?" or "Where did that go?")

- ☐ Having no knowledge of things I am reported to have said or done.

- ☐ Abnormal anxiety or fear, for example, of attending events, of being with a large group, or of performing in some way.

I experience:

- ☐ Flashbacks to traumatic events resulting in fluctuating or conflicting feelings about my self-worth.

- ☐ Feeling at times as though I am two different people.
- ☐ Overwhelming feelings of hurt, rejection, pain, grief, and/or hopelessness.
- ☐ Feelings or expressions of anger disproportionate to the present situation.
- ☐ Distrust of anyone or anything, myself especially, and including God.
- ☐ Being engrossed in television program(s), movie(s), or music.
- ☐ Uncertainty about whether I have done something or have only thought about doing it.
- ☐ Difficulty paying attention during sermons or Biblical teaching.
- ☐ An unusually high tolerance to physical pain.
- ☐ Feeling fatigued most of the time.
- ☐ Not recognizing myself in a mirror.

If 11 (25%) or more of these 44 statements have been marked, the possibility exists of some level of common dissociation. If 22-33 (50-75%) or more of these 44 statements have been marked, there will be some level of common dissociation.

Trading Faces

Procedures

This section of the Appendix is primarily geared for ministry facilitators. The content of this section will help a facilitator prepare for, facilitate, and document a formal ministry session. However, individuals walking out their personal healing journey will also benefit from the information that follows.

Facilitating a Formal Session

Prepared facilitator

As a facilitator of inner healing ministry, you are a bridge between the ministry recipient and the healing power of Jesus Christ. You are an ambassador of the love and acceptance of the Lord. History of relationship with the Lord builds authority and confidence to represent him to others. History of relationship with other ministry facilitators builds mutual trust and increases your ministry experience, knowledge, and skills. Combined, these relationships develop a heightened sensitivity to the Holy Spirit and God's guidance for facilitating individual sessions.

Offering inner healing is not about a "counselor" applying learned techniques to a "patient." Inner healing is an interactive exchange that brings about renewal of the mind, restoration of the soul, redemption of loss, and reconciliation of relationships. One component of healing is vulnerability before the Lord and before others. This is best experienced in an atmosphere that is safe and built upon the principles of mutual ministry in a genuinely caring environment. Therefore, it is important for facilitators to have received, and be continually open to receive, personal healing themselves. It is not uncommon during a session for a facilitator to be "triggered" by something the recipient shares or to experience some measure of personal insight, help, or healing. However, during a formal ministry session, the primary focus is to be on the recipient who has come for healing. A facilitator's needs may be tended to during a separate, scheduled session of his own.

Facilitators must be pray-ers. "Pre-prayer-ation" for a session can never be overemphasized. Team members are encouraged to pray together for one another and for those who are to receive ministry. Confidentiality is imperative. If you have more than one ministry team, it is not necessary for other teams to know who one another's recipients are. Fasting on behalf of the recipient, while not a requirement, may help focus your prayer as well as heighten sensitivity to the Holy Spirit. Facilitators should review a recipient's file prior to a session, familiarizing themselves with the recipient's status.

First impressions are important. Your appearance, tone of voice, and attitude will all communicate something to the recipient. Facilitators should be well groomed and practice good hygiene. Comfortable, modest attire is recommended. Avoid apparel with loud patterns, t-shirts with messages, and other types of clothes or accessories that could be distracting to the recipient.

You may or may not know the recipient previously, although there generally will be some prior contact, at the very least to have made the arrangement for the session. A recipient will typically arrive to his first session nervous, possibly fearful of what might be experienced. The two dominant questions in his mind are, "Can I trust this person?" and "Will he accept me?" Welcome the recipient and reassure him as needed. Thank him for his preparation. Assure him that the session is strictly confidential, that he will not be judged or condemned, and it is the Lord's work, not man's, that will take place in the session.

There is wisdom in working as a team, typically two facilitators together with one ministry recipient. Facilitator teams have the advantage of mentoring one another, learning together, and holding one another accountable. Recipients tend to be more relaxed with two facilitators than with one. At least one facilitator should be of the same gender as the recipient. It is imperative to guard your integrity. By virtue of association with needy people, you are at higher risk of moral failure. Do not fool yourself into thinking you will be the exception. Eighty-seven percent of caregivers (doctors, pastors, counselors, etc.) admit sexual attraction to someone they have worked with. Forty-eight percent get sexually involved with a client. It is prudent to avoid all physical contact with someone of the opposite sex and all behavior that could be misconstrued. This is especially important when dealing with issues regarding sexuality. One safeguard a ministry partner provides is a witness in the event of litigation. Ministry partners of the opposite sex should not spend time alone with each other without appropriate, third party supervision. This includes the intimacy of praying together. Common sense and accountability will help intercept the enemy's attempts to damage relationships within the ministry team, as well as to individual facilitators.

Prepared recipient

In all my years of facilitating inner healing, I can only recall two times that recipients arrived expecting their healing to be an event, not a journey. Having led me to believe they had thoroughly done all their suggested preparation, I was taken back when they demanded that their problems be "fixed" – *now!* – an impossible request. Some have come with a history of regular therapy. They may have experienced marginal recovery yet remain stalled in fear and shame, confusion or addiction. Others stumble upon us frustrated by the rejection of the local church or those they thought were friends. People have come from across the street. One even came from across the world! With the possible exception of the two mentioned at the beginning of this paragraph, I believe all will testify to having experienced some level of healing leading to singleness of mind and inner restoration.

The two common denominators to a productive inner healing session for a ministry recipient are his motivation and preparation. Our ministry requires that people first complete an application form. This document stimulates introspection of personal, family, and medical history as well as spiritual background and beliefs. It confronts unforgiveness issues. It reveals lies and searches for hints of dissociation. The potential of being under curses or demonic influences is explored. Optional reading is urged. Before a person can schedule a ministry session, this application must first be returned. There are four primary reasons for this document. First, it will quickly determine a person's seriousness about being healed. Regrettably, there are many wounded people whose brokenness makes them special. They thrive on living out of their pain, consuming the time and energy of others, but really never wanting to be healed. Second, the application process will bring a person into a level of personal examination that, while potentially painful, will motivate them to seek healing. Because working through the application tends to stir up a lot of issues inside a person, it is important to receive him for ministry as soon as possible after he has submitted the form. Third, it will tend to thwart a person with ulterior motives. Not everyone wanting to come to you may have personal healing as his objective. Do not discount or be ignorant of the enemy's scheme to attack, discredit, or destroy those committed to setting captives free in Jesus' Name. Finally, the application gives an overview of the recipient to ministry facilitators and aids their prayerful preparation to meet with him. The application might never be directly referred to in a session, although the foreknowledge it provides may help expedite the ministry process.

As with the ministry facilitator, the most important preparation the recipient can do is pray. Fasting is suggested but not required. The enemy does not want a person healed and restored. He may try everything possible to hinder a person from keeping an appointment. Out of my years of experience, there is only one person who was so fearful of coming that she simply could not bring herself to show up. (She did, however, reschedule and later experienced some great healing!) The prayers of the facilitators, in conjunction with a person preparing to receive ministry, become a powerful force to stand against any plot of the enemy to stop what God wants to do in a session – starting with hindering a person's arrival.

Prepared environment

The duration of a ministry session will be determined by the availability and restraints of the facilitators. Rather than subscribing to the traditional one hour weekly format, our facilitator teams generally commit a day to a recipient. The average session is five hours long. Regardless of the duration of a formal ministry session, a prepared environment contributes to a positive experience. Whether in an office, a home, or some other setting designated for ministry, the three main things to provide for the ministry recipient are privacy, lack of distractions, and no interruptions.

Always welcome recipients into a room that is clean, attractive, and comfortable. Arrange seating so no one is looking directly into a window or light fixture. Because of potential sensitivity to allergies, avoid using fragrant candles, potpourris, or other scented decorations. Adjust the temperature of the room. Use a small fan to help keep the air circulating and an air filter if needed. The following checklists will guide your preparation.

Prepare the room and yourselves:

- ❑ Arrive in advance of the ministry recipient to prepare the room
- ❑ Arrange seating (facilitators side by side, opposite recipient)
- ❑ Play quiet worship music (as able)
- ❑ Pray together (as appropriate)
- ❑ Display a "Do Not Disturb" sign on door (if needed)
- ❑ Turn off phones and pagers

Have within easy reach of the ministry recipient:

- ❑ Tissues
- ❑ Trash can
- ❑ Small pillow
- ❑ Water
- ❑ Mints

Have within easy reach of the facilitators:

- ❑ Clipboard/s with notepad/s
- ❑ Pens
- ❑ Bible
- ❑ Anointing oil
- ❑ Other ministry resources

Other:

- ❑ Clock (take period breaks; track session time)
- ❑ Bathroom (convenient to ministry room; freshened and prepared for use)

Documenting a Session

Documenting a session is an important component of providing ministry. Notes are recorded chronologically during a session and help ministry facilitators stay on track. Session notes are to be kept secured in a recipient's confidential file. The following tips are categorized by topics. These also may serve as an outline for creating a session summary for recipients as a helpful follow-up to a ministry session.

Note-taking tips

Suggested materials

Recommended:

A yellow 8½" x 11" pad on a clipboard; a pen that will write fluidly and not smear. Use one side of the paper only. Record legibly and concisely, yet thoroughly. Leave space as needed between recording memories or lies for subsequent notes to be inserted as needed.

Draw a 1½" to 2" margin line on the right side of each sheet of paper before you begin recording on that sheet. You will use both the left and right margins during the session, as noted below. In the left margin you will code memories, lies, curses, and dissociation with symbols for ease of locating and referring to on each page.

There should be one primary note-taker for a session. The main facilitator may also prefer to have a separate pad and clipboard for taking abbreviated notes, or he may refer to the notes his ministry partner is taking when addressing memories, lies, etc.

Documentation

In the upper left corner of page one record:
Names of facilitators
Full name of recipient
Today's date
Starting and ending time

In the upper right corner of each subsequent page record:

Recipient's initials

Page #

Overview

When providing the recipient with a session summary, state in 2-4 sentences a synopsis of the session.

History

Pertinent, general, or historical information shared by the recipient may be recorded throughout the notes in conjunction with a memory, a lie, etc.

Themes

Note any identifiable themes of the enemy that appear to be a pattern in the recipient. For example, bullying, invalidation, sabotage, a particular addiction, etc.

Memories

In the left margin, note and number the succession of memories a recipient visits.

M#1   12yo (i.e. 12 year old); summer cabin at Benton Lake; alone with uncle Scott; etc.

M#2   8yo; grandfather's farm house; left there with sister for an afternoon; etc.

Memories are personal and a facilitator's impressions are never to be imposed upon a recipient's recollection. It is important to realize and accept that, because of trauma, data may be fragmented, scattered, or incomplete. Never press for information that is not there or cannot be readily recalled. Always pause to allow the recipient time to reflect and "look around" in the memory for information. Allow for silence to give the recipient time to think about, reflect upon, and connect with the memory. To aid recall, it may be helpful at times to ask non-suggestive questions to draw out information about what is happening in a specific memory. For example:

- **How** "How do you feel in this memory?" (List emotions: afraid, dirty, alone, small, helpless, etc.; Probing to specifically identify emotions may help clarify lie-based statements held by the recipient in relation to a memory.)

- **Who** "Is there anyone else in this memory?" (List name(s) and/or relationship to the recipient: mom, neighbor, sister Sue, friend Joe, teacher Mr. Smith.)

- **What** "What is going on in this memory?" or "Is there anything else you see, sense, hear, or feel?" (Record information as it is shared.)

- **When** "How old are you in this memory?" (Note the age of the person in the memory; A recipient may not recall an exact age but may recall a general time frame related to a place lived, school attended, etc.; If significant, list dates, years, ages of others in this memory, etc.)

- **Where** "Where are you in this memory?" (Note the location: house, room, outdoors, at the store, etc.)

- **Why** "Do you know why this is happening?" (Note what precipitated the trauma event.)

Lies

It may take some trial and error to pinpoint the exact wording of a lie-based statement. Ranking a lie on a scale of 0-10, with 10 being high, may help the recipient indicate to the facilitator the intensity of emotional response linked to a lie. Articulating a lie often leads a person to the original memory where that lie was embraced as a truth.

☐L☐ Identify in the left margin the location of lie-based statements by a boxed, capital "L".

Once the lie has been recorded, ask the recipient to verbally state the lie back to you and to get in touch with the feelings he has associated with the lie. Record the ranking after the lie by circling the number. Note: a single word or phrase may make a big difference in how "true" the lie feels. For example:

☐L☐ It is my fault I let it happen. ②

☐L☐ It is my fault I let it happen again. ⑥

☐L☐ It is my fault I didn't tell anybody. ⑩

Ask the Holy Spirit to take the recipient to the original memory where this statement was first believed to be true. Encourage the recipient to get in touch with his emotions in the context of that memory.

Invite Jesus to reveal truth in that memory however he chooses to do that. Quietly wait upon him. Record any insight or impression he is giving to the recipient. Do not make suggestions or attempt to force this in any way. It is the Lord's prerogative to reveal truth to dispel lies associated with a memory.

When you sense the Lord has done his work in a memory, have the recipient restate the lie verbally and rank it again on the 0-10 scale. Record the difference, by drawing an arrow from the first ranking to the revised ranking:

☐L☐ It's my fault I didn't tell anybody. ⑩ ☐ ⓪ (new ranking after revisiting the lie)

Demonic

Address the demonic as it comes up. When you identify a demonic spirit, underline the name of that spirit in the body of your session notes so it can be found easily on the page. For example, two of the most common spirits you may encounter are <u>confusion</u> and <u>mockery</u>. The enemy will try to incite <u>fear</u> and <u>failure</u> to discourage you from proceeding or wanting to be involved in this ministry. As needed, pause to pray and take authority over the enemy in Jesus' Name.

Curses

Identify a curse by writing and underling the word <u>curse</u> in the left margin of the session notes. A recipient may be under a word curse, a self-curse, a generational curse, or a soul-tie curse. (See *Pointers: Curses* in the Appendix)

Examples of how a curse may play out in all four categories of curses:

<u>curse</u>   "You are as stupid as your mother's side of the family." (Generational)

<u>curse</u>   "If you weren't so stupid, I wouldn't have to beat you." (Word)

<u>curse</u>   "I am stupid." (Self-curse; Note: this is also a lie-based statement)

<u>curse</u>   "My dad always said I was stupid." (Soul tie curse with father)

Dissociation

In the left margin, place a "P" with a circle around it anytime you are accessing a dissociated, wounded part of a person. Seek to identify his age and the circumstances of the memory when formed. The identity of a person's wounded part(s) will typically share the name of the true person at the age he is stalled. For example, the name may be:

- Six-year-old Billy. This may hereafter be recorded as 6yo (six-year-old) Billy

Ⓟ 6yo Billy; a crybaby who holds pain of being beaten by his father at age 6

If an alter identity, place an "A" in the left margin with a circle around it. Ascertain when and how he was formed, how he prefers to be identified (what name), and what his function is (to protect, control, present, or a combination).

The name of a person's alter may be identified and recorded as:

- a distinct human name, nickname, alternate name (e.g. Butch)
- a function name (c.g. Angry Bill)
- a symbolic or other type of name (animal, character, etc.)

Ⓐ Butch; despises crybaby 6yo Billy; protects Adult Bill from acting like a baby

Right margin notes

The right margin is reserved for notes to identify:

- <u>feelings</u> next to a lie or in a memory

(In the memory) 6yo Billy feels worthless, scared, helpless, rejected, intense physical pain

- notes of <u>resolution</u> in a memory

6yo Billy senses Jesus bent over him, taking the brunt of his father's blows; Jesus says "It's okay," "I'm here to protect you," "I won't leave you," "I love you"

- notes of <u>forgiveness</u>

6yo Billy forgives his father for beating him, lying, cursing him, causing fear, not protecting him

6yo Billy forgives self for hating his father

6yo Billy forgives Angry Bill for bullying others to protect him

6yo Billy forgives Butch for treating him mean and not letting him cry

6yo Billy asks God to forgive him for rejecting God and for fearing God would never accept or love him

Note: Any other overflow notes may also go into the right margin.

Note: Facilitators may use the last page of the pad for any personal notes to themselves they need to record during a session. This will help keep distracting thoughts from interfering with the session. (e.g. Pick up bread on the way home.)

Assignments

Assignments are optional and may be negotiated with the recipient as a session draws to a close. Assignments flow out of the experience of healing and are not given as attempts to provoke, create, or sustain healing. Assignments may be given to serve as a bridge between inner healing sessions. They may also be helpful to reinforce what has been experienced during a session. Assignments are personal to a recipient and therefore will reinforce or augment the experience of healing received during a session.

Précis

A Summary of Trading Faces

1. Dissociation is a normal mental process
   a. to cope with the mundane (e.g. "spacing out").
   b. to protect the mind of one who has experienced severe trauma.
   c. to aid survival.

2. Dissociation is a relational dis-order with spiritual implications due to relational separation
   a. within oneself.
   b. from others.
   c. from God.

3. Dissociation is a common condition found in many people and in varying degrees, from mild to complex.

4. The goal of inner healing is
   a. renewal of the mind (to singleness).
   b. restoration of the soul (putting things back the way they were intended to be).
   c. redemption of the loss (that which has been missing due to dissociation).

5. Dissociation typically occurs at the time of trauma or extreme stress. The conscious mind "looks away" as
   a. a wounded part goes into hiding in the subconscious mind, along with trauma memory data.
   b. an alter identity forms to protect the wounded part from re-traumatization; an alter is created without the choice or awareness of the conscious mind.

6. Alter identities primarily function to protect by avoiding both hidden and present pain. They also control or present as ways of protecting wounded parts of a person.

7. Alters are not demons. Alters are mental defense mechanisms the mind creates to protect the person. Demons are evil spirits assigned to destroy a person.

8. Once dissociation occurs, the door is opened to demonic influence, whereby Satan can set up schemes, themes, and strongholds against a person.
   a. Satan is a real enemy who steals, kills, and destroys, and thwarts the things of God.
   b. Demons, demonization, and demonic influences are real; demons are attached to lies people believe about themselves.

9. Psychiatry and self-effort, at best, provide only a measure of tolerable help and coping tools for dissociated people through therapeutic, medical, or other remedies.

10. There is true victory over dissociation through the power of Jesus Christ. Faith, hope, and love overcome doubt, despair, fear, and failure.

11. Dissociative identities (wounded parts and alters) function in three "camps." They will be either dominantly God-focused or self-focused. There may also be neutral "regulators" who help monitor and manage dissociative activity within a person's system.

12. It is the Light of Truth (Jesus Christ) that dispels lies, illumines darkness, and restores fragmentation in the mind. Accepting his truth leads to renewal of the mind.

13. There are numerous "keys" to help release a person from their personal prison of pain and dissociation, as well as to help set others free.

14. Once dissociation is discerned, it is possible to dialogue with it in ways that will lead toward restorative inner healing. This includes acknowledging and affirming alters, accessing wounded parts, and communicating the love, truth, and power of Jesus Christ.

15. An individual functioning in dissociation is a microcosm of the Body of Christ (the church) and also depictive of disconnection in other relationships.

16. There is hope and healing for those who are dissociated.

Trading Faces

Post Script

Although the book ends here, the journey toward inner healing does not. In fact, your journey may just be starting. Perhaps it is in progress. At whatever point along the way you find yourself, may you be encouraged by the following reminder that you are not alone:

"Therefore since we are surrounded by such a great cloud of witnesses, let us throw off everything that hinders and the sin that so easily entangles, and let us run with perseverance the race marked out for us. Let us fix our eyes on Jesus, the author and perfecter of our faith, who for the joy set before him endured the cross, scorning its shame, and sat down at the right hand of the throne of God. Consider him who endured such opposition from sinful men, so that you will not grow weary and lose heart."

Hebrews 12:2-3

Trading Faces

Glossary

A general study of dissociation will soon bring one to realize there are some terms that are commonly used while others may be coined or specific to a particular individual, group, or organization. The following glossary includes terms that are helpful for understanding dissociation as a relational dis-order with spiritual implications. Therefore, some definitions may differ from those conventionally used. As necessary, distinctions will be made that will enhance clarification. This is not an exhaustive glossary, but it includes terms found in this book.

Abreaction: Reliving a physical memory of trauma as though it were happening in the present. Abreaction may occur in varying degrees, from wincing at the thought of what is happening to a fully engaged body "re-enactment" of the experience. (See *Body Memory*)

Alter: An encapsulated and separate identity that forms in dissociation which holds its own memories, thoughts, feelings, attributes, and characteristics. An alter's primary role is to protect the person in order to avoid both hidden and present pain. Psychiatric terms for such identities include "multiple personality," "alter identity," "alter personality," or simply, "alter;" i.e. a distinct, alternate personality of someone diagnosed with Dissociative Identity Disorder. (See *Dissociative Identity Disorder*)

Amnesia: A protective mechanism of selective memory often exemplified by the inability to recall certain information such as time, place, people, sequence of events, etc. in the trauma data held by a wounded part. Amnesia walls may be internally erected that prevent parts, alters, and the true person from being co-conscious. (See *Alter; Co-conscious; Part; True Person*)

Bible: The Bible is the holy Christian Scriptures written in two main sections, the Old Testament and the New Testament. Numerous authors, under divine inspiration, wrote the Bible, believed to be the Word of God.

Besetting Sin: This is often experienced as an overwhelming, repeated compulsion over which the True Person seems to have no choice but to succumb. Dissociation is present when a person is struggling with patterns of besetting sin. Typically, urges intensify to the point a person feels driven to find relief. This usually culminates in some act and results in a sense of shame or guilt. Afterward, the true person may be remorseful and feel even more wounded, fearful, confused, shameful, dirty, or guilty. A pattern of besetting sin may cycle around in somewhat predictable time periods, perhaps weekly, or monthly, or every few months. (See *True Person*)

Body Memory: This is a past physical sensation that accompanies a memory, or a memory that returns because of a present recurrence of a sensation connected to the memory. For example, in a memory of abuse a person may physically feel pain in the stomach, which is what was experienced while being abused. (See *Abreaction*)

Co-conscious: Literally, to share consciousness. This is the condition when the conscious mind is aware of other areas of the mind. Entities are also considered co-conscious if, for example, one or more alters within a person have awareness of another alter or alters and/or of wounded parts hidden in the subconscious mind. Evidence of co-consciousness may be that alters "hear" what other alters think, they share or have knowledge of other alters, they feel emotions of other alters, or a combination of these. Co-consciousness is not necessarily reciprocal; e.g. Alter A may be aware of Alter B, but Alter B may not be aware of Alter A. (See *Alter; Entity*)

Confidentiality: It is imperative that confidentiality be strictly kept between a facilitator(s) and a recipient. The recipient's name is not to be referenced outside an inner healing ministry session, or any details of ministry that would violate his trust. If a recipient wants to discuss details of his session and how the Lord has brought healing, that is his prerogative and his alone. (*Note: The exception being a recipient's disclosure of information of an illegal or life-threatening nature that by law needs to be reported to authorities.*) (See *Facilitator; Recipient*)

Confusion: That which is against fusion, or opposes restoration and unity of a person to wholeness. Confusion is a typical demonic manifestation the enemy, Satan, may bring upon a person who is seeking inner healing. Confusion may be experienced as foggy thinking, scattered thoughts, jumping erratically between memories, blurring of vision, or a feeling of mentally shutting down.

Deliverance: "Classical" deliverance is the process of identifying demons, or demonic influences and afflictions, and expelling them from a person's life in Jesus' Name. A more traditional term for deliverance is exorcism.

Demonized: The New Testament Greek verb, *diamonizomai*, means "to have or to be afflicted by the presence of a demon." This definition is more accurate than "demon possessed," as possession implies ownership. Demonization occurs when a door for the devil's activity is opened, allowing evil spirits access into a person's life. (See *Spiritual Abuse*)

Desertion: One of the three extreme outcomes of dissociation, the other two being insanity and suicide. Desertion may occur when double-mindedness becomes so torturous that a choice is made to abandon significant relationships or responsibilities to pursue self-focused, often compromised lives. Friendships, marriages, businesses, churches, and reputations may be destroyed through desertion.

D.I.D.: Acronym for **Dissociative Identity Disorder**.

Dissociate: By definition, "to separate from union; to disunite; to subject to dissociation."

Dissociation: By definition, "the act of dissociating, or state of being dissociated (separated, separate, disunited)." Dissociation is the common solution of the mind to avoid pain and aid survival in the event of trauma. By psychiatric definition, dissociation is classified as a mental disorder. This book views dissociation as a relational dis-order with spiritual implications. (See **Separation**)

Dissociative Identity Disorder: *The Diagnostic and Statistical Manual of Mental Disorders (DSM), Version IV*, Section 300.14 identifies "Dissociative Identity Disorder" (formerly Multiple Personality Disorder) as a mental disorder. The essential feature of Dissociative Identity Disorder is the presence of two or more distinct alternate personalities within a person that recurrently take control of the person's behavior. Each alter identity may be experienced as having a distinct personal history, self-image, and identity, including a unique name. When viewed as a relational dis-order and from a spiritual perspective, dissociation and Dissociative Identity Disorder are far more common than typically recognized or accepted. (See **Alter; D.I.D.; DSM-IV; M.P.D.; Part**)

Dissociative System: This term refers to an individual's internal system of dissociation made up of wounded parts and alter identities. (See **Alter; Entity; Part**)

Double-minded: This is "the condition of having different minds at different times; unsettled; vacillating; also, deceitful;" in its literal sense, "two-souled" or "double-souled," as though having two independent wills.

DSM-IV: *The Diagnostic and Statistical Manual of Mental Disorders (DSM), Version IV.* This publication of the American Psychiatric Association is the handbook most used in diagnosing mental disorders in America and other countries. The DSM-IV, which may be found in a local library, includes a compilation of dissociative disorders. (See ***Dissociative Identity Disorder***)

Entity: An entity is used to refer to either a wounded part or an alter identity, or collectively to both (i.e. entities), within a person's dissociative system. (See ***Alter; Dissociative System; Part***)

Empowered Multiplicity: This is a term coined to describe people who are multiple but do not feel they fit into the classic definition of Multiple Personality Disorder or Dissociative Identity Disorder. Empowered multiplicity promotes the concept that there are literally many real people sharing the same body, each with independent wills, emotions, abilities, interests, and rights. They do not seek nor require therapeutic diagnosis because they do not consider themselves to be disordered. Rather, they have learned to take responsibility for their lives and behaviors in ways that maximize the strength and potential of their multiple selves.

Facilitator: A trained ministry team member who facilitates an inner healing ministry session is referred to as a facilitator. To facilitate simply means to "make easy." The facilitator's goal is to be led by the Spirit of God in order to "make easy" God's ability to have his way during a session and among all who are present. The best way a facilitator can do that is to "get out of the way" of what God wants to do. *(Note: A ministry facilitator is not a counselor and does not provide counseling. Because of legal ramifications the term counselor cannot be and is not used. Rather, facilitators simply act as representatives of the true*

Lord Jesus Christ to minister his love, healing, deliverance, and renewal by the leading of the Holy Spirit and the power of God.) (See **Recipient**)

False Memory Syndrome (FMS): False memories can be highly vivid recollections of events that have not actually occurred or are a distortion of an actual experience, often of abuses in childhood. Some therapists regard dissociated people as victims of misguided suggestive therapy techniques. False Memory Syndrome (FMS) has been linked to wrongful accusations of innocent people who have been fabricated as abusers, perpetrators, and tormenters. FMS is not recognized in the DSM-IV. (See **DSM-IV**)

Freud, Sigmund: Freud developed a method of mental investigation called psychoanalysis to bring to light hidden and underlying causes of behavior and to determine their effects upon an individual's life. Freud, an atheist, had abandoned not only his Judaic heritage but all religious beliefs. He did not accept the things of the Spirit of God; they were foolishness to him (See 1 Corinthians 2:14).

Inner Healing: Inner healing is the process of renewing the mind and restoring the soul to its original intent of wholeness and peace. (See **Restoration**)

Integration: Integration is the healing goal of many therapists and generally defined as "joining separate alter identities back together into one whole person." However, from a spiritual perspective, integration is not the objective of healing but rather a result of renewal of the mind and restoration of the soul. Integration is often used to describe two different aspects of the restoration process. One aspect is that of alters and parts coming to co-conscious self-awareness. As this happens, entities learn to dialogue, cooperate, and share their memories and information with each other. The other aspect of integration is that of actual merging, or fusion, of separated entities back to wholeness within the true person. Integration is a process, not an event. It is a part of the inner healing process that happens in God's timing and in his way.

M.P.D.: Acronym for *Multiple Personality Disorder*.

Merging: (See *Integration; Restoration*)

Multiple Personality Disorder: (See *Dissociative Identity Disorder; M.P.D.*)

Part: When a person is traumatized, part of the true person's mind may fragment and "go into hiding" at the subconscious level, along with pain experienced during the trauma, as well as scattered memory data. Functionally, this wounded part of the true person "stalls" at that moment and in that memory, even though the person overall continues to mature. (See *True Person*)

Post Traumatic Stress Disorder (PTSD): An anxiety disorder associated with serious traumatic events and characterized by such symptoms as survivor guilt, reliving the trauma in dreams, numbness, lack of involvement with reality, or recurrent thoughts and images. This is associated with a number of anxiety and mental disorders, including that caused by the stress of active warfare.

Program Based Mind Control: The deliberate conditioning of a person's mind through repetitive trauma events. These are designed to impart a belief that can be used later to get a person to do something he would not normally do and at the same time not remember what he has been through or done, thus creating the ultimate slave and spy. (See *Satanic Ritual Abuse*)

Psychiatry: Psychiatry simply means "soul-doctor." Psychiatry is a branch of medicine that studies and treats mental and emotional disorders. Psychiatrists not only have a strong background in psychology and counseling but also are required to hold a medical degree.

Psychology: Psychology is simply "the science of the mind." Psychologists have extensive training in therapy and psychological testing but not the medical qualifications that distinguish a psychiatrist.

Psychoanalysis: (See *Freud, Sigmund*)

Recipient: An individual who receives inner healing. A recipient is not a "client" or a "counselee" but a receiver, or beneficiary, of all God wants to do to renew the person's mind and set him free from the bondage of the enemy. (See *Facilitator*)

Restoration: The goal of ministry to dissociation is the restoration of the soul. This includes renewal of the mind and redemption of loss caused by dissociation. Entities that have been separated unite, their strengths are joined, and the soul operates from a position of wholeness and peace. Simply put, restoration is putting things back the way they were originally intended to be. (See *Entity; Inner Healing; Integration*)

Sabotage: The furtive work of Satan that seeks an opportune time to attack a person, bringing malicious injury and destruction.

Satanic Ritual Abuse (SRA): SRA is programmed abuse created with the intent to gain spiritual power and control over another person through traumatic events that are ritualistically designed. Such rituals may involve torture, maiming, rape, demonic activity, cannibalism, and murder. (See *Programmed Based Mind Control)*

Scheme: The plot and plan of the enemy, Satan, to "steal, kill, and destroy" (John 10:10).

Self-awareness: As a person's dissociation is revealed, he becomes aware of who his parts and alters are as well as their history, function, and purpose.

Separation: The outcome of dissociation is that a person becomes separated, or divided within himself, forming distinct wounded parts and alter identities. (See ***Dissociation***)

Soul Tie: A soul tie is a relational connection with another person through the bond of family, friendship, marriage, and other types of association. Soul ties may be godly or ungodly. A soul tie curse is one acquired through an unholy, unnatural, or ungodly relationship and the corresponding transference of demonic influence from one person to another. This may happen through a range of relational connections including generational inheritance, illegitimate sexual union, occult connections, abuse, and trauma.

Spiritual Abuse: A form of abuse which violates a person's spirituality. In relation to dissociation, spiritual abuse may occur when a well-meaning person mistakenly identifies another person's dissociation (i.e. a wounded part or an alter identity) as a demon and attempts to cast it out. Dissociated parts are not demons and therefore cannot be killed off, sent away, or exorcised. (See ***Deliverance; Demonized; Part***)

System: (See ***Dissociative System***)

Switch: When one entity switches place with an alter, with a wounded part, or with the true person. Indications of switching may include changes in appearance, posture, voice, attitude, or behavior. (See ***Alter; Part; Trigger; True Person***)

Theme: A destructive theme in a person's life may be identified by repeated, characteristic patterns exercised in ways that bring harm.

Trigger: A trigger is a type of "code" or prompt that may take a person in his mind to the trauma event hidden in the subconscious mind. A trigger may be a word, phrase, threat, sight, sound, aroma, touch, object, experience, or anything else that suddenly stimulates a memory or feeling associated with a trauma memory. Usually a "trigger" will cause a "switch," allowing a dissociative identity to surface. For example, a trigger may activate an alter identity to respond, react, or present. Not all triggers are negative or lead to negative responses. (See *Switch*)

True Person: This is the actual person who has been born and presumed to be the "original" person in whose subconscious mind wounded parts are hidden and alter identities have separated. Others may refer to the true person as the "authentic person," "core personality," or "original personality." (See *Alter; Part*)

Wounded Part: (See *Part*)

෴ Praise for *Inner Healing* ෴ *Prayer Ministry*

"People struggling with almost any issue can find lasting freedom and healing through this Biblically sound and highly effective method of ministry."

Michael ෴ Oklahoma City, Oklahoma

"The peaceful, accepting atmosphere opened my heart to be healed. God's healing works!"

Brian ෴ Boulder, Colorado

"After engaging in traditional therapies for approximately twenty years, at long last I was released from the dark prison of dissociation and fear. The result of this approach has been key to my re-entering the world as a more confident, whole human being."

NJ ෴ Stillwater, Oklahoma

"I can now detect dissociation in others' lives, which has given me greater patience and love for them."

Frances ෴ Los Angeles, California

◌ Praise for *Inner Healing* ◌ *Prayer Ministry*

"The ministry environment was emotionally safe; the facilitators were accepting and nonjudgmental. This was a huge plus."

Becky ◌ Houston, Texas

"The answer to the question, 'Why is my life a mess?' is found in this type of healing."

Larry ◌ Stillwater, Oklahoma

"I did not feel like I was in a clinical setting. The environment was spiritual and God-focused, allowing me to be truly set free from my struggles."

Rick ◌ Portland, Oregon

"Since being helped to get to root issues, I don't walk around so wounded and defensive."

Erin M ◌ Norman, Oklahoma

Made in the
USA
Middletown, DE